Education of a Hospice Doctor

Gregory L. Phelps MD

Parson's Porch Books

www.parsonsporchbooks.com

Education of a Hospice Doctor
ISBN: Softcover 978-1-951472-42-9
Copyright © 2020 by Gregory L. Phelps MD

Much gratitude to **Katie Baker** of Baker Advertising & Design for the design and creation of the cover. You may contact her at 704.574.1155, 1810 Country Garden Drive, Shelby, North Carolina, 28150.

Education of a Hospice Doctor

CHAPTER ONE

I was in a Panera's taking a quick minute between patients to scarf down some food. Sitting alone, I was surrounded by the buzz of couples dining and friends meeting -- including an animated threesome of middle-aged women at the table next to me. My phone rang; it was one of my nurses calling about a patient in pain. I asked a few questions and then said, "OK well increase the morphine to 60 milligrams three times a day and add another 5 mg of methadone to the current dose that she's taking. As I rang off, I realized it had suddenly gotten quiet around me. I looked up from pocketing my phone. The threesome of matrons was glaring at me. Cockroaches get more benign stares. The woman closest to me curled her lip, it was clear she could see the large MD on my ID badge clipped to my lapel. "What kind of a doctor would hand out those kinds of medicines, are you one of those 'pain doctors?" she spat at me. Her friends nodded. Clearly, the public campaign against pain clinics and their doctors was having its desired effect.

I spread my hands apologetically, "I'm a hospice doctor, my patient is dying, and she is in pain. What would you have me do?" The effect on the trio was almost instantaneous. A sagging of shoulders, raised eyebrows, looks of concern and empathy. "Oh, that's so sweet!" one cooed. "A hospice doctor! You guys really have a hard job. I don't know how you do it."

That is a common phrase. Just a few weeks later, I was caring for a surgeon's mother. We talked both personally and professionally. As he walked me out of his mother's room, he patted me on the shoulder. "Man, I couldn't do what you do, but I am grateful you're doing it." He started to walk away. I reached out a hand of my own for his shoulder, unexpectedly stopping him for a word of explanation.

"Weird as it sounds, I love what I do." His raised eyebrows encouraged me to continue.

"I come into people's lives at the worst time for them. They and their families have gotten the direst news possible- impending death. They are in pain and suffering. I cannot cure them, but I can treat their pain, their nausea, their SUFFERING and make their lives a lot better. I'm helping both patient and family find some calm, meaning and purpose as life closes down." He nodded, patted me absently again and says, "Well, I'm just glad you're here. "

Shortly after this encounter, I'm speaking in front of a class of Family Medicine residents for their noon conference. I do a lot of educating for physicians, nurse practitioners, nurses, and other professional groups. Educating around end of life care is my passion. It is not so much about the ending, as the living beforehand, about which I want to evangelize. I also often speak to church groups and civic groups. I joke that I'll even do weddings and bar mitzvahs, but right now it is medical education. Young doctors and medical students are looking at their notes, fiddling with phones and chatting as I'm introduced.

I step to the side of the podium and with great drama announce, "Life... is a terminal illness!" A few heads snap up as I continue, "It is also sexually transmitted, so be careful." A snicker turns to a guffaw, then the group begins to laugh. I have them now, as I begin to expound on my passion.

"It is not so much about death and dying," I explain. "It is about how you want to live your life. Each birth certificate is stamped with an invisible expiration date. Life is limited that is why it is precious!" My voice gets a little louder. You've heard that country song- "Live Like You Are Dying?" A few heads nod. "This is it, 'your life' not a dress rehearsal for your perfect 'real' life to come." We doctors do something meaningful, even sacred in caring for people. Einstein once said the "best life is serving others." This is our gift to our patient....and ourselves, but there is more." I continue.

"My older son is a banker in New York City he's about your age. He's young in his position and works 80+ hours a week like many of you do. Heads nod. When he tells me how hard he's working I say, 'Son remember what I do for a living. No one ever died saying "I wish I'd spent more time at the office.' But he loves his work."

"Dad" he tells me, "I'm having a blast. The projects I work on change companies, change lives and end up on the front page of the Wall Street Journal." He assures me he is working hard, but finding meaning, having fun."

In 2008, I quit my job as a Chief Medical Officer of a large health system to go back to school at the age of 55. After eight years as the CMO, I was no longer having fun. My mother had died a year before in hospice. Her death kindled what had been a casual interest in end of life care. After long reflection, I resigned to go back to school for a fellowship in hospice and palliative medicine. What ensues is the tale of what I learned, before the fellowship, during and after. It is a personal memoir of returning to school when most doctors are thinking about retirement, as well as insights, and perspectives on palliative care, hospice and end of life.

I include several caveats in this writing. The first, is that I am a "thief of parts." By that, I mean in order to protect the innocent and the guilty, as well as patient privacy, all of the actions and activities in this memoir are true, however I have borrowed bits and pieces from one patient or staff worker and comingled them with another so that no one's reputation, other than my own could be injured. Names assigned to staff and patients are all aliases. Likewise, the extensive quantity of staff and faculty have been consolidated into a manageable number of pseudonyms. On the rare occasion I use a real name, mostly of family members, I try to indicate the fact.

The second caveat is, as we say in East Tennessee, it is an awfully thin board that only has one side. To that end, these are my recollections as best I can recall. I took extensive notes during my fellowship and thereafter, but all memory is subjective. Conversations are replicated as accurately as I can recall, with rare exception to make the telling more comprehensible.

Third, most of this story is about the year I did my fellowship. However, it is not possible to write this story without applying some of the lessons from both before and after the fellowship.

The fellowship is like beginning in the middle of a larger story, in medias res in Latin. So, there is some meandering to attempt place significant events and insights outside the fellowship year into the greater context.

The final caveat involves my fellowship diploma. It has a disfiguring stain. The day I graduated, I tossed the diploma in the foot of my car not knowing that the window had been cracked, and the carpet was wet. When we got the diploma out of the envelope a few days later to show friends, we saw the stain. Katie Baker, (her real name) my wife's best friend, is a graphic artist. When she saw the disfiguring blot, she said, "How awful, all that work." She grabbed the diploma from my hands and said fiercely, "I can fix this." She took the diploma home, scanned it, and worked her computer graphical magic on it. A few weeks later, she returned an unstained version. In fact, she returned the diploma in three versions, on better paper stock with original and different color schemes. Touched as I was with all her hard work, it was the stained original I framed. It seemed emblematic of the year.

The story most of us would like to tell is how we succeeded- how we triumphed and slammed the ball in the end zone and did our victory dance. This, regrettably, is not that story. I did the hospice and palliative medicine (HPM) fellowship, kept a journal of who I saw and what transpired. I had a vague idea to write about the experience. At the end, I was so close to defeated that I put the journal away and went on with my life. I had a job to find, a specialty board to pass and was just too damned exhausted from the year and all that had happened. I couldn't imagine going to a keyboard and reliving it. Moving back to Knoxville, in the unpacking, the journal and notes disappeared into one of many shelves in the basement. Later cursory searches for the journal and notes were unsuccessful.

A few years later, my church put a request for contributions for a Lenten reflection journal. The prompt was "the most challenging time in one's life and how we got through it." I wrote a two-page piece detailing a few of my challenges in my fellowship. I sent it in and didn't think much more about it until publication. Then I got an outpouring of comments and support. It was mostly along the lines: "We knew you were gone for a while, but we didn't realize how much you struggled. Wow, what an experience. You should write more!"

Still more time elapsed. I do a lot of public speaking about end of life, hospice and palliative care. I began to weave in anecdotes and personal stories, often with a humorous take. More people began to say the ever popular- "You should write a book!" The final push to get back at the keyboard came from my youngest son who found my notes in his closet... (who knows how) and said: "I thought you were going to write this year up, what happened?"

A few words of explanation of my career to this point. I began practice in a small town in the Piedmont region of South Carolina, after my Family Medicine residency. Chester was home to a classmate, fellow resident, and friend Dr. Sam Stone, his real name. Sam and I practiced for some years together with his father before I joined another practice a few miles away, in an even smaller town. Collectively I practiced in Chester for almost 9 years. A poor mill town, a medically underserved area, it was but a wonderful place to practice the full range of family medicine. I delivered babies, treated heart attacks and did some low-level procedures. But, the life of a small-town doctor is a very, very hard one. Constant calls, emergencies and crises often complicated by poverty. One year, after losing two partners, I found myself in solo practice. I was on every night call including OB and ER. (The ER doc went home at midnight!) One horrible week, I averaged less than 4 hours of sleep a night. (Five to six was the norm) I staggered in Monday following a brutal call weekend and told our pharmacist/administrator "Don't ask me any hard questions. I'll probably start crying." Still, I couldn't go home- the patients were sick.

Another time I'd had a persistent cough for two weeks. The staff confronted me in the hall and said, "This cough has gone on long enough. You look terrible and you're scaring the patients and us. We think you need a chest X-ray. We think you have pneumonia. Are you going to make us hold you down? "Sure enough, the chest X-ray showed a whited-out lung of 'walking pneumonia.' The staff gloated, "See, we told you!"

"Wonderful" I replied sarcastically, trying desperately not to cough. "So, we close the office. I go home and go to bed and no one gets seen and no one gets paid for a week or so?" Slightly chastened, the staff and I negotiated that I'd take antibiotics and keep working. When I'd first come to town, I'd asked my new partner, Sam's Dad, how he decided when to take vacation. "Oh, I usually work until my ulcers bleed so bad that I'm vomiting blood, then I'll take a few days off." At the time, I'd thought he was kidding.

So, how did I get to hospice and palliative medicine and the fellowship? I used to think I had a grand plan for living my life. Since then, I've learned if you want to make God laugh, tell her your plans. After over forty years of practice and sixty plus years of living, I've discovered that so much of life is determined by random, chance encounters, by accident or mistake or divine inscrutable plan. An early example, shortly after entering practice- I made an administrative mistake involving workers' compensation. The employer wanted to know about the patient's care, which was his right under workers' compensation law. Ignorant of that fact, I refused to even admit I knew the patient. Workers' comp just came with the practice, and I hadn't thought much about it until that point. A few minutes later I got a genuinely friendly phone call from the helpful local attorney who educated me on the rules to which I had been oblivious. Legal matters, other than malpractice were not taught in residency or med school. Chastened, I realized there was a lot about workers' compensation and occupational and factory illness I hadn't learned in medical school or residency.

Shortly thereafter, I was presented a puzzling case of a lady with a rash from a chemical at work. I dimly remembered a professor, Dr. Stan Schumann, also his real name, from medical school, who had once lectured us on the specialty of Occupational Medicine. I did some digging to find his contact information and called for help. Stan Schumann's boundless enthusiasm included a two-hundred-mile drive to visit me a few days later to investigate the case. Stan's energetic devotion, plus my recent gaffe, led me to a field I knew little about- Occupational Medicine. (Stay with me, I know this is eventually about hospice!)

The mark of an educated person is someone who acknowledges the scope of their ignorance. My encounter with Dr. Schumann demonstrated I had volumes of ignorance about something we all do that impacts our health--Work! My developing default mode became dig in, buy books and study.

Thus, began a pattern of recurrent returns to education. Now let me say this was not a hard journey. I was the nerdy kid in school with horn rim glasses, often beaten up. A compulsive reader I did so many book reports in fifth grade that my stars ran off the sheet of poster board and onto the wall. Eventually I was banned from giving book reports to let other kids try to catch up. If there was a full-time paying job description for 'student." I'd be first in line to apply.

So, it was I was led to one of the very first online master's programs in the country in 1984, a Master of Public Health in Occupational Medicine. Notice the "on-line" part. At the beginning of this program, I didn't even OWN a computer. AOL was in the future and dial up was pretty high-tech stuff.

Studying at night between house calls, and hospital runs, I had to learn both technology of the internet and study the course work at the same time. Looking back, it is amusing that the computer had to be jury rigged to the otherwise incompatible local phone company wires by a techie neighbor who worked a computer job in Charlotte. The internet accelerated my path as a perpetual student. Using my MPH degree, I managed to grandfather the Occupational Medicine/Preventive Medicine boards. The result of this new degree led me and my family to Macon, Georgia to start an occupational health program as part of a family medicine residency. If I hadn't gotten the training in school, I was going to bring it in now! I also practiced and taught Family Medicine, ultimately rising to Associate Professor. Similar educational enthusiasms led to a certification in Medical Management which led to administrative jobs as a Medical Director of a large primary care group and eventually a hospital system.

That health care system was Catholic and that led to another Masters in Catholic Theology related to health care ministry. The irony here is that I'm not Catholic. "But who better to explain mission to the doctors than a doctor with education in both fields," explained the nun who authorized me entering the program. You, gentle reader may begin to see a pattern developing.

I brought home abandoned baby birds as a child. The abandoned and lost have always had a piece of my heart. So, I have long had an interest in people on the margins. Little explored topics in medicine have intrigued me. Being a child of two alcoholic parents, led me to a certification in addiction medicine, as well as treatment of addicts for many years. These people often exist within the fringes of medicine, often only as an irritant to the ER and staff that must put up with them at their worst. But nonetheless, alcoholics and addicts are people desperately in need of medical care, as I learned from painful family experience.

Another group on the margins are those nearing the end of life. Until very recently these people were only spoken about in whispers and euphemisms. Too often, when the possibility of a cure or success becomes elusive, medicine loses interest and withdraws. I had long been interested in the conundrums and quandaries of the dying. Over the years I had taken several classes and seminars on death and dying. Some of my interest came as early as college.

My college roommate's mother was diagnosed with terminal cancer in our junior year. We both lived in the same small South Carolina town where my mother was the county librarian. At that time, we often didn't even mention the word "cancer" to the patient. It was, in some ways, considered a shameful diagnosis though I could never figure out why. My roommate's mother, I'll call her Mrs. Wallace, was a local high school teacher. Once diagnosed, Mrs. Wallace declined over the next year or so. At that time the concepts of end of life care and hospice did not even exist in the US. Fear of even the mention of death crosses many cultures. Take for example tetraphobia, the fear of four. In Chinese culture the word for death resembles to the word for number four. So, the number is not used much in addresses, room numbers, especially in hospitals or even elevator floors! As I said, Death is not a topic for polite conversation.

The first hospice began in England in 1967. Cicely Saunders, a young nursing student took up the cause for a better way to die with a bequest from a dying patient. When no one would listen to her, she next became a social worker. Still she made little progress, so with determination I can only admire but not replicate. Cicely went to medical school to become a doctor and started her own program which continues today- St. Christopher's Hospice in London. Hospice was in part, a radical counter cultural response to the expanding invasive technology of intensive care units and equipment that isolated and confined patients, often in their dying moments.

The very first hospice in the US began with little fanfare in 1973 in Connecticut, about the time Mrs. Wallace was diagnosed. So… like everyone else, she went to the hospital for "treatment," which was really a euphemism, a cover for dying, though no one ever said that. As she declined, she became confused at times. Some days were good, others not so good.

I was working as an orderly at the hospital that summer between college and medical school. One steamy day I came into her room one afternoon to look in on her. The curtains were pulled, the room warm and dim. I asked her how she was. "Oh, you know, same old, same old. I know what you're here for." she continued. Since I was just on the hall and thought I'd stop in, even I didn't know what I was there for. So, in a playful tone, I asked.

"Oh silly," she said, "I know you're here to kill me and get this over with." shaken, I said "Oh no, I would never do that.!"

"It's OK, honestly. I know what really goes on here. I'm ready, go ahead," she seriously replied, then began to doze again.

Not knowing what else to say, I slunk silently out of the room and didn't return for days.

My mother, knowing my roommate like an extra son, went to visit Mrs. Wallace. It was supposed to be a short visit, but it was hours later when Mom came back looking a little rattled.

"How'd it go?" I asked looking up from my book.

Mom flopped down in the chair across from me and lit a cigarette, blew out a plume of frustration and relayed. "It went well until I asked one simple question."

"And that was…" I prompted.

"Well" mom said, "She kept hedging around like she wanted to talk about her illness. She's gone downhill so much since I saw her last, And I just blurted out the obvious question…"

"Which was….?"

"What does it feel like to have cancer and be dying?'"

"Oh, and then," I asked.

"Well no one had even admitted to her that she was dying, though it is pretty obvious. She said she was so frustrated that every time she brings up the possibility of dying to family and friends, they quickly shut her down and say, 'Oh no, don't talk like that, you'll be up and out in no time.'"

Another cigarette was lit and a final sigh, "So, anyways, two hours later, she finally finished telling me what she's wanted to tell everyone else about her life, her illness, and her impending death. "Mom looked up reflectively at the smoke streaming up towards the ceiling. "I am so glad I asked, and at the same time, so sorry the question had to be asked."

My mother is a central part of this story I'm to tell here. It is from her, a librarian, I got my love of reading and education. But it was only at her death that I decided to pursue a new career in hospice and palliative care. Many staffers in hospice will tell you their personal story was what brought them to hospice. In hospice, due to the context and often spiritual nature of the care, it is often said that hospice workers are called, not employed. My mom not only provided my impetus to study, she died in hospice. Also, through inheritance, she provided the funds for me to be able to quit my job and return to school yet again. What follows will tell how I made this decision and how I happened to make this choice, upsetting my career, wife and family.

My youngest son was approaching the end of college. I had had the idea of a fellowship in Hospice and Palliative Medicine (permanent students remember?) rattling around in my brain for a month or so. I'd been the medical director for a health system for eight years. It was very stressful, and I sometimes felt under appreciated. This came to a head a few months earlier at medical staff meeting at one of our rural satellite hospitals, where the sole hospitalist had abruptly quit. It would take weeks to months to find a replacement. The hospital staff physicians were angry blaming us and saying if administration didn't get a replacement quickly, they would quit using the hospital. Since I came from a rural hospital background I was asked if I could help. I went to our system CEO and asked if I could temporarily cut back on my duties at the main hospital to help fill the gap. She fixed me with a baleful eye and said, "I have no idea what the hell you what do here anyways, so do you need to." While I was glad to be able to fill in, after having worked for her for seven years, this was to say the least, a bit disheartening.

A few months after that we had a meeting of the area hospital medical directors at a local restaurant in Knoxville. I'd been wondering if I could find a local study program to bring me up to speed on hospice and palliative medicine. As we were leaving, I turned to my friend, Jack, the chief medical officer for the University of Tennessee Hospital system and asked. "Have you guys happened to have started a fellowship in Hospice and Palliative Medicine?

Knowing my interest, Jack shook his head and chuckled. "Don't we all have fantasies of going back to school and being young again? But, "he continued," Who among us does not have kids in college, a mortgage to pay, let alone enough money to quit working for a year? "I stopped dead on the restaurant steps, momentarily blocking an elderly couple trying to edge around Jack and I. Epiphany! I held up fingers one by one "Last kid is in his last semester, no mortgage, and recently inherited enough money to quit for a year! I can do this!" Jack shook his head in bemusement and wandered off, calling over his shoulder "Maybe you think you can quit, but have you tried this idea out on Gayle?"

Ah yes, Gayle, my wife now of 40 + plus years and a nurse. We met when she was a nursing student and I was a struggling medical student, she is the mother of my children, and the love of my life, but we are a study in contrasts. I am a glass is half full person, while she is the glass is half empty person, plus 'the glass is dirty and is that a crack?' The love of my life is the hard-headed realist in the family. She is my loving family's curmudgeon. After several decades, Gayle and I have developed a relationship probably best called "lovingly sarcastic." Case in point, on a Saturday morning I brought up coffee to where Gayle was finishing her shower. (My weekend nickname is Coffee boy.) Gayle's gaze sketched between the two cups. "Which one is mine?" she queried.

Borrowing a line from the Princes Bride I quipped, "Doesn't matter, I poisoned both of them"

"Works for me," she said grabbing and hoisting one to slurp from.

As I had been developing this idea of a return to school, I had a private fantasy that Gayle and I would be empty nesters. We could pick some place new to live for a year while I studied, and she worked as a nurse. I particularly thought that Boston might be an attractive place. My brother Rick lived there for years and we loved going and visiting him. I thought we could live in Boston and on weekends tour the Northeast --just the two of us. To that end, I searched for fellowships in the Boston area. (Notice! Conversation with Gayle has not yet occurred.)

I may be the only person ever to apply to Harvard by accident. I had seen a Hospice and Palliative Medicine fellowship listing at the Dana-Farber Cancer Institute. I had read good things about its' culture of improvement following the death of a famous journalist there. In talking up quality improvement for our medical staff I had used them as the poster child for process improvement. Now I could go there and learn from them. I wrote a letter of inquiry to Dana-Farber. To my surprise, Harvard answered back, asking for a formal application which I hastily provided. I should have guessed, but it had not occurred to me that as a world-famous cancer center in the same city, the institutions would be affiliated.

You might think after being married more than 30 years that I would have been smart enough to elaborate ideas on my educational diversion with my wife first. I had this fantasy of just the two of us together, like newlyweds. So, it was only after the application had been mailed, that

I mention my thoughts of our year of togetherness to Gayle. My treasured escape is met with a snort of disbelief.

"You've got to be kidding me," she snarks. "I don't want to move to Boston or New York or anywhere else. My family is here. What happens if our daughter gets pregnant and has a baby? What happens if my mother gets sick or even dies?" (Given that her mother is on the north side of 90, this is not necessarily a rhetorical question.) "Still," she continues, putting the metaphorical nail in the coffin, "it's Harvard, I don't think I have to worry about anything." End of discussion, temporary end of year long adventure fantasy.

Astonishingly, it was only a few days later that I heard back. Harvard wanted to know how soon I could come interview. I set a date for the following Monday. And then… I had to tell Gayle. I can only attribute how I said it as petty revenge for her previous comment above. (And yes, I can be an ass.) We were out driving to get dinner. I told her I had heard from Harvard and that the news 'was not good.' She tried hard to hide a smile that was both a smirk and a sigh of relief. "I'm sorry, I know you wanted that."

"Oh" I said airily, "I didn't mean it was bad for me, but more for you. They want me to interview on Monday." The look on her face should have served as a final warning.

OK, it was probably cosmic karma getting revenge for that comment that awaited me in Boston. I arrived on a beautiful fall day, a tourist fantasy with the leaves in full color. A delightful secretary with whom I had bonded on the phone, had arranged the interviews and provided the appropriate agenda and information before I arrived. A member of the faculty met me for dinner at an atmospheric Italian restaurant. She presented me with a full schedule of interviews for following day. As we chatted over the meal, she casually asked me the question that would be a harbinger of disaster for the coming interviews:" "Do you think it might be difficult to come back to school after being a successful physician and executive?"

As it turned out that concern would be the principal focus of every interview I had. The clear implication was that it would be very difficult to step down from successful executive and experienced physician to lowly fellow. Nevertheless, I persevered. I talked about my previous educational efforts that included the two earlier master's degrees. I talked about the servant leadership culture in the Catholic hospital where I worked, that saw no job, no duty as beneath ones' worth.

At one point, mentioning my Master's in theology degree, I was told I was probably 'too religious' for Boston life. "You don't understand," I was lectured, "there are many more religions, and mostly none at all here in Boston. We're not like the South; you'd probably be offended." I told them I thought that unlikely. As an added off-hand comment, I offered that I thought the movie Dogma (a sacrilegious comedy that included Rufus, the 13th, black apostle and a "shit demon") was funny. Ironically the reference sailed over their heads and they thought the reference more evidence of my presumed religiosity.

"There! You see," they said as if that clinched the argument. "You even argue in religious terms." It went downhill from there. In another instance, it was strongly suggested I was too old to learn. Another yet questioned my health and my stamina. I am a little shocked at these questions and I'm wondering to myself, "Have you ever even heard of the Equal Employment Opportunity Commission? In yet another exchange they told me of a requirement to see a psychiatrist regularly to monitor my mental health. It appeared they thought this required introspection might scare me off, but I shared that my brother was a PhD psychologist, and that would be fine.

I'm shuttled all over Boston during the day. The chaotic afternoon ended in the basement of Massachusetts General Hospital with a senior member of the faculty almost shouting at me that I couldn't possibly return to school my age. As I struggled to get a word in edgewise, his wife, also a physician, has joined us and was tugging on his elbow and saying, "let the man speak! "I ultimately left the interview with the less than reassuring words: "We'll get back to you."

I called the secretary with whom I had so many pleasant conversations. My opening comment was "Well that didn't go the way I thought it would." She'd heard about the shouting match and agreed things had gone disastrously and to not keep my hopes up. To her, I wondered why I had even been invited. She said she honestly didn't know. Still, it took three months to get the official word. Gayle wisely but just barely chose not to say, "I told you so." In the meantime, unbeknownst to her, I had already started on plan B.

Believing my newest scheme would be more palpable to her, I looked at other fellowships close enough to allow me to get home some weekends. There were other HPM fellowship programs in Alabama, and Kentucky which were only a few hours from Knoxville. The problem with one program was, while it was on my old search list where I'd found Dana Farber, it was not on the newest list. So, I called to ask why it was not listed anymore. The secretary there told me that there had been several departures, including the medical director, and there was no one available to be the program director. With only a hint of slyness in my voice, I said "I may not know much about hospice and palliative care yet, but I know an awful lot about being a medical director. "Perhaps we could work something out." Her voice was chilly enough to freeze a jalapeno pepper as she said, "I don't think that would be practical," then she promptly hung up on me

The next closest program would be the University of River City-a pseudonym for this tome. I had reached out to them even before going to the interview in Boston. They were interested in talking with me. They were curious however as I could grandfather the hospice exam without a fellowship, why did I not just go that route. I said although I had been caring for hospice like patients in a limited fashion while working as medical director, I wanted to make sure I learned the full spectrum of comprehensive end of life and palliative medicine as a specialty.

I wanted to put the administrative role behind me for a while and get back into patient care. I joked about being a hospital medical director, stuck between administrators and physicians, "sometimes the only people who really liked me, were the patients." So, after the Boston disaster, I arranged for a visit to River City to follow a system wide Catholic hospital management confab in Ohio. It would be a one-hour detour in four-hour drive back to Knoxville.

The people in River City were very welcoming in their arrangements for me. I was excited to be coming for the visit. It was a trip I would not get to finish. The required management meeting was finishing the second of four days, I had dinner and a drink with a colleague of mine that evening. Over dinner we compared notes on the management challenges we faced. It was a cold evening, and after dinner I went to my room for some reading and an early bedtime.

It was about 4 AM and I woke up with a sense that something was not right. I just felt funny --. it felt like a catfight in my chest. It took me a few moments to realize that my pulse was racing. I didn't feel bad, I wasn't short of breath; I had no chest pain, but my heart was racing. Reflexively, I grabbed my watch and my wrist to check my pulse. It was flying, I clocked my pulse for a few seconds and did the math…Wow. I did it again for a full minute. 170 beats a minute. It's a truism that doctors are notoriously bad patients. I shall now demonstrate.

Deciding there was no immediate threat, I laid back down in bed and went back to sleep. The next morning, I approached a close friend and nurse manager, Doug. I knew he'd had problems with rapid heartbeat. I ask to borrow several of his beta blocker pills. Reasonably he asked why, and I casually reply 'my heart seems to be running just a little fast' in such a tone as to discourage a follow up question. Then, I spend the day in meetings, swallowing these pills and checking my pulse. I see Doug giving me occasional surreptitious looks. Naturally, he is a bit concerned and after checking my pulse himself, encourages me to go to the hospital. I demur.

"Are you doing the stupid doctor thing?" he asks. Sheepishly I nod and return to hoping it will all go away. Gayle is from tiny Denmark South Carolina and she doesn't do well with interstate travel or large cities. I do not want to call Gayle and tell her I am having heart problems in a large city she'd never been to, several states and four hours away. Nonetheless the following morning with my heart still racing I finally decide it is time to go to the hospital. I felt fine but, this wasn't normal, and it wasn't stopping. Since I know the cardiologists back at St. Mary's, I decide to drive home.

I am two hours into my drive, when Doug calls me. He is still concerned, "This is bullshit!" he exclaims by way of opening the conversation, "You're a doctor. I saw you taking my pills. You know that you should go to the hospital. I'll drive you."

"Not necessary," I tell him cheerily, "I'm on my way."

"Which one," he asks, "I'll meet you there." I tell him I'm halfway to Knoxville. There follows another burst of profanity. He berates me for being stupid and promptly hangs up. This becomes a recurring theme, as the nurses at the hospital, the ER doctor, and the cardiologist I called to meet me in the emergency room, all agree- I'm an idiot. During the trip south, I called the staff and faculty in River City University and said I might not make the meeting as I appear to be having some heart trouble. The irony of this, after the accusations of age and possible ill health from Harvard that I had pooh-poohed, are not lost on me.

The cardiologist I had called, meets me at the emergency room. The ER doctor, who knew me well, stops by to say hello and kindly asks if I want him to call Gayle -- who is working just a floor or two away. I wave the offer away. The ER nurses then repeat the offer. However, I decline, wanting to know what is wrong first. My strong preference after 30 something years of marriage is to have the problem solved before mentioning it. Yes, it is sort of amazing I'm still married,

The cardiologist is telling me that I will need to be admitted. I resist, hoping to be cardioverted and discharged. He is having none of that and is doggedly writing admission orders, pointedly in my presence. When our CIO arrives in the emergency room saying, "Hey Greg, I heard you were down here and having heart problems," I realize the gig is up.

"Oh, crap. Give me a phone to call Gayle." You may have heard of the HIPPA, the patient privacy law? I promise it does not work in these circumstances where you are part of the 'hospital family' and having cardiac arrhythmias. Gayle quickly arrives in my cubicle in the ER, having already been briefed by her fellow nurses. She now stands like an avenging fury at the end of my gurney, arms crossed, trying not to shout, "Seriously? You drove yourself all the way home?"

The first cardiologist consults another cardiologist who specializes in electrophysiology and arrythmias. The second cardiologist now bustles in looking surprisingly cheerful. "We may not need to electrically cardiovert you" he starts. Having never had, and really not wanting to have, my heart shocked back into rhythm, I am all ears. Realistically, who doesn't want to avoid medically sanctioned electrocution. He wants to try me on a brand-new medication. Better yet, he is excited to have someone as a guinea pig on whom to try it out. However, he notes, as an aside, it does have a rare side effect of more cardiac arrhythmias and death. Gayle looks a little non-plussed, but I gamely declare, "first time for everything, let's have at it."

So, although he kept checking in and saying everything was fine, just great, he was in and out over the next hour as the infusion ran in, checking on me frequently. Success! Even though my arrhythmia converts, it is decided, over my head and with Gayle's collusion, that I would indeed be spending the night in the hospital. This led to a parade of doctors, nurses and staff, escorting me by gurney, through the main halls -- in a hospital gown -- past multiple employees who know me. Most blinked and say, "are you okay? Oh Dr. Phelps what happened?" It is never as much fun to be the patient, as the doctor.

The nurses on the floor are alternating between concern and berating me, as Gayle regales the staff with my sordid tale so far. As I slide from gurney to bed amidst the hubbub, the cardiologist leans over and said *sotto voce-* "I think I'd have done the same thing." He assures me again that the event is probably a "one off" and unlikely to happen again. How I wish he had been right.

The interview in River City is put off a few weeks. I initially planned this second fellowship application as a fallback when I'd initially done it. I had not undertaken it with any gravity. In fact, I joked in my essay, that having a background in addiction treatment would be an excellent complement to learning pain and palliative care. I quoted one of my favorite comedians, "It would be, like the veterinarian that got his taxidermy license, his motto would be 'either way you get your dog back'. Amazingly, after the essay and hospitalization, River City still wants to talk to me.

The day of the interview day arrives, and I drive up to River City the night before, where I'm put up in one of the city's venerable old hotels. There are a few concerned questions about how my heart is doing and then straight into a quick tour, then the round of interviews, the format this time is different. One of the faculty is starting a management degree and he is very keen on utilizing his coursework. We sit at a roundtable with all the faculty. A piece of paper with what I assume are a variation of 'best management interview questions for new hires,' begins to be handed from staff to staff to pick a question.

I note, with the exception of the management trainee, who is of my vintage, that the majority of faculty could stand in for my daughter's older sister. As the paper moves from hand to hand, there is a little awkward pause as each person scans the sheet to pick the question they want. As the sheet is passing by me to the next person, I snag it, and comment with a small amount of attitude, "let's just make this simple I'll read the questions and answer them, then we can go from there." They are slightly taken a back but agree it would speed things along. Then there are a few individual interviews, only at the last one, was I asked the question for which I'd been waiting. 'Do I think I would have trouble going back to being just a fellow again? To their surprise, I bust out laughing and explain the significance of the question from my previous interviews. When I leave, it is with the impression there would be a spot for me if I wanted it.

I've been the chief medical officer of a hospital system for eight years. You wouldn't think it would be hard to get an appointment to tell my boss I was leaving, but it was. She kept having emergencies and cancelling my appointments with her. This may have been some of the reasons I figured it was a good time to leave. Three times her secretary shrugged helplessly as I came in for an appointment saying, "I'm really sorry, she had to run to Lafollette/ Newport etc. What is so important that you keep trying to get in?"

Pledging her to secrecy, so I can deliver the news myself, I tell her I'm leaving. The next day I get a call from the CEO's office. "So, you're leaving" she begins without preamble. (So much for secrets) "Come on over and tell me why?"

I tell her my plan to go back to school. "I've lost my passion for the job here" I explain, "It is time to try something new."

"Humph," she responds reflectively, "that's not unusual, I'd guess half your co-workers in administration have burned out and lost their passion too. I wish they'd take the hint from your example and move on like you."

A few months later it is getting almost to time to leave. The nuns with whom I've had a close and supportive relationship, decide to have a service of farewell for me. I am touched beyond measure as they celebrate and anoint me for the coming venture in the hospital chapel. So, I'm a little surprised when I come into my office to find my administrative assistant giggling as she hangs up the phone saying, "No I promise he's not dead, he's just fine; in fact he just walked in the door."

Seeing my quizzical look, she says, "Well you know the sisters had this service of farewell for you. Apparently, there is some confusion about what kind of farewell it is. That's the third call today asking when you died. The good news" she said pensively for my behalf "is, they all sounded upset."

After eight plus years in administration I've acquired a substantial collection of keys. I spend a day or so sorting out what goes where, to make sure they are properly returned. In the end, I have three orphan keys that I couldn't place but had been toting around for years. I give up and take them home to hang them on the cork board, inside the back door where we put doctor's appointments, pins, cards and other stray keys.

Earlier in the season, Gayle and I spent a weekend looking for apartments. I wanted to be downtown near the medical complex, preferably within walking distance. Gayle was looking for small, utilitarian and cheap. I suspect there was some penitential/punitive object in mind for my dwelling. We looked at a variety of buildings in neighborhoods of varying quality. We finally found a single bedroom apartment on the sixth floor of a building that was an odd combination of private school and apartments. It was only three blocks from campus. I would discover over the year, quite a few of my fellow denizens were medical students and residents.

Rental agreement signed; the building manager handed me a set of three keys to take home pending my move in date. A few weeks later, my son-in-law helped me move the big furniture. We opened the apartment and used the freight elevator to bundle the heavy items in, then returned home to put the three keys back on the cork board to await a final move in day a month hence.

What happened next was emblematic of the upcoming year. After work one day, I was running late, Gayle and I hastily loaded the car with clothes and small items, kitchenware, lamps, pillows, linens etc. I grabbed the three keys off the corkboard and off we went. We arrived in River City late that evening. Given the urban neighborhood, we decided to unload the car in segments where we could keep an eye on my possessions. First, car to elevator, elevator to apartment door, then haul all the stuff inside. It took an hour to get everything to the door. It was almost July. We were sweaty, we were stinky. As I rummaged in my pocket for the apartment keys, we good-naturedly argued who got the first shower. I pulled out the keys and put the first key in the lock. Nothing happens, the next and the next. Gayle's glaring at me a little frustrated. I stare hard at the keys, all three of them, just like the three left over from the hospital, also on the cork board. Realization of my error leads to a loud and sincere litany of profanity. I then explain to a bewildered Gayle what has transpired.

I thought Gayle would kill me then and there. I'm positive the thought went through her head but luckily, she bursts out with a laugh that has a slightly hysterical edge. I am however, reminded repeatedly of my failings as we reverse the process and schlep the pile of belongings back to the car. We check into a motel across the street, awaiting dawn when the building manager lets us in. I then endure Gayle telling our children of our move in adventure in gleeful and sweaty detail once we arrive back home. After that episode I designed a series of key copies and fail safes to ensure I could always have a key available.

CHAPTER TWO

When I was an intern over thirty years ago, orientation consisted mainly of a breakfast and presentation of a lab coat, a beeper and a printed sheet with the intern assignments, the name of the resident leading the service along with that of attending physician. This was followed by a vague wave in the direction of the hospital that loomed over our family practice center. The morning of my final year as a resident, I recall a new intern wandering into the call room a little before lunch, looking a bit confused.

"How do you dictate a death summary?" he asked plaintively.

"Already!?" I asked, "you've only been here two hours?" He nodded dumbly; shell shocked already.

"Wow" I said sympathetically, "I think that is a record." Then I showed him how to do the dictation.

No more. We had already had several days of general orientation. July begins with more orientations. I'm learning my way around the two hospitals in which I'll spend most of my time - the VA and University hospitals. Each hospital has its own computer system that must also be slowly and painfully learned. University Hospital has a unique challenge in this regard. Each floor (!) has something different on the computer. Some floors only do orders, some make notes, some have vital signs and others don't. To make matters worse, tech savvy I am not.

I also go out to the VA for orientation there that largely consisted of getting a government issued ID. I'm met by Ralph, a huge but genial security guard. Ralph is a former Army MP and he takes down my information as we chat in his cramped office. The phone rings at one point and he answers and asks a few cryptic questions then levers his bulk up telling me to stay put he'll be back soon. So, I settle back, pull a paperback out of my pocket and start reading. A longish interval ensues before Ralph returns plops down behind his desk and resumes as if no time at all has elapsed. I raise a questioning eyebrow to him, and he responds with a snort. "Some knucklehead called in another bomb threat for the building. It happens, but we have to check each one out," he says nonchalantly. I of course, am sitting there thinking, "OMG, he left me here IN THE BUILDING!"

One new bit of technology for the fellowship does catch my interest. This is yet another a computer system that tracks our time to ensure that we don't spend too much time (!?) in training. This was a luxury I sorely missed as a resident. Back then, days without sleep were considered a mark of honor and a badge of acceptance into the fraternity of doctors.

I remember being up two days in a row as resident, then moonlighting in a rural ER till midnight. Gayle had gone along for the ride. Halfway home, I asked Gayle if she saw the large elephant about a half mile down the road. She looked confused and said "No, what elephant?" I was already pulling over.

"I'm done, I'm tired, I'm so tired I'm seeing things." I never told anyone at the residency about this elephant encounter as it would have been noted as a mark of shame to buckle.

Now, I'm given a new white coat, it says Palliative Care. I'm not a fan of white coats. I remember as a medical student I couldn't wait to have my first white coat. The coats lengthen in relationship to the wearer's importance to the system. So med student, short coat. Interns and residents got a coat a bit longer. Fellows and attendings got the full-blown, almost floor-sweeping, white coat. The white coat is a century old as a marker for physicians. When medical education underwent sweeping reform at the beginning of the 1900's it was a signal of a new emphasis on "science."

Up until then, physicians wore mostly black suits, for everything - including surgery. Since residency, I've always owned a white coat but, rarely wore it. I mean they're white, they show every stain. They also scare the patient's as in 'white-coat hypertension.' Yes, that's real. I find white coats tend to create distance and disparity between physician and patient, so I tend to avoid them. I also don't like large white coats because I'm fat. I would leave the coat unbuttoned and flapping, only to often get snagged on the door handle walking into a patient's room.

Nothing builds a patient's confidence in their doctor like me coming in … "Hi, I'm Doctor……" Yank! Bang! as I'm brought up short hung on the doorknob. When I practiced in a small town in South Carolina, I usually wore khakis and a polo shirt. One doctor pointedly asked me once if I'd ever heard of the book <u>Dress for Success.</u> "Sure," I said, "I own a copy and read it."

"Didn't take, I take it?" he commented dryly. For years I owned one suit, mainly for funerals. I wore it to a job interview once. The interview was supposed to last a day. They asked if I could stay to meet the CEO the next day and I told them no, I only had the one suit! They thought I was kidding.

When I moved into my first administration position. I finally bought a few suits. These lasted almost three days. I was meeting with a new doctor's group who dismissively referred to the administrators as "the suits." From then on, I went over 20 years of wearing a sports coat. If there were a big occasion, I'd put on a tie, frequently a cartoon tie. Patients love these.

All this to say that here I am at River City University Medical Center on July 1st in a white coat and tie for the first time in years, with my name and "Palliative Care" in red print. My mother would have been so proud, I finally looked like the doctor she had in mind.

My first two months of fellowship will be at the University Hospital. I was supposed to be at the Veteran's Administration Hospital, but there's been a glitch with the other fellow who will be coming a month later, so here I am at River City University Medical Center.

This hospital is a sixties modernist concrete building, now showing its age with too small double rooms. Things are slow as we edge up to the fourth of July holiday. We have four patients to start. I quickly reacquaint to the routine of patient rounding, as they still use the format I learned as an intern 35 years ago. We have a list of patients to see. Our team of attendings, residents, medical students and fellows augmented with a psychologist, chaplain and social worker, follow the list wandering from floor to floor of the medical center.

For each patient, the team crowds in and someone- resident or student recites the information while we cluster around the patient and occasionally family. A brief exam by the attending confirms physical findings. Unusual findings are shared and re-examined. Occasionally a team member is left behind to deal with new issues as the rest of the team moves on. As most of our patients face serious and often life-ending illnesses, the chaplain or social worker are most often left behind to offer consolation, aid and help with family and existential issues.

Our attending physician, the first three days of my fellowship, Marci (Not her real name) is young. A few years older than my daughter. In fact, many of our attendings had completed the same fellowship in earlier years. Her youthfulness causes some awkwardness, as I am visibly, by far, the oldest person in the rounding group and many patients assume I am the attending. Patients and family direct their comments and questions to me instead of her. In response to her only partly hidden annoyance, I learn to hang at the back of the group.

On the second day, I have my first exposure to something new in our rounding- the family meeting. I will later learn that this is one of the key elements to palliative care and is as stylized as a kabuki dance. The meeting is an orderly exercise that may take an hour or more. We probe for what the family and patient understand about the diagnosis, get them to tell us about the patient and what is important to them, and then slowly edge towards understanding what the patient would want in these circumstances.

I've been a doctor over thirty years. I had never heard of a family conference. The idea of regularly orchestrating a compassionate give and take to get to the core of the patient's desires, dreams and goals was both foreign and yet extremely appealing. I have never witnessed such a genuine investment in the non-medical needs of the patient and family by medical people, and I am entranced!

In the first three days, we do several of these conferences, and I feel that THIS is what I came here to learn. I love the patient and family stories. The routine begins to set in. After morning rounds and conferences, we head over the skybridge to the office. Here we check the fax machine for new consults. A few days in, a new wrinkle. I vividly recall the day our attending picked up a morning fax.

"Oh, Walter is back!" our attending coos. Walter has been a patient of exceptional longevity for a service such as ours. He suffered an abdominal catastrophe two years earlier and bounces from hospital to hospital. He is on his second or third generation of palliative care fellows.

As Walter is well known and liked, our group troops off en mass to greet him. Turns out that Walter is not in his room, and there is a brief confab. Our attending who had Walter as a patient when she was a fellow, recalls that Walter likes to sneak out to and smoke. Sure enough, she pursues him into his hideaway, a wind protected corner in the lee of the hospital, hidden by a large concrete planter. There he is, exceptionally tall and rail thin, cigarette in hand. As we round the corner, Walter smiles in chagrin as he unfolds stork-like from his ledge. A floating haze of smoke wreathes his mane of long, curly, dark but graying hair. Self-consciously, he hides the cigarette behind his back, a small plume of smoke continues to rise. We are introduced one by one to Walter.

Our attending repeats the circumstances of Walter's plight. A vicious case of ulcerative colitis and a combination of medicines and surgery have brought on an abdominal catastrophe of multiple fistulas. These bowel openings cross connect in a hodge-podge, from the stomach to loop after loop of bowel, short-circuiting his ability to get nutrition. Several fistulas connect to the outside though his abdominal wall. Unselfconsciously, Walter hikes up his hospital gown to show the collection of ostomy bags draining fluids from wounds that pucker his abdomen.

At present, he is recovering from yet another infection from a central IV line. His condition presents a terrible paradox. He needs the IV lines to maintain his precarious nutrition, but they keep getting infected, and they need to be removed and replaced. We will see Walter again and again.

The next patient has lung cancer and has developed a salt depletion complication called Syndrome of Inappropriate Anti-Diuretic Hormone or SIADH that that happens with some cancers. Marci asks that when rounds are done, I go back to back and pull the newest labs from the computer. "No problem," I respond cheerily pulling out a pen and marking an 'L' for labs on my wrist.

"Wait, what is that?" she asks.

"It is what I do to remind me of something to do. The 'L' is for labs

"But why your hand? That's nasty. Use a piece of paper."

"Ahh, "I respond, "but in all these pockets" gesturing to the lab coat, "notes get lost and only found in the wash. I don't take off on wrist or lose it. I've been doing it for years."

"Well it still looks nasty and I don't want to see you doing it." Chastened I dip a quick nod.

I love hearing the stories of the patients and their experiences I always have. So, I'm stunned when the anesthesiology resident gets frustrated as one patient pours out some memories of the Korean War. I listen fascinated. The resident is polite…until we step out of the room at which point he opines tersely, "You know the problem with some patients is they're awake and do not have an endotracheal tube in their throat so they can talk , like this one did. Jeez.!"

I had thought I'd wanted to be a surgeon when I got into medical school until the first few weeks. We became immersed and overwhelmed by anatomy and physiology and many other topics with very little clinical connection to actual patients. We had one break. The newly formed specialty and Department of Family Practice was presented to us.

They announced, "we know when you go home at Christmas and the holidays even though you are first year med students, your family is going to begin to bombard you with medical questions. We're here to help make you not feel too stupid." With that they handed out binders with topics in several brief pages that included heart failure, hypertension, diabetes and many clinical entities with the promise to give us a lecture each week we could then talk about with our families. We medical students were thrilled. Finally, REAL MEDICAL STUFF.

The following week in medical school we showed up with our binders to hear about the first topic- heart failure. To our surprise and dismay, the family physicians told us there had been a terrible mistake, and we needed to hand our binders back in. There was a fair amount of grumbling and hands up trying to ask why, but the faculty were implacable.

Once all our binders were taken up, the family medicine faculty handed out new, seemingly identical binders to all of us. Same topics in the same order. Now we were really confused, until the chairman of the department took center stage. "Ladies and gentlemen, we are family doctors, we don't treat diseases. We treat patients and their families. If you'll notice, heart failure is now the PATIENT with heart failure. We family physicians believe in the bio-psycho-social model of illness and no patient or illness stands alone. We will now begin with the patient with heart failure." I was hooked to both the patients and their stories.

The next day in the fellowship though, I was hoping to see Walter again to hear more of his story, but I am sent to do an evaluation on Macy, a nonagenarian with dementia. Looking through the chart, I see Macy has been in a nursing home with profound dementia for years with multiple hospital admissions and is nearly unresponsive. She'd been brought in from a nursing home with yet another urinary tract infection which made her even more confused. This was her fifth admission for the same problem.

The hospitalists elected to ask palliative care to initiate a conversation with the family about the utility of keeping this demented soul in this world when she seemed to be trying as hard to pass to the next. I reviewed her chart as I went down the hall to her room. A nurse was changing her linens and struggling to move Macy, who was essentially dead weight, around in the bed. After I introduced myself to both the nurse and to Macy, I helped the nurse roll Macy from side to side, helping tuck sheets, while sneaking a listen with a stethoscope to what would have been her inaccessible posterior lung fields.

Many years before, having worked as an orderly at the Marion County Hospital between college and med school, the rhythms of rolling and tucking came back, and the nurse and I chatted. I continued my exam of Macy as the nurse fluffed and tucked sheets and pillows, and then we both headed back to the desk. I was writing notes in Macy's chart, I looked up to see Macy's nurse and several nurses staring at me.

"Who are you?" they asked.

"Oh, hi," I said putting my pen back in my pocket, "I'm Greg Phelps one of the new fellows on palliative care."

The nurses looked at each other, and Macy's nurse explained the huddle looking at me, "In all the years I've been here, that's the first time I've EVER had a doctor help me change a patient...ever." The other nurses nodded emphatically: a row of bobbleheads.

I'm embarrassed for my profession." Well, I've been well trained; I've been married to a nurse for over thirty years."

As I started to swell with a bit of pride, another nurse further down the desk interrupts, "He doesn't count. Those palliative care docs aren't like the others." She warms to her subject, "these types sit up in their offices, hold hands and sing Kumbaya until someone down here needs help. It's not normal," she says nodding to the others. The bobbleheads nod again.

The conversation with Macy's family occurs later in the day. Having done the exam and reported to the team, I'm a bystander, as the attending leads the family through diagnosis, and likely prognosis. Then I'm out of the hospital for even more orientation. The area hospice is sponsoring a segment of the program that is a bit more touchy-feely. Cultural diversity, ethnic sensitivity and personal reflections make the list of topics. Attending the meeting at the hospice headquarters, I add a third ID badge to my growing collection. After the morning seminars, I'm to meet with the medical director for the hospice. His secretary rises to apologize as she meets me. She explains he has a crisis and doesn't have time for me today. So, with abject apologies, she has a new assignment, hooking me up with a now married, former Catholic priest, who works as a chaplain.

Together we chat as we roam River City doing spiritual house calls. We pray with the patients and listen to their individual concerns. We see a WW II vet who shares his firsthand reports of sights and sounds of the war. Realizing, I am face to face with living history, this part of the job quickly becomes one of my favorites. Another chaplain visit: 92-year-old homebound woman whose spouse recently died. Hospice and its staff are her only links to the world. She is looking forward to joining her husband.

The chaplain explains as we peregrinate through aging neighborhoods, "It is not so much religious work, as hearing and supporting the patient. If we lift their spirits, I've done spiritual care." Again, I'm reminded how much I love this work with its multi-disciplinary outlook and value, not only the physical or medical but the emotional, spiritual and psychological aspects of patient care. My journal notes it as "a grace-filled day." I'm glad the medical director was busy.

I live alone the entire time I'm in River City, so spare time away from work is a bit of a challenge. One of my longstanding problems is that of weight- I'm fat. I've always been big. I can and have lost 100 pounds, but the *avoir du pois* always finds me again and usually brings friends! My usual time-wasting default is sitting, reading and snacking. Not this year! The city's downtown YMCA is only a few blocks down the street from my apartment. In the early weeks of fellowship, before routines begin to calcify, I drag myself the few blocks to enroll at the Y and begin a regimen of diet meals and workouts. I also bring a bicycle that I keep in the stairwell (illegally) with all the others.

The next few weeks of July pass quickly. Consults include a young melanoma patient in his 30's who is declining. His family can't bring themselves to give up. He may soon be on a ventilator. We also see several more end-stage cancer patients and another unfortunate with liver failure. We are having more family conferences. The other services and attendings like this service because we have the time and inclination to deliver the bad news they wish to avoid. At a later doctor meeting at the hospice, we debate whether this makes us 'enablers and/or co-dependents.' The discussion gets a bit heated before Howard, the medical director I'd missed earlier, steps in, ending the discussion declaring. "It's what we do, it's what you signed up for. We do the work that no one else is willing to do, so let's get on with it."

Along with our rounds and patient care are 'didactics' AKA lectures. These include formal grand rounds for whole departments, as well as smaller lectures, discussions, and even role playing. A few days later, we are gathered in a conference room in the hospital basement. We are gathered for the small group palliative care education. Despite the "small group" designation, the table in room is jammed with students, fellows, faculty and residents. Howard rises from his end of the table. "There are two ways of learning, "Howard says with enthusiasm.

Warming to his pedagogical topic, he continues. "There is knowledge," Howard continues as he turns and walks around the table where we are clustered "which can be read from a book and with careful study; one can become an expert in a body of knowledge without ever being exposed directly to the subject matter." Howard slows and looks over his shoulder to make sure we are all taking notes. "The other way of learning is skill," he says as he turns a corner of the table and starts back up. "Skill," he continues, "must be practiced, it must be handled, processed and then repeated over and over before one becomes proficient."

Howard retakes the seat at the head of the table. His gaze sweeps the room trying to make eye contact. The room gets quiet, most of the residents and students study their hands in earnest, a successful skill many students pick up in medical school.

"We've been talking about critical conversations with patients" Howard continues. "We've talked about it, you've watched us do it, and now we're going to practice on each other."

I've been out of the game too long, my reflexes slow. I look up. I feel doom settle next to me, as Howard makes spots me, smiles and sidles over. Across the conference table from me is Ted. Ted had been faculty in Internal Medicine and helped out with the Palliative Care

Service. A week earlier Ted had been promoted to Chief Medical Officer for the University Hospital. Howard hands Ted and I each of us a piece of paper.

"Greg here, is going to tell Ted some devastating bad news." Howard consults his notes. He then reads the written narrative aloud. "Ted has seen Dr. Greg for abdominal pain. Earlier tests were inconclusive. Dr. Greg sent Ted for a CT scan of the abdomen. Ted is here about the results. "Gentlemen," Howard says, "please begin."

Ted swivels his chair to face me, a sunny smile on his face. "Hi Dr. Greg," he says sounding hopeful, "that stomach medication you gave me really helped. I'm sure the test results looked good too."

Ted is playing it straight; I glance down at my paper. It's all pretend, but suddenly it all feels real. Over thirty years of personal experiences when this has gone badly for me, suddenly crowd my mind. The piece of paper I hold in my hand says, "Ted has come back to you for his CT results. CT scan shows unequivocal evidence of a large pancreatic mass. It's almost certainly cancer. There's also evidence of metastasis to the liver." The report goes on to describe the masses and sizes and locations. If it was real, it means almost certain death.

I look at Ted. He looks at me expectantly. "So, what did the scan show?" he prompts.

My mouth goes dry. My mind races, there is an algorithm for sharing bad news. The multiple algorithms I've just begun to learn compete to crowd my thinking. Begin with introductions, set a calm time and place free from distractions, silence beepers and cell phones. Everyone is sitting down. The holder of bad news should be seated at a 45-90-degree angle from the recipient of the bad news and within reach of the person for a personal hand on the shoulder if necessary....

Ted is still sitting looking expectantly, smiling. I shift my chair slightly to the 45-degree mark. I am aware not only of Ted, but the rest of the room watching intently.

"Gee Ted, the test results were a bit... of a... surprise."

"A surprise," Ted responds, "but still okay, right?"

"Well Ted, I wish I had something better to say about this report, but it doesn't look good." I nearly flinch as I try to look him in the eye. "The report shows a mass in your pancreas."

Ted looks confused, troubled. "Pancreas, what's a pancreas? What kind of mass?"

Apparently, Ted's slip of paper says, "Go for the Oscar!"

Flustered, I try again, "It looks like there's cancer in this scan. It also shows that it has probably already spread to your liver."

Ted leaps to his feet. Clearly, it's Oscar time, the chair behind him hits the wall with a noisy thud. "Cancer???!!" he shouts, "Oh my God, are you sure?"

I gape. I can't look at Ted. I'm blank now. I stare harder at the piece of paper in my hand. "The report," I read, "says a mass in the head of the pancreas measuring 3.4 x 5.8 centimeters with adjacent lesions in the liver, most likely adenocarcin…."

"Bzzzzzt!! Whoa! time out!" Ted yells, doing the referees' signal. "You panicked dude," he says. A nervous titter echoes from the others at the table.

"This usually happens the first time," Howard explains, "You broke eye contact and started reading the report, you lapsed into jargon." Howard motions for Ted to retake his seat. "Now let's try it again. Ted?"

Ted retakes his seat. He feeds me his line…. Cancer, are you sure?" Ted looks at me intently, willing me to get it right.

A deep breath and sigh, I look him in the eye and say, "Yes Ted, I'm sure. I wish I had something better to say. In fact, it doesn't really look good right now." I wait for Ted's reaction. He simply stares at me.

"We'll run some additional tests to confirm the diagnosis," I explain. I think about putting my hand on his shoulder, but chicken out. I do manage to say, "We will be with you on this journey."

Howard calls time, and I slump back drained. The expressions from the residents and students suggest they all think they could have done better. At this point, I would have to agree.

Howard gives me a friendly pat on the shoulder, "First time is the toughest, thanks for volunteering." I nod, a little dejected, even I think I should have done better. Some discussion follows, and then residents, medical students, fellows and faculty all pick their way out of the crowded room.

It may be surprising, but medical students in palliative care are something of an oddity. The University has gotten a grant to begin teaching end of life care/palliative medicine and hospice to medical students with some exposure in each year. We are one of six medical schools to get this grant. Up until now, medical students have been getting the same one hour 'Death and Dying' talk derived from Dr. Elizabeth Kubler-Ross that I got way back in the 70's. It may seem astonishing but as I write this years later, hospice and palliative medicine is not a required topic at the majority of medical schools.

Now we have medical students on the floors. Three of them, new, fresh-faced and terrified. I find them in our nook in the hospital where we hang out awaiting consults. Entering the room, I make eye contact with two of the victims. "I'm Greg Phelps, the palliative care fellow," I start by way of introduction. "I assume you are our first students for the end of life care program?"

They nod silently. "Well, we have a patient who is dying, and you are going to sit with her. Have you ever heard of NODA?" The nods turn to head shakes. As eyes widen as they digest what I just said.

"NODA is no one dies alone." I want you to sit with the patient, hold her hand and keep her comfortable."

"But we haven't had any lectures or in-service, or anything…" they bleat.

"You are absolutely right; the problem is that she is dying now, not later, and I'll in-service you afterward." I resist sarcasm in the face of their terror. "Just pull up a chair, be calm, and be nice. This isn't a medical thing, but a human thing. I lead them into the room. The patient is barely conscious, not speaking, just moaning occasionally. I situate the students, one on each side and introduce them saying "Cynthia, this is Doug and Jon, they are medical students, they are here to keep you company for a while." I get the faintest of nods. I've probably scarred them for life, but they come back shortly to report the patient's death. They are subdued and thoughtful and thank me for the experience. We then in-service and debrief. It is clear they had never really thought of death as something real and tangible. For both it is their first patient to die.

A few days later, Polly the young melanoma patient, has been on the ventilator for a few days as we check in on her. The family asks for another family meeting with us. They've succumbed to what is obvious to us, but rarely to the family. After many tears and reminisces, they all agree that she would not want to be kept alive like this. The meeting is almost as hard on me as on them, as I have a daughter only a year or so younger. They ask when we can stop the ventilator.

One of the key parts for hospice and palliative medicine education is that I am required to document how many "ventilator withdrawals" I do as part of my training. This will be my first.

We arrange for the family to gather and have time with their daughter without us. Meanwhile, I dig out and review the protocol. The goal is to give the family time with the patient, administer enough medication that the patient is comfortable, but we do not shorten the patient's life with an overdose. Additional medicine needs to be immediately available if the patient shows signs of distress. The respiratory therapy tech is rounded up to deal with the endotracheal tube and ventilator. My attending is in a back corner of the room. This is my show. She's there to bail me out if it goes off the rails.

When the family finishes goodbyes, hugs and hand holding. They nod to me, we begin. First, we deliver the initial dose of medications, usually a small amount of morphine and a benzodiazepine such as Ativan IV. Next, the nurses disconnect the alarms and monitors. The respiratory therapist does the same with the ventilator. The goal is to have the family with the patient, not staring over her head at the tracings and O2 monitors but to be "present" with the patient.

After the medication has had time to take effect, the therapist uses a syringe and deflates the Endotracheal (ET) balloon that holds the tube in position in the trachea. Loosening the anchoring tape, she then slides the hose-like contraption out onto a waiting pad where the gooey tube is cleanly whisked away. I stay to watch for signs of distress. There are none this time. Breathing slows over a few minutes, then stops. There are a few muffled sobs, a last embrace and the family turns and gravely shakes my hand and thanks me for all I've done. I'm moist-eyed and thank them too.

The irony that they are thanking me when I just facilitated the comfortable demise of their daughter is at the top of my mind. Frankly, I'm grateful no one accused me of murdering their child. My attending, silent up to this point, gives me a quick nod as she exists. "Good job" she mouths as she leaves. Somehow, I don't feel like I did a good job. I wonder if it ever becomes routine and at the same time, I hope it never does. Concluding my work at the hospital, I blow off steam taking my bike on a six-mile ride. Four miles out, I blow a tire and walk back two miles. Perfect end to a miserable day.

The next days are spent trying to track down families of patients for conversations. Most families are desperate for information and time with the doctors. But some families simply can't face us. They avoid our calls and hang up when we identify ourselves. Nonetheless, it is my task to track them down.

It seems some families believe "as long as palliative care can't talk to us, nothing bad can happen. If we don't communicate, we can deny that death is approaching." I catch one small family walking out of the room of a dying patient and try to lead the group to a place where we can talk. To my surprise, they hastily shut down the conversation saying they are just now leaving town. They turn and speed walk stiffly down the hall. At loose ends now, I spend a short while quizzing the medical students on what they are learning. The students have become enthusiastic about what they are learning with us and wonder aloud why there's not more education on end of life since- "every patient dies at some point."

They have a point, current medical clinical curriculum mandates a minimum of 300 to 600 hours of everything from psychiatry, OB and pediatrics to medicine and surgery in the final two years of school although a psychiatrist may never gain deliver a baby professionally. However, ALL doctors will have patients with which they will confront death. We all hope for cures but in the end the death rate remains 100%.

There is still some of the afternoon left. I remind myself that I need a life outside of medicine as well. "Work/Life balance" is a mantra I hear with our younger faculty. I walk a few blocks down to the River City main library and request a library card and get my bicycle tire fixed. I still have some time, so I head to the Y for a workout.

I'm learning that the Y is a mix of two classes. First are the yuppies from the downtown, gentrifying apartments. The second group includes more 'urban' toughs, one grade above street toughs. Somehow, we make an occasionally uneasy group.

I'm working my rounds on the weights. Down the row, a huge young man drops his weights loudly and announces loudly he can "beat any mother f*#ker in here." This must have happened before because surprised, I'm the only one who looks up, he glares at me. I smile, unthreateningly, and nod, and by doing so, I confirm his status. Placated he goes back to his weights.

July is ending, our chairperson spends a few minutes reviewing the month with me. The results are positive. She tells me the nurses are still talking about the palliative care doc who helped change a patient's bed. I continue to find it a little embarrassing that treating the nurses kindly is that big a deal.

The new month of August starts hot, too hot. I'm already sweating through my white coat from the three blocks walk to the medical center. Only a day or so in, I'm asked to have a goals of care (GOC) discussion with a new family. The GOC is similar to communicating bad news and sometimes contains the discussion about end of life but is often broader, focusing on what is important to the patient- 'what matters most.'. The protocol varies depending on the circumstances. These are living, continuing discussions with different people, so sometimes the conversational string can be calm and straight forward, threading the needle with ease. However, that same conversational thread can easily get twisted up in a wooly knot in a heartbeat! There are a variety of guidelines and plans for clinicians to facilitate this conversation that I briefly alluded to in my earlier practice attempt.

One guideline written in 2000 by Dr. Walter Bailes and company is called SPIKES. This acronym stands for: Setting, Perceptions, Information, Knowledge, Emotions and Summarizing. We learn a variety of other schemas range in detail from sparse suggestions to excruciatingly picky detail. Vitaltalk.org is an institute devoted to teaching communication skills to professionals. Pulitzer Prize winning journalist Ellen Goodman also has a website called www.theconversationproject .org for families having these conversations.

Now with the benefit now of over ten years' experience, let me show how I teach medical students, residents and other physicians, goals of care and end of life discussions. While I tend to follow this outline numbered 1-10, I tend to pepper my educational talks with some of these anecdotes to help make the points memorable.

1. Awareness- know the patient and clinical setting as best you can. Don't limit yourself to just clinical specifics. Keep watch for any family dynamics you can get out of the nurses, or others on the floor. The family dynamics may include loving family, disgruntled heirs, dutiful children or estranged children. Keep an eye out for both the decision maker and particularly, the troublemaker. A typical case. 'Sis' has dutifully cared for widowed Dad since his wife died ten years ago. He is now over eighty and has struggled for years with emphysema, and in this hospitalization has been diagnosed with stage IV (the worst) lung cancer.

Palliative care is being called in to talk about the end. Sis calls her brother, well let's call him 'Bubba'' and says, "Dad is dying, they've called in the palliative care people to come to talk with us tomorrow about the end." (Sis is a sharp cookie!) Bubba who has twenty years of unresolved differences to deliver, hops the red eye flight arriving just in time to make everyone's life miserable. Bubba is formally known in hospice literature as the 'dreaded child from California.' I've personally had two families involved in fistfights at this decision point in the clinical care. I've been threatened with lawsuits and worse. One family, refugees from the Balkans placed a huge hunting knife, almost a sword, on the coffee table between us in their home. They described their beloved patriarch we'd come to talk about, interspersed with comments about violence they had been involved with in fighting in the Balkan wars!

2. Semiotics- Paying attention to the setting and the non-verbal language. "What I do, says so much more than what I say." Studies show 70% of communication is non-verbal. So, we are intentional about all our communication. We make an appointment to talk with the patient and family-This is not a drive-by 'diagnosis bombing', followed by a quick getaway. When we make an appointment, we set aside a conference room if possible, mute beepers, and cell phones. We all SIT DOWN! Studies have shown that a patient's estimate of how long the doctor spent doubles if the physician just sits. The lead doctor should sit close to the decision maker, preferably within arm's reach, at a 45-degree angle. The angle and distance deter us from staring at them the entire time, but arms reach allows for a pat on the shoulder or arm if needed. Tissues are available discreetly at the side

3. Introductions- Begin with introductions, each of the participants, who we are, and what we are responsible for. Amazingly, a New York Times article, telling entitled "Doctor, Please Shut Up," detailed that fewer than 25 % of physicians introduce themselves. In these days of hospitalists and specialists, even fewer patients know who their doctor is. Make sure the other doctors and specialists attending the meeting are prepared as to the nature of the conversation. Once when I failed to do this, the specialist,

 clearly irritated and in a hurry, at the end of introductions blurted out- "I don't know why we have all this rigamarole, you mom has end-stage cancer and these new docs are taking over to keep her comfortable until she dies." Then he stood up and left, leaving everyone shocked.

4. Format-is "Ask, tell, ask." Encourage families to talk. Most families grade the success of the GOC discussion not by how much the doc talked but how well they feel they communicated about the patient. This was a bit of a jolt to me. As a family practice resident many years ago, I was given clear and detailed instructions on how to limit, guide and minimize patient discussion to "just the facts ma'am."

For most doctors, the hard part is to be quiet. After inviting the family to "Tell me about the patient," studies show the average doctor will interrupt within 16 -19 seconds. We ask what the patient/ family knows about the illness. Their responses give us a starting point for imparting information. Often the results would be comical if not inherently tragic. I had one patient's daughter promptly exclaim, "They say dad has a neoplasm (tumor) in his thorax (chest) but thank God he didn't have lung cancer!" I was so surprised, that I blurted out, "but that IS lung cancer."

Often the family dutifully memorizes the formal name, the jargon of the illness or disease, but with no idea what it entails. Studies show more than half the US population is functionally, medically illiterate. This lack of knowledge compounds the patient and family's stress. I see nurses and medical students struggle with unfamiliar, polysyllabic medical phrases. So, my heart goes out to the many patients who try to master the terms for what afflicts their loved one. I remember one dutiful daughter who painfully enunciated, tongue to the side, eyes staring at the back of her left sinus, "they say he has Addd... Deeno carcinoma of the Pan... creatic head."

To which I gently replied, "What does that mean to you?" She shook her head in despair, "that's what they say he's got." Generally, words of three or more syllables will not stick. If it's cancer, we have to say cancer and not hide behind neoplasm or adenocarcinoma and similar jargon. Studies show that people have more difficulty understanding bad news than good. We need to be able to help them hear

5. Warn- firing a warning shot. In this step I use a 'wish' statement, as in 'I wish we didn't have to have this conversation. I wish things had turned out differently.' The subtext here is- Pay attention, I'm about to ruin your life. Simultaneously, the statement shows empathy. 'I know what I'm about to say is terrible, and I wish I didn't have to say it.'

6. Explain- Deliver the diagnosis. If the patient is dying, say so and be explicit and avoid medical jargon. This is really HARD. We doctors are human. The patient and family don't want to hear it. We don't want to say it, and often won't. Once we deliver the dreaded news, it is hard to stop. The tendency at this point is to speed up, gloss over and make plans for more tests and specialists. God forbid we give the patient and or family a chance to cry or get angry

7. Validate-(emotions) Let the family react, express their emotions be it tears or rage or resignation. Some will threaten malpractice suits or worse. I've learned to take the heat and redirect it. My response is to say "I can see you're angry, this is a big shock. If you need to sue, you can do that later. But today, right now, we need to know what care your dad would want to have. Do we need to take a break and get a drink in the cafeteria and reconvene? By validating and normalizing the family's emotions we're able to empathize with their feelings and help them begin to come to grips with the shock of the diagnosis and prognosis. Studies show bad news is often not well heard, so it may need to be said again, and again.

8. Plans- Does the patient have a life care plan? Are then any potential strategies for circumstances like this? Is there a living will or advanced care plan? If I'm talking to the family, I'm looking for what ethicists call 'substituted judgment.' I'm looking for what the patient would want, not the family. No child (Well, almost none) wants his or her parent to be "allowed to die" But the same parent, may be sick and tired of being sick and tired. I'll say, "I know you want your mom to live forever, but if she could hear us talking and leaned over your shoulder, what would she be saying?" When a family member is hammering the table and saying, "We want this for our dad," I have to bring him (usually him) back to the reality of the patient's wishes asking - "but what does he want?"

I often recommend the book Nudge by Thaler and Sunstein, to health care providers and ethicists. It is about choice architecture. While it is nominally about economics, it fits well into medical decision making. (After I 'd been recommending it for several years, Richard Thaler won a Nobel Prize for their insights.) If a patient comes into the emergency room with end-stage cancer at 4 am, the harried hospitalist will perfunctorily ask, "If your heart stops while you're in here, you want us to re-start it, right? "The most common response would be 'hell yes!'

A more thoughtful approach is reviewing the clinical history and prognosis and asking, "in the face of this likely fatal cancer, if the time comes, would you like us to allow a natural and peaceful passing?" Surprisingly, when the question is re-worded and given more thought, the answer is again, likely to be yes. Sadly, too often these desperately ill patients have gotten close to death without anyone telling them the likely outcome. A 2008 study in the Journal of the American Medical Association in showed only about a third of oncologists had discussed the care terminally ill patients would want in their final months. "So, let me get this straight" an angry hospitalist told me one time. "This patient has been seeing their specialist for two years, all the while they are slowly dying. The specialist NEVER told the patient their illness is fatal and they're dying. Suddenly, it's two am, the patient comes in crisis and you want ME to tell them? Good luck with that." More recent follow up studies to the 2008 article find little to minimal progress in promoting those discussions.

9. Cardiopulmonary Resuscitation (CPR) Getting to the facts. Most families, at least initially, want CPR even in the face of terminal illness. Often their preferences are based on what they've seen on television. The trouble is the media is not even remotely close to reality. A New England Journal of Medicine article documented watching hundreds of hours of TV and found the success rate for CPR was 65-100%This rate of success for CPR makes sense, of course, to drive the plot. If 'beautiful, but estranged Taylor' is electrocuted in a bizarre accident and the CPR is not successful, she won't be seen joyfully reunited with her one and only! Failure of CPR then leaves the directors with a lot of show time to fill! (Note this never seemed to be a problem in Game of Thrones!!)

Actually success rates for CPR is a lot less impressive than on TV. Most studies show out of hospital CPR about 10% successful and in-hospital CPR under 20%. In the cases of success, close to half the survivors have significant brain injury or other injuries that may later confine them to nursing homes. Likelihood of survival diminishes further with the patients with multi-organ failure or end-stage metastatic cancer often to a survival rate of zero to three percent. And then as I point out to patients, "they still have the cancer/heart failure/emphysema and will have to die again."

CPR is an often an exceedingly brutal exercise in futility in end-stage patients.

Early on in my fellowship, I had a family insist on CPR for their 87-year-old stick thin mother with end-stage Alzheimer's disease. Her bent over spine emphasized her osteoporotically fragile bones which look likely fracture in a hearty breeze. Had I been perhaps, further in the fellowship I might have posed a compassionate and insightful, open ended question such as- "tell me a little about how you see CPR playing out for your mother."

But no, incredulous and insensitive I blurted "Do you know what you are asking me to do to your mother!?"

"Well yeah, we see it on TV all the time."

"What you see on TV has almost no relationship to what actually happens. For a little old lady like your momma, it is close to torture. I'll give you a scenario. Image they call a Code 99 on your mother right now. I race into her room and establish she is in cardiac arrest. I jump up on the bed…" I pause here looking down at my paunch, "Well I'm kind of chubby, so I climb up on the bed, straddle you mother, link my hands together (I demonstrate) and start doing compressions. On TV, it looks like a mildly vigorous massage. In real life, I have to 'mash' her heart between her breastbone and her backbone to pump the blood out. It takes a lot of force, and about a third of people can get broken ribs."

My voice gets a harsher edge, "I've seen your momma, and I know my size. I would break her ribs with CPR. Then as I continue CPR, I'll feel her ribs crunching under my hands." My attending, yet another a youngish woman only several years out of training herself, gets a slightly alarmed expression on her face.

I continue- "As soon as someone else comes in, I'll pass compressions off to them, so I can place a breathing tube down her throat. Have you ever put your finger down your throat?" I ask rhetorically. "Makes you gag and gasp and want to vomit. It can do the same to the patient, so we blow up a balloon to hold the tube in place and protect the airway and breathe for the patient.

The alarmed look on my attending's face is getting a little more pronounced as I glance at her and momentarily hesitate, but now I'm in full on 'education' mode. Retrospectively, I think she was morbidly curious as to just how far and how graphic my description of CPR would go.

"Meanwhile, "I continue, "The nurses have started IV line to give medications and then if we can, we try to shock the rhythm back to life. Now on TV, they say 'clear.' There's a buzzing sound, and we go to the next scene for the reunion of the patient and family. In real life, it is like being electrocuted. It is not a buzz but a bang. Anyone touching the patient or bed will be knocked to the floor.

"Now the first jolt usually doesn't do it," I continue, "so we double the voltage and we do it again; then if we need to, we double the voltage and do it yet again." I've already told you only one to three people in a hundred like your mother will respond. For most end-stage patient's it is a painful way to die." I take a deep breath and survey the family and conclude theatrically- "NOW is that what you want me to do to your momma, or when the time comes shall we let her go peacefully? The family opts for peaceful.

The attending and I leave the room and start down the hallway. We get just out of earshot when she pulls me up short. "Wow," she says shaking her head as if to try clear hearers of what she just heard." That was the single most graphic description of CPR I have ever heard... Do you think you can tone that down a bit? I appreciate your candor and don't deny the reality of what you said but still... Even I feel queasy after that."

I shrug, "I wanted them to know what they were asking for."

"Just the same," her tone stiffening, "dial it down a few notches. OK?"

I assent somewhat stiffly, "you're the boss."

10. Summarize: Record the Meeting; put all this on paper. Who was there, what was talked about, what decisions were made, how were any goals, plans or wishes noted? This is vital when the dreaded child from California arrives that night and knows nothing of the conversation.

It took the full year of practice and then some to be able to navigate this this ten-stage mine field comfortably. In the meantime, back in River City, it is with this paradigm, studied but still hazy in my head, that I go to meet with the next family.

Lawrence, "not Larry!" is an elderly gentleman, in his 80's. He has suffered a sudden, massive, catastrophic bleed in his head. He's been on a ventilator for several days with zero improvement. Atypically, the family, not the treating team, has asked for a meeting with the doctors. The neurosurgeons think the palliative care team is the best set of candidates.

I set up a meeting for an hour or so later with the daughter whose sitting vigil by her father. She doesn't want to talk until the whole family is collected so I just sit with her as we wait for her family and my team to gather.

The smallish conference room is designed for six, but it is packed. Lawrence is clearly a popular and well-loved man, the seats are filled, and the walls lined with several daughters, one son, a niece and nephew, several friends. There is also me, Lawrence's nurse, and a resident crammed into the room. Lawrence's wife of 61 years died just a year or so ago. The neurosurgeons have briefed me but begged off claiming 'too busy.'

We begin with introductions and purpose, "tell me a little about your dad," I encourage the daughter who was earlier sitting vigil with me and is apparently in charge. She has clearly given this some thought.

She begins with a clear and firm affirmation. "Dad is a pilot. He flew in, Korea and Vietnam and then for a commercial airline." He loved to fly… he lived to fly." She pauses, swallows, trying to hold it in. "A little over a month ago, he developed a heart arrhythmia and was put on a blood thinner. He'd been flying the week before. 'Can't fly with atrial fibrillation,' they said. It is the arrhythmia that killed him when they grounded him. This bleed in his head is him giving up." Her relatives nod in agreement. She takes a deep, calming breath and continues," Dad would never want to be like this. He'd be appalled to see himself now. We believe he would want to be off the ventilator and allowed to die; that is what all of us we want for him. He lived fully, fought in two wars and never feared death. Can we stop the machine…? now, and let him go?" Having completed what she needs to say, she ends with a sob and tears begin to flow

Wow, in a few well-chosen words, she covered most of the necessary paradigm and impressively honored her father! Not for the first and certainly not the last time, I find myself wishing I could have met my patient before his final days. All eyes are on me. I mentally adjust. The neurosurgeons had lost interest when surgery became impractical, they were fine with de-escalating treatment, turning off the ventilator and allowing the patient to die.

After a moment's pause, I agree to withdraw the ventilator. The family seems a little surprised by my quick assent. I think each of us had thought we'd need to convince the other of the necessity of allowing this death, but they rally. Together we plan for them to contact remaining family to come to the hospital to ensure everyone who needs to, can say goodbye.

We agree to meet in the ICU in 45 minutes

Again, we get the respiratory therapist, silence machines, monitors and alarms. We give the comfort medications, with a daughter on each side holding his hands. We turn off the ventilator. Nothing. Not a sigh, not a gasp. After a minute, the daughters turn and gravely thank me. Wiping tears, the family files out.

However, more frequently, these conversations don't go so smoothly, and the result is not so peaceful. The matriarch of another family has terminal liver disease. While her organs were failing one by one, her labs continued to deteriorate, and her eating consisted of pushing food around the plate, she would nevertheless bravely say "I'm feeling a little better today." She is bright yellow with her jaundice and her cheekbones are jutting out, she is visibly wasting away. She presents a stark contrast to the robust woman portrayed in a family photo on the stand beside the hospital bed.

Our team meet with the extended family of sons, daughter, and cousins to try to explain the severity of her illness. We needed to work on plans for end of life. Her family appears willing to listen, but our words seem to slide right off them. The next day we meet again. Her people are farmers from the country and while polite, they just do not seem to want to understand. I try different terms and phrases; round and round we went. The family continuing to smile and nod in the face of the grim news I'm saying. When I ask them to tell me back what they are hearing from me about how Mama is doing, they seemingly ignore my words and revert to; "Oh she'll be fine, she said so."

After an hour, I give up and suggest we meet again in a day or so for an update. The family thanks us for our time and files out of the room talking amongst themselves. We watched them as they dwindle down the hall, as we still sit in the conference room. Just before stepping on the elevator I hear the eldest son say: "That Dr. Phelps feller is a really nice doctor. If Mama ever got seriously sick, I'd want him to take care of her." I stare out the door at the closing elevator door.

"Okaaaay," I note sardonically to the residents and students, "clearly not the sharpest tools in the shed." Another resident counters with, "maybe a few fries short of a Happy Meal." We grin and leave the conference room. Little do I realize that with those few words, the seeds of a year's worth of trouble for me have been planted.

I head back to Knoxville for the weekend. Originally, the fellowship was supposed to have a weekend call obligation about once every four to six weeks, but the faculty feel sorry for me with my wife steadfastly planted in Knoxville. I end up rarely taking a weekend call. I drive the several hours back over the mountain to Knoxville, arriving at nine in the evening. Gayle is done with dinner and sitting in the kitchen reading the paper. The dogs are jumping around my feet in delirious joy. Gayle glances up, then back at her paper.

"I'm home" I cheerily and unnecessarily announce.

Gayle snorts dismissively. "So, I see" and goes back to her paper. She is still livid about my taking this fellowship. Coming home to a disgruntled and irate wife is to be the pattern to repeated for the next eleven months. Even when the fellowship is over, it takes her a year to get over her anger.

Beverly is the other fellow in our year-long program. Several undescribed mishaps delayed her completing her residency, and she is starting the fellowship program a month late. We've been exchanging emails for over a month. She tells me she plans to rent an apartment out in the countryside near the VA. Her husband is going to stay in Washington state, and she wants a place outside of town where she can think and paint. So, at the end of July I hear a cheery voice on the phone, "Hey Greg, didn't you say you could see the YMCA from your apartment?"

"Yes, I can." I answer, leaning towards my window to verify the truth.

"Great! I can too. We must be near each other." I'm surprised by her location, decidedly not the distant countryside, and we quickly make arrangements to meet on the patio of a nearby bar.

I'm telling my daughter Tiffany about the encounter, while home the following weekend, admitting I was a little nervous to meet Beverly in the flesh

"Oh," Tiffany asks, "why is that?"

"Well, you know your mom has been mad at me for months now. Beverly is leaving her husband in Washington state and moving to Louisville. Turns out she's in the apartment building next door. We'll be together...a lot. Things could get...messy?"

Tiffany stares at me and bursts out laughing," Dad, you and mom have been married over thirty years. You've never cheated, I'd know. Mom would know. "

Now I'm suddenly, slightly affronted. "How do you know I've never cheated? Your old man could still have a secret or two.

Tiffany laughs again. "Dad, you are the most honest person I know. You couldn't keep a secret like that for more than about ten minutes. It'd be all over your face." (This is true, when I was chief medical officer for a hospital system, I once had a Joint Commission physician surveyor tell me how much he enjoyed inspecting my hospitals with me. Said he, "If I ask a question you don't want to answer, you turn red, stutter, sputter, then give me an honest answer you really didn't want to give. My advice to you is- never to play poker.") Still, my pride is wounded a little.

Tiffany prompts me, "Well what were you hoping for when you met?"

"Me? "I'm hoping that she's stone cold ugly and when I see her coming, I can say 'Oh thank God,' any hint of temptation avoided." I continue the story. "I get there first, I'm out on the patio nursing a beer, when she comes around the corner…"

"Well? Then what?" Tiffany prompts again. I smile, "Beverly had described herself as tall with long red hair. She comes around the corner and I wave her over. As she walked over, sizing me up, I'm pretty sure I heard her mumble "Oh thank God." Tiffany stares a moment, and bursts out laughing.

Like most of us in Hospice and Palliative Medicine we have a story as to how we came to this calling. Bev's was particularly poignant. Bev had been a factory worker and rafting guide when a child of hers was killed. She spent a lot of time with a grief counsellor recovering. Coming out of the grief process she discovered her purpose in life which was to help people like she had been helped. This required going to college which she did with a goal of becoming a grief counsellor. To her surprise she blew through college and decided to press on to go to medical school and then become a family doctor. Then she worried she'd wandered from her original goal. Then in what she called a 'BFO-blinding flash of the obvious' She decided to spend one more year coming full circle by doing hospice and palliative care.

Back in River City after the weekend, I begin to fret about my spiritual life because weekends are now almost exclusively with family, and I've been missing church which has been a large part of my adult life.

I was active in the Episcopal church as a teen. Like most college students I drifted away. Only when our first child, Tiffany came along did I come back to the Episcopal church, mainly to get her baptized. Then I never left again. I've done everything in the church from lay reader to senior warden, even starting a daycare center at the rural church where I first practiced. I find myself missing the church fellowship and prayers. As I traverse a variety of routes to the medical center, I discover the Episcopal Cathedral only a few blocks from my apartment. I also find they offer a Wednesday seven am service.

I arrive the first morning in August to find a small group of homeless people asleep in the garden fronting the church door. I pick my way around the inert sleeping bags and into a small side chapel just off the nave. Five other communicants look up curiously and smile a welcome as I sit behind them. It is an intimate service. Rotating priests serve these Wednesday Eucharists.

Today's clergy has a unique ministry which consists of riding up and down the Ohio river on tugs and barges delivering spiritual care to transient sailors. He devotes his homily to describing the ride, his ministry and the sailors' loneliness on the river. The six of us take communion standing in a circle passing the bread and chalice. Revived and at peace, I complete the two-block trek to the medical center.

We are all working to help orient Beverly. I'm a little jealous that she missed the extensive and mind-numbing orientation I got. Still, there's a good amount of catching up for her to do, and I feel a bit protective for her. We both spend August at the University Center.

There are a variety of conferences that we are either required or encouraged to attend depending on specialty and topic. The Grand Rounds, the biggest are open to all and are usually sponsored by a department. Then there are specific topic presentations for our palliative care department and then general discussion rounds for the team. Next there are cross discipline topics such as the ethics committee, cancer committee and finally, off site conferences. After a grand round on Elder Abuse in early August, Bev and I join the palliative care faculty at a two-day conference at the VA in a neighboring city. I spend our downtime with Bev, continuing to give her the low down on the program. It helps that we are spending the rest of the month on the same service. Among other things, she soon learns of our team's regular frustration of being called only when it is painfully obvious that that the patient's end is nigh.

As death gets closer, it becomes increasingly obvious. Then death becomes a self-fulfilling prophesy. If we only get called in the final hours and days, we somehow seem to carry the blame for the patient's death! Again, and again this delay deprives the patient and family of the supremely important opportunity to plan, to share and to address the existential and family and relationship questions we'd all like to devote ourselves to in our last weeks and months. Instead, we can often only intervene in the final hours or days. It is never enough.

At the end of the month, our team examines a patient dying of lung cancer. The end is coming quickly. It looks like maybe a day at the outside, maybe less. The medical resident from the team that consulted us shows up late. In the crowded nurse's station, he gets the Reader's Digest version of the consult. He asks for the bottom line- 'how long'. Aware of the numerous people around me, I make a frustrated shrug and make a discreet circling motion with my finger as my hand falls to imply the patient is 'circling the drain' and death is imminent. I accompany the gesture with a *sotto voce*, "Hours."

His face clouds a moment, then he thanks me and rushes off. We're all in a hurry. Our team heads on to the next consult. Again, I wish we got called a little earlier. Our mantra as the fellowship continues would become: 'it is always too early, until it is too late!' At the very minimum, get the patient comfortable and pain controlled.

Speaking of pain, it will likely surprise non-medical people that physician education places minimal emphasis on pain and pain management. Medical students get a few lectures in pharmacology in the second year of medical school. These lectures involve dense diagrams of molecular structures and side effects. But the patient in pain? Who gets what and why, and why not? Almost never. Instead, it's pain diagrams and C un-myelinated neuro fibers. The most common exposure to the use of pain medications was during residency by watching people who cause pain- surgeons.

Surgeons, when I was in training, were most commonly using Demerol and hydrocodone for acute surgical pain. So, it was often 'monkey see, monkey do.' The problem is family doctors and others are often dealing with other kinds of pain, usually non-surgical, chronic pain. It hasn't been until the ongoing crisis in prescription medication abuse- AKA- the opioid crisis, and rising overdoses that the profession began to focus on pain medications. Even then, it is often only to demonize opioids.

Society's approach to pain prescribing is analogous to paddling a canoe. We paddle a little on the right, then a little on the left. When I graduated from residency in 1982, pain was something you put up with. People wanted chronic pain meds, but they weren't often prescribed. People wanting pain meds were "losers," "addicts." Nancy Reagan was pushing "Just say 'NO". Then the pendulum began to swing back with Bergman v Chin, a famous malpractice case where a physician allowed a dying patient to suffer ten out of ten pain for three weeks before finally expiring. The settlement was well over a million dollars. This case and others like it helped sparked a backlash about not treating pain. This counter movement was assisted by generous funds from pharmaceutical companies that were providing subsidies to speakers and groups to help get the word out. Eventually the health care certifying agency- The Joint Commission joined in promoting a program - "Pain as the Fifth Vital Sign," urging patients to try to quantify their pain from 0 to 10.

Oxycontin was heavily promoted as a non-addictive and safe medication. (Purdue Pharma producing Oxycontin as widely reported paid an unprecedented fine of $634 million for that whopper. This case is still reverberating today in state lawsuits and family accusations.) In response to the lawsuits and growing opioid crisis, regulators are now paddling on the right side of the canoe. As prescriptions for pain meds went up, unsurprisingly, the number of overdoses pretty much paralleled it. Even now however, as prescriptions are falling in number, overdoses continue to rise, and patients return to un-regulated street drugs.

My personal introduction to the concept of palliative care came many years ago by way of a surgeon. This was way before I had any experience in pain or palliative medicine. I did however have a certification in addiction medicine and had moved from Chester to Georgia to teach Family Medicine. I also started an occupational medicine clinic, and when word reached me that the hospital was getting ready to close their recovery center for lack of a medical director, I volunteered.

Dr. John Arthur was central casting's Southern Surgeon. He was tall, autocratic and proud of his profession and his role in it. He stood ramrod rod straight, with a shock of white hair combed straight back. He drove a huge, bright red (Georgia colors) Cadillac with a double pun license: "Sir John," that played off his self-reported English aristocratic pedigree. He also lived up to the primary care doctor's joke: You can always tell a surgeon…just not much." Doctors in our department tended to avoid him due to his well-known temper. I didn't think he even knew who I was, until he called me one day. I also don't know how he found out I had some expertise in addiction medicine.

All I know is my pager calls me to a floor of the hospital, and Dr. Arthur answers the phone. "Phelps" he begins brusquely, "I got Billy, an addict up here, always driving me crazy for more drugs. I want you to do something." I take down the pertinent name and room number and after a few more patients amble off to the surgical floor. I introduce myself to the nurse at the nurses' station, and what I am there for. Her face tightens a little, and she says she'd be glad for my help. She hands over a very thick chart in its blue plastic binder, and I sit down to read the story of Billy Soames. Billy is 52, a smoker but no history I could see suggesting alcohol abuse or addictions. (Keeping in mind most physicians don't ask effectively, and the patients almost never volunteer this information.) What Billy does have are two separate cancers and lots of surgical procedures. The first cancer is in his kidney and has now extended into his back. The other, a usually benign 'basal' cell skin cancer that Billy has ignored for years until it has eaten into his sinuses.

I go in the room to interview Billy. The room is dark, and there's only a smallish hump in the bed that moans. I turned the lights on and tell Billy I am there to talk about his pain medication. That gets him out from under the covers. My face must have shown my surprise. A good part of his eyebrow and forehead has been eaten away, and a reddish drainage seeps through the bandage that is sloughing off the wound. I do a medical history, and physical and then concentrate on the history of drugs and alcohol use, using some addiction screening tools. Nothing. Nada. I couldn't find any evidence that Billy has been abusing drugs. Then we talk about his pain… which was severe. "Ten of Ten-all the time." Finally, back at the chart, I review his hospital consumption of Demerol a common pain medicine. He is asking a lot but getting very little. He's getting Demerol a low dose, maybe 25 or 50 mg, ordered only as needed every 6 hours. Although not highly educated on Demerol pharmacology, I know that the medication wears off in about 3-4 hours. So, he is having two to three hours with essentially no pain medicine in him! I also know that after weeks he'll develop some tolerance to any opioid. This doesn't mean addiction; it just means it'll take more as time and the condition progresses. Finally, I know the doses I'd use would be closer to 100 mg.

From my addiction training, I am familiar with a condition called 'pseudo-addiction' in which people act like addicts due to untreated pain. I am pretty sure what's going on, so I write for INCREASES in his medication, both in frequency and strength to reflect this. Then I ask the nurse to give an extra dose... now. Her look should have told me I was entering dangerous waters. But as I watched Billy get the extra higher dose, I saw him sigh and melt into the bed. "Thanks, doc. This is the first time I haven't hurt in three months."

I then write what I think is lengthy and erudite note about the confusion with pseudo addiction and how to continue to effectively treat his pain. Twenty minutes later I get a page back to the floor. Thinking the staff had a question, I quickly dial back, and get an enraged Dr. Arthur. "GODDAMMIT!" he roars, I swear I could feel the hair on my head blown back by the blast, even through the phone. "I asked you for help with a junkie, and you gave him MORE F*#KING DRUGS! I had to come back here and cancel all the crap you wrote! "Don't you ever see any more of my patients! "I promise him I would be happy not to see any more. Billy, I hear later died…

in pain a few weeks later. Dr. Arthur glared at me for years later whenever he saw me in the hall. In retrospect, I should have done a better job of communicating. My only excuse is that as a family doctor I was much more comfortable asking for consults than giving one. I answered his request, treating him as I would have wanted to be treated. I should have called Dr. Arthur and spoken with him before making changes. Maybe it would have gone better. Somehow, though, I doubt it.

It is with that incident in the background that I begin treating pain during my Fellowship. We have an outpatient clinic at the VA one afternoon a week. We have the lectures; we understand how to convert from one pain medicine to another. The algorithms call for 25/50/100% increases based on both the amount of long-acting pain medication the patient takes, as well as how many doses of short-acting pain medications he takes. Then, we we're told to factor in the reported level pain. It was with all this in mind that I met John, a grizzled Vietnam veteran at the clinic. He had metastatic lung cancer and was miserable." Doc," he said" I don't know if I can hang on like this. ´ He was taking 30 mg of long-acting morphine known as MS Contin twice a day. He also had ten mg of liquid morphine he could take every four hours, and he had taken all six doses available to him in 24 hours. He reports his pain is a ten out of ten He looks like it, misery written large.

I do the calculations carefully. One of our faculty members recently told of how she'd been interrupted once writing the prescription. When she resumed, she used the already multiplied amount as the baseline and overdosed the patient. So, I did the calculations extra carefully; then I did them again. Then I did them again on paper.... with a calculator. According to the algorithms, being conservative, his long-acting pain medicine would jump from 30 mg twice a day to 60 mg three times a day. His breakthrough medication would jump from 10 to 15 mg every four hours. It was late in the day and no one to review my math.

I wrote a prescription and crossed my fingers. I have to admit I was worried. I stayed awake all night concerned that I might have caused harm. I literally stared at the ceiling a large part of the night. The following morning, I couldn't stand it. I was still at River City

University Hospital. But I took a break at lunch and swung by the VA early. Arriving at the VA, I scooted up to an empty computer terminal and pulled up his records.

There was his phone number. With some trepidation I call John at home. He answers on the second ring, when I asked for him by name, he says, "yeah, speaking." I can feel the tight spot I've nurtured all night slacken with relief. Whew, I thought, he's still up and talking. I'm elated, almost giddy that I didn't harm him. But we're not done. I introduce myself and say I am just calling to see if the medication changes helped. "Doc," he enthuses warmly. "This is the first time in six months I didn't wake up groaning in pain. I can't thank you enough. This makes my life worth living." I relax a little, the algorithms work, the patient is better.

Back at University Hospital an interesting problem arose for one of our own staff. A resident from the Middle East is trying to get his mother home. She was diagnosed with colon cancer in Egypt. Her son, an international medical graduate, is doing his residency here in River City Hospital. He persuaded her to come to the US for treatment. Unfortunately, some things can't be stopped, and she is declining towards death.

Palliative care is summoned to officially inform the patient, medical resident and family of the bad news. A decision is made quickly to fulfill the desire for patient and family to return home for the end. The palliative care team is further pressed into duty to see if we can keep her comfortable on the trip. We also help to prep for what happens if she declines or even died on the journey home. Carrying controlled substances through several countries is a challenge in and of itself. Our social worker researches the regulations and has us writing notes to go with the bottles. The patient and family know she could die on the way and all are ready to take the chance. It is a full team effort! The flight from River City will have one US stop in Chicago, before the jump to the Middle East. A new question arises: what happens if she collapses before the international flight?

Fortunately, I have an old faculty colleague Bob in Chicago. I look him up and give him a call. "Greg," his voice booms out followed by a few affectionate obscenities. After some catching up, questions and comments; he agrees to quarterback problems in Chicago…. should they arise. With all our notes, the chart and Bob's phone number, they are off. I hear some month's later that mom made it to Egypt and died a few weeks later, comfortably. For our team that counts as a roaring success.

I've been in River City for six weeks. Gayle is coming up to visit for the first time since I arrived. We set out across the state on a bourbon tour visiting a variety of distilleries. Each distillery has a similar patter about how once the grains and mash are lovingly distilled, the leftover mash is fed to the cows and other livestock. Each distillery insists they have the happiest cows in the country. Back home, we go out on the town for dinner, then Gayle heads back to Knoxville, as I set out to the YMCA to play catch up on my exercise and work off the previous night's barbeque.

Monday, we are slammed with consults at University Center. Lung cancer, stokes, more cancer. Our rounding group looks a little ragged as we trudge from floor to floor. At times we peel off one or two members, usually, the psychologist or chaplain, who are needed to spend more time with the patient's and their families. A practice referred to internally as "Who do we throw under the bus so we can keep up with the volume of consults. My turn comes as I'm left to work with the steadfast daughter of a lung cancer patient. She tells me the rest of the family are coming in later for a family meeting and don't understand the gravity of her dad's condition, so we spend a short while in a quiet conference room war gaming the best way to present information and deal with the blowback. She declines my offer to help with the discussion. When we finish, I emerge, page the group to catch up with them. The grind continues another few more hours.

That evening Bev and I get together for our once a week dinner and beer. We find we've both wanted to learn Spanish and that the university discounts classes for residents and fellows, so we plan to sign up. (I told you I'm a compulsive student!) A few days later we watch together as Barak Obama gives his acceptance speech for the Democratic nomination. Bev and I discover we are both closet liberals. In a rural southern state, we don't heavily advertise that fact. Bev and I also get word that as palliative care fellows we are being drafted to the hospital ethics committee. I'm delighted, Bev, not so much. I pleased because I have spent years at my last job chairing and co-chairing ethics committees. The Catholic sister at St. Mary's had sent me to St. Louis University for a week to learn ethics some years ago. It was not a part of my position I'd anticipated.

I was new at my job as medical director for the hospital when Sister Elizabeth (her real name) came to tell me she was signing me up for ethics training. I asked why. After all one might wonder when you start a new job and a nun tells you that you need to study up on ethics what exactly she might have heard about you. Note, I didn't object, in a very short time at St. Mary's I'd already learned refusing was not an option to a Sister, so I just asked why. She said, "I'm in charge of the hospital and church mission, so ethics falls under me." Her eyes twinkled a bit, "You see if you don't go, I have to do it." I went; I enjoyed the ethical exploration and attempts to discern a path between bad and worse options. I have been on ethics committees pretty much ever since.

We're back at the University hospital in ICU. The patient has had a massive stroke. His kidneys are failing. He has gangrene and endocarditis; tips of his toes are rotting off. If he doesn't get amputations now, it is just a matter of time until he dies. Probably even with the amputations. We get the wife in. We talk amputations.

"No amputations!" she says firmly. "Do everything." We also talk about his failing kidneys and I explain that with his stroke and multiple other failing organs, dialysis might not help much. "Sure, it will" she asserts. "I've done it at home." Now we are confused. I am shot some angry glares from others on the team as if, I somehow missed the fact he was a home dialysis patient. Before the gap underneath me can widen further, the wife asserts that she knows dialysis at home is easy because she is a kidney doctor. In her dirty housecoat, missing teeth and general demeanor we begin to look at each other with a dawning realization that maybe it's not us, but her.

"The biggest problem," our attending continues, trying to pull the conversation back to the patient, "is that he's had a massive stroke." He has a very little brain left." Now the wife confirms our dawning suspicion.

"Well, then we're just going to have to get a brain transplant, "she declares with the authority of Moses on the mountain. "I've done them before. It's not that hard." We agree to consider her 'input' and slink off to call legal and ask for a court order.

The consult service is drying up as August winds down. Only Walter remains in the hospital, already on his second admission in my brief tenure here. Finally, on the last day of the month, his symptoms are sufficiently controlled that we can send him home, reasonably secure in the fact that he'll be back soon. I've really enjoyed spending time with Walter and his wife. They've shown me pictures of life before the catastrophe: boats, mountains, a happy couple doing what happy couples do. This becomes a recurring refrain for me: "I wish I had known you before you got so sick!"

Almost the end of the month, our attending for this day is a sly octogenarian of the old-school: Dr. Utterback. Dr. Utterback asks an esoteric question of a fourth-year medical student. It's intended more to plumb the student's ignorance than showcase his learning. As the student stutters and struggles for an answer, Dr. Utterback, slips me a slightly crooked smile and a wink, in this we are, despite differences in rank, co-conspirators. Addressing both of us, he quirks a grin at me, "you know about pimping, don't you? This is an effort to expose 'medical learners' deficiencies. It's also intended to humiliate and encourage further learning, time honored technique, now somewhat frowned up. If you don't believe me, see the AMA Journal article on the 'Art of Pimping.' Right Phelps?"

"Yes sir," I reply. "Long-standing practice in medical education initially codified in the New England Journal back in the 80's. The bane of my life until I learned how to cope."

"How did you deal with it back then?" he asked. I turn my own smirk back to the students.

"Find an obscure disease that has many vague symptoms, and then know everything there is to know about it. I chose porphyria. The more I was asked, the clearer it would be that I knew more about this than any attending soon they'd go pick on easier prey."

Dr Utterback lets out a satisfied grunt, "Yup, teaching by intimidation…Ahh, the good old days. They won't let me do that much anymore." The residents and students look a little relieved.

I can't help but continue, "I find a more effective way these days is to admit a mistake. You know healthcare now is focusing on 'non-punitive culture. So, I use my own teaching method, I call it- Dare to be Stupid." Dr. Utterback cocks an eyebrow at me and gestures with his head for me to continue, so I do.

"DTBS is admitting that we're all fallible. By admitting our errors, we allow others to admit to their own, and everyone learns from them. We work toward a learning culture that accepts mistakes and works to engineer them out of the system. As a medical director of a hospital system, I found the biggest problem for doctors, nurses and others involving our mistakes was trying not to admit our humanity in the face of error."

"I'll give a personal example." Intrigued, Dr. Utterback indicates I should continue. Our administration was trying to come up with a blame-free method to admit and correct medical errors. It was intended to be nonpunitive. In a few days, we were to have a meeting in front of the senior clinical leaders about unrolling this new initiative when I screwed up." I see I have the attention of Dr. Utterback, the residents and students and continue, "It happened that particular day that our new CEO had been to her allergist for a follow-up visit. She accosted our chief nursing officer, Ellen, and me, the chief medical officer in the hallway."

"You two," she barked, "come here quick." We looked at each other in askance and followed her into her office where she closed the door and produced a box from her purse. "I'm supposed to start new allergy medicine—today. I need a shot from the vial marked number one," she said as she proffered a small brown box.

I took the box and opened it. "Hurry up," she barked, "I've got a meeting in two minutes." I took the box as Ellen took out a plastic baggy of syringes and alcohol wipes. I opened the box and out rolled a small vial marked number one with a red label. I dug my finger in the box looking for instructions but set it down when our CEO reasonably pointed out "there's the vial it's number one. It is a 10th of a CC... get to it." Ellen cleaned the vial with alcohol and drew up the amount and held it out to me to confirm. As Ellen injected the serum, I returned to the box still looking for instructions. Tipping it up, out rolled nine vials, three in each color labeled 1 thru 3.

A quick perusal of the instructions revealed the lowest starter dose, was vial one in the yellow, then green and the strongest dose intended for months later would be the red one's vials one through three.

"Well crud," I murmured pointing at the instructions, "Ellen, this is awkward."

"F*#k!" said Ellen whispered less delicately.

Pulling her shirt sleeve back on, our CEO noticed our somewhat stricken expressions said, "What?

What's the problem?" We explained the problem was an inadvertent overdose of allergy medicine.

We felt like two kids called into the principal's office.

"So, let me see if I've got this right," she asked in acid tones. "My chief nursing officer and my chief medical officer just gave me an accidental overdose of my allergy medicine in the hospital's administrative suite?!" We nodded in unison.

"Well first things first," she asked, "is it going to kill me?"

I answered a question with a question, "how do you feel so far?"

She ruminated for a moment, experimentally tested her tongue for swelling, took a breath and paused. "So far, I feel fine. But I've still got this meeting in a few minutes. I've got stuff to do." It was decided I would sit in a folding chair outside the meeting in case she had a bad reaction. As she strode towards the door, she paused and turned back.

"Hmmm," she said reflectively, "awkward situation, time pressures, unfamiliar medication and procedure with interruptions. Sounds like what we've been talking about with medical errors. She turned to face the two of us squarely, "And when we talk about nonpunitive error reporting to the clinical staff, you two are going to use this example and this patient," gesturing to herself, "plus the fact you both still work here, as an example of what we're talking about." Ellen and I nodded like bobble heads in relief.

Dr. Utterback tips his non-existent hat to me and says, "I still think pimping is more fun, but now, for the residents, you have dared to be stupid, in an impressive fashion. Good story."

Friday, we have a Grand Rounds for medicine department, the topic is on asthma. It's a free lunch, so I head over. The lecture is good, but I should have stood by the fax machine where the consults had been coming in at an impressive rate. There is massive pile of requests and records heaped up in the rack of the machine. I'm busy until evening. I'm even later, because I spend two hours picking dead tissue off a one patient with a particularly nasty skin cancer. I'm trying to get down to viable tissue, picking and picking to find tissue I can put a dressing on. The earlier dressings had just been covering dead tissue without providing any healing benefit. To get a dressing to do any good, we must get down to decent tissue. No one had done a decent job of debriding her wounds up until now because it was so painful. So palliative care was asked to help minimize symptoms.

I've made sure that the patient's pain is well controlled before I start. Up until then, they would simply let her scream and shout as they tried to peel her. The patient and I just chat amiably about her illness and her family as I hunch over her wounds and pull strips of scab and slough. The patient expresses her gratitude for the extra pain medication.

Finally, in the darkening sky of late evening, I make a quick a quick stop by my apartment to clean up, then make the several hour trek back to Knoxville. I'm caught in a storm and am late getting in. Gayle is in a slightly better mood than most Friday eves, as family friends have come in for the weekend. The next evening, I blow the communal goodwill. We were talking about going downtown to see fireworks for Labor Day. I beg off tired. I soon wish I'd just gone. Gayle is livid that

I just want to stay home and veg out. She and our visitors leave in a huff for the holiday display without me.

September

September soon brings the first wave in what will become a series of mounting disasters, and it all begins on my birthday. But to understand what happens next in my fellowship, I have to make a detour into more distant past. Bear with me.

I am the second son. As you may gather during this writing, I was always closer to my mother with whom I shared a love of reading and learning. My father was a Naval WWII veteran with PTSD (we learned much later) who focused mainly on my older brother and sometimes my sister. Despite his challenges, including never finishing high school, dad was probably a certifiable genius who as a teen built his own full-sized glider and flew it…once into a tree. At age fourteen, he completely rebuilt a Model A and according to family legend, drove it from Detroit to Chicago and back to prove he could.

During World War II, Dad saved his ship that was flooding from a hull breach in battle. The pumps could only pull up 22 feet, and the hold was down was over thirty feet. Dad had the bright idea to lower the pump 21 feet into the hold so the pump could pull 21 feet then push 20 feet. It worked. They gave him a medal for that. He was a big, bluff man given to frequent loud dogmatic statements about how things should be. He swore like the sailor he'd been.

Dad was into projects, and my brother was always his willing helper. Me, I was the goof-off. I would much prefer to sneak off with a good book. This of course, caused some friction and occasional shouting with my father and me. (Mostly in my direction) In my teen years, as Dad spiraled into alcoholism that would prematurely end his life at age 43. Our paternal relations just got worse and worse. The marriage concluded with a drunken tirade ending with us being chased out of the house and around the neighborhood. Dad went back home to sleep it off while we hid out at the neighbors. Mom who had been at church doing marital counselling with our pastor came home collected us three kids and fled to Canada (not far from Detroit where all this happened) while divorce papers were filed.

Near the end, divorced and a second marriage failed, he was largely a broken man living alone in a small one-bedroom apartment. He spent his time trying to catch us outside in the yard to tell us his side of how Mom had done him wrong. Near the end, we lived in fear for Dad's orange Mustang cruising our neighborhood. (This was before restraining orders were common.) He said he just wanted to talk with us, but sometimes it was more sinister.

On one mid-winter visitation to his apartment, he became very drunk and threatening. "This isn't right what your mother did to me, stealing you away." Older brother Rick tried to calm him down and they went in the back of the apartment. My sister Kathy and I took the opportunity to slip out and walk two miles home in the evening winter's snow. Dad, and Rick showed up an hour later. My tiny grandmother dragged my brother inside and stood my father off at the door. It a was a profane David and Goliath shouting match, and again David won. It would be 20 or 30 years later, that I learned that my father held a gun to Rick's head and debated about killing both my brother and himself.

The following winter, my sophomore year in high school, following a worsening smell, Dad was found dead in his apartment. I received the news dry eyed from my mother. I didn't mention the fact when I went to see my girlfriend that evening. The following school day my girlfriend strode up to me, eyes blazing and slapped me hard. As I stood there bewildered, she half sobbed and shouted. "Why didn't you tell me your father died!?" She soon broke up with me. I went off to college and buried all those issues. All of this left me with issues around father figures and authority.

Many years later I was teaching in a family practice residency in Georgia all this forgotten. We were assigned a new administrator I'll call Jim, for our program. Jim was large and loud. He hid his bulk in impressively well-tailored suits. His relationship with the doctors was at times caustic and fault finding, other times fawning, and results focused. He had been tasked with getting the program closer to profitability as well as getting a stalled computer system and automated phone answering program up and running. These systems were universally loathed by our faculty physicians who complained often to Jim. But our complaints seemed to fall on deaf ears.

One disastrous evening, the practice had a series of a patient calls to the phone system that it failed to forward to the on-call physician. The next morning, we doctors clustered round the machine listening horrified, as the calls from one patient became more and more desperate. I was tasked with follow up. I did some calling and found out that the patient had survived by calling an ambulance that whisked him off to the emergency room and was quickly admitted to ICU with heart failure. A new set of doctors admitted him, as he wanted nothing else to do with us. I'd had it and rebelled. I sent a blistering email, not well thought out, to the hospital system CEO demanding that "this electronic abortion be removed before it kills someone."

That afternoon, I am out by the front desk talking with staff when Jim blasts through the doors. He'd just had his posterior reamed by the CEO for my email about the phone system. He couldn't wait to pass the 'love' along,' he says as he grabs me by my lab coat. "You and I have to have a talk about your email habits," he snarls and drags me stumbling behind into his office to dress me down. (Mind you, I'm forty he's fifty, both ostensibly adults). Slamming the door to his office he rants and threatens many things including firing me. He excoriates me about what the CEO said about my email. To my stunned shame, I don't yell back, but I embarrass us both by turning red-faced and then to my horror, tears begin to drip down my face.

His anger swiftly dissipates, turning to dismay and then true regret as he tries to comfort me. I am, of course, mortified. I pray to have the floor swallow me up. When that fails, Jim retreats to his desk, I bolt for the door. My face is red, tear stained, and worst of all my nose is running like a reverse geyser. I pass staff in the hall as I plunge blindly towards my office, past my secretary who gets a second's chance to say, "what the hell?" before I slam the door and collapse in my desk chair. I am both embarrassed and bewildered by what happened.

I have a few moments of privacy before a tentative knock and our department chairman, George comes in. ("Kill me," I'm thinking, "I really don't need this!) George, awkward and embarrassed both for us, keeps it short. "Phelps," he says and stalls, alternating between looking at me, his feet and the ceiling, "Phelps, there seems to be a problem. I'm not sure what the hell just happened but, shit happens." He puts a note on my desk with a name and phone number and says "This is a psychologist named Edith Williams that used to be on faculty here. I think a lot of her, go home, get yourself together and don't come back until you have an appointment." I take the note and slink out the back entrance.

I make the appointment. Edith probably spurred on by George, agreeably schedules it for the very next day. Edith is thin, 60s, short grey bob. She takes me through the incident and my reaction and then asks the obvious question. "What triggered all that?"

I flop back in the chair and spread my hands and shrug," I do not know. I think I was surprised as Jim was." (Keep in mind gentle reader, you have the paragraphs above to infer a cause. I had to spend some months in therapy to get to that same conclusion.) Starting at the beginning, Edith begins with family and childhood. I talk about my mom who raised us as a single mother, my brother, and sister.

At a lull in the conversation, Edith observes "You haven't mentioned your father once."

"There's not much to tell," I respond. "My father died of alcoholism when I was a teen."

"And yet when I mentioned him, you hunched in and crossed your arms," she comments archly. I opened my mouth to object, but she cut me off. "I think that is enough for today. Think about your dad, authority figures and we'll start digging there, next time."

So now we're back to the worst day of my fellowship program. It's my birthday. We are a little over two months in. Things seem to be going well. Noon conference is ending, as we stand up to leave the table where we had our discussion. Lugubriously pulling himself to his feet, because we share a similar girth, Howard motions to me, "Hey Greg, can we have a second? He motions to a small conference room across the hall, and the other faculty follow. I assume they're going to wish me a happy birthday and following Howard's gesture of entry, cheerfully precede the group into the small room. It is only when they close the door, and they look meaningfully at each other, that I realize this might not be the case. Howard gestures for us all to take a seat.

I randomly note that I'm in the far corner, farthest from the door and escape. It may have been their intention. "I suppose you're wondering why you hadn't seen your evaluations on the computer yet," Howard comments. I shake my head wondering where this is going. (In all honesty, I hadn't known there would be formal evaluations. Marci had said at the end of July things were going well, and I hadn't thought about it again. In my residency 30 years ago, evaluations were only made if they were unhappy with you. I certainly hadn't learned to look in a computer file for them. (As I'll note again, I was not particularly tech savvy.)

Howard, still standing, looming over us, shuffles uncomfortably and looks down at the table. I realize this must be the case at this point. Howard confirms this by saying "we held back an extra month to see if things got better."

Now I'm flustered, I can feel my face heating, no one has said an unkind word to me in two months. "Well, what seems to be the problem?" I ask. That is apparently all the cue they need to start in.

One of the newer young faculty jumps in. "Well," she begins, "To begin with, I'm not sure your sense of humor is appropriate. You made a derogatory comment about a family's intelligence, 'a few fries short of a happy meal,' or something like that?" she says accusingly then continues gaining speed. "In another case, when asked about a patient's prognosis by a resident, you made a circling motion indicating they were going down the drain." I sit back chagrinned.

I realize the times have changed. The black humor that was so prevalent in my residency is no longer used or approved. The comments continue to build in force and number. I can feel my face begin to redden as I try to respond. "However, in both of these incidents," I point out, "I was only in the company of other residents; where no family could hear."

"That doesn't matter," she snaps back. "It showed disrespect for the patient and offended the residents." I'm embarrassed and humiliated.

"Okay," I promise, "absolutely no more shows of humor."

"Oh no," Howard jumps in confusing me. "Humor is a good thing in end-of-life care but just not with the patients." Since that was what I had avoided, I'm a little confused. The comments keep coming from around the table as the apparent conversational dam is broken.

"And another thing," another faculty member snipes. "At times you seem scattered, occasionally confused about this patient or that patient. It doesn't seem like you have them all in your head." Ruefully I agree and point out that I am 55 today. There are scattered looks of surprise around the room. I don't know if they didn't know it was my birthday or that I was that old.

"You also forget things. I ask you to check a lab and you don't report it." I debate mentioning that I've been banned from using my longstanding habit of writing on my hand to make sure I don't forget things. I decide in this torrent of complaints that rebuttal is not going to help me. So, I hunker down and try to nod and smile, but I can feel my face slipping. These criticisms continue and eventually, after the event, takes the form of a written critique, I'm to return.

Years later I still have the minutes of the meeting they provided me after the review "We told him that he passed his two rotations, but he was not fully meeting expectations and needed to demonstrate improvement… Dr. Phelps was visibly surprised and dismayed…and asked appropriate clarifying questions." Reviewing these notes for writing this memoir I can still feel my face tighten. The comments continued for what seems like an eternity but checking my watch later it was about 30 minutes.

"Anyway," the department concludes, collectively nodding with Howard, "we would like to see an action plan around how you plan to address keeping up with your patients better. We would like that by Friday." I'm not even sure what an action plan would look like, but at this point, I'm certainly not asking.

By now, I am thoroughly humiliated. To my horror, I find myself near tears, and my face is beet red. I furiously wipe my eyes. It is almost as bad as Jim years ago. Worst of all, unshed tears are causing my sinuses to fill, and my nose begins to run.

Like Jim some years ago, they back up a little bit and offer some small false consolation by saying, "Oh, but we still think you're doing a great job. And the patients seem to like you." Their collective expression is like they just witnessed someone beating a puppy. That of course, makes it worse. With that, they get up and file out of the room. Howard looks a bit chagrined at how things went. He pats me awkwardly on the shoulder in passing. "Well, I'm sorry, I guess that wasn't the birthday greeting you were thinking of getting." I am left to go home to my apartment and stew for the night. I came across a bible verse that night that fit the day to a T, From Psalms 55, "Had it been an adversary who taunted me, then I could have borne it…But it was you, a man after my own heart, my companion, my own familiar friend."

Why did it hit me so hard? I still don't know. I've faced down angry neurosurgeons and been screamed at by cardiologists and didn't turn a hair. My dad died and I shed fewer tears. So why did this hit me again so badly. Maybe more "daddy" issues, maybe that I really shouldn't have taken the risk and gone back to school at this age. Maybe I really am getting too old for more school? Maybe I perceived it as an attack on my self-worth and ability as a doctor? Whatever it was, it started a downward spiral that would persist for months.

Thus, begins September – This month is dedicated to hospice and palliative care in nursing homes.

It quickly becomes apparent now that I'm tainted and under suspicion. I am assigned a small, hyperactive physician named Gerda who rockets from one nursing facility to another. She does this on the interstate while working on her computer and managing phone calls and slaloming through heavy traffic. I hang on for dear life and pray hard.

"Satan or Saints" she spits out the side of her mouth as I cringe in traffic. I pause in my terror to look up in askance. "That's what we are in most nursing homes. They either see us as saints who come to help relieve their suffering patients who are crying out all night. Or," she continues, dodging a minivan, "we are Satan, and they are convinced that we are only here to end their patients' lives as quickly and cost-effectively as possible. To them…. we are scum, murderers… Satan!"

Thus, we begin days of rounds at a variety of nursing facilities of varying quality. It turns out there are a lot of nursing homes in River City, and I think I saw them all. It is in one of these facilities that I encounter the fundamental difference in what is called curative care versus hospice care.

Annie B is a sweet 92-year-old with severe dementia. Demented patients seem to go in one of two directions. They either become the sweetest, but most confused people you'll ever meet, or they become mean, cruel and suspicious. They wait for you to get within range and then attack with claws, bites, and pinches. Often mute with dementia and colored with rage, they do what damage they can, usually minimal, in the time they have before you can drag yourself away.

One creative lady waited until my stethoscope was lodged in my ears and the bell planted on her chest. She then grabbed the stethoscope tubing and dragged my face down to spit in it. It makes some sense for the demented. They are robbed of rights and possessions. They can't know they put their purse in the fridge. To them, someone must have stolen it, and the 'thievery' gets worse as their minds deteriorate.

Annie B is none of that. She smiles a sweet and serene smile despite the fact her hip is broken.

Like many demented patients, she's forgotten that she can't walk. She has also partly forgotten what food is for, and only grudgingly nibbles bites if food is pushed in her face. Because of the broken hip she is in pain every time she moves. And she forgets that it hurts, so each move is a new and fresh pain. We are consulted to "keep Annie comfortable." To me with almost 30 years' experience, the answer is obvious. Although a total hip would seem a bit much, a simple hip pinning would seem the obvious answer. Stabilize the break and minimize her pain. To my evident surprise that is NOT the way, we are going. The plan is more pain medicine.

"But then she'll just lay in the bed!" I exclaim in objection.

"She was doing that anyways' I'm told. "But if she just lies there, she'll probably get pneumonia." I try again. Gerda nods agreeably. "Yes, probably. Would likely happen either way. Our job is not to make her live longer. It is to keep her comfortable until the end comes. We don't take life, but we don't try to extend it either. Keep in mind that for a third of elderly patients, hip fractures are the beginning of the end. They get pneumonia, urinary tract infections, or worst of all, bed sores that become infected, and then they die from sepsis." Somewhat to my surprise the family agrees with Gerda's plan. No one thinks Annie would like a long bed bound existence and the family would like to be kept comfortable."

We round every few days. Annie is indeed comfortable and dreamy. As I predicted, in about two weeks, Annie indeed has pneumonia; what doctors in older times called the 'old person's friend.' We keep her comfortable, but withhold antibiotics and Annie become more obtunded and drifts off not awakening a few days later.

After the events of my birthday, I get the recurring feeling that I'm now damaged goods. I work with extravagant dedication to try to redeem myself. but every error, every slip seems to dig me in deeper. At one nursing home Gerda hands me a pile of records. "See what they did about the cancer treatment on this one?" she asks and wanders off. I pore over the records noting medication and chemotherapies I'm not familiar with. I summarize what I found. "Did you see what they did about the hypercalcemia?" she asks. I admit no, I didn't see that medication mentioned. With exactitude, she pulls a single page out and points. "Zolmeta, they gave him zoledronic acid." Since it was then a newer medication, I hadn't known what it was and didn't recognize implications. The look on her face implies I'd struck out again. I feel my face flush and wander off to look at another chart.

A few days later, I get a call from my wife. Gerda and I are at yet another nursing home on the outskirts of town. Seeing my wife's number in mid-day, I excuse myself to step outside to get a better signal. As I stand in the parking lot, Gayle provides running commentary on the C-section birth of my first grandchild looking thru the operating room door. However, she is not IN the delivery room where she wants to be, having been barred from the delivery room so the two parents can greet their new baby alone. As Gayle is both an experienced OB nurse and the new Nana, she is supremely frustrated to be excluded. So, the commentary is part awe and wonder and part anger at being excluded. I try to cheer her up by pointing out that I'm even farther away. "Yes," she snipes, "but you chose to leave us." Ouch.

Still, I'm all grins as Gerda steps out of the building looking for me and we get in her car. "Congratulate me," I said. "I'm a new grandpa." Gerda flashes a brief smile, more of a grimace, and off we go to the next nursing home, she is barking orders into her ever-present phone. Me still grinning looking out the window.

Two nights later I wake up confused in the dark. There's jumping, wrestling in my bed and for a moment I blearily wonder how a squirrel got into my bed clothes. Then I realize, it is my heart again. It feels like a catfight in my chest. This is the third time this has happened since I got to River City, though the first time it has happened at night. In the dark, I grope for my pulse and feel it hammering in the classic rapid irregularly irregular fashion of atrial fibrillation. In general, the wisdom is that it is only after 48 hours that the heart is likely to churn up a stroke-inducing clot. I look at the time and lay back down.

Sleep is beyond me though. The other two episodes were brief, and I can feel when they start and stop. This one churns on through the next day. I go to work and say nothing. Surreptitiously I check my pulse from time to time, still hammering. Once or twice the residents note I'm not my usual cheery self. "Didn't sleep well," I curtly reply in a tone that discourages additional probing.

Back home the hammering pulse continues into the evening. I know that if it is still going strong by the following morning, I'm going to need cardioversion. Like many docs, as I've already demonstrated, I hate the thought of being a patient more than I fear death. The following morning, at 4 am. I find my pulse still hammering. I'm coming up on 48 hours

I get up from another sleepless night. I figure the ER is probably slowest now. I trudge out of the apartment building and over to the night-shrouded garage next door. I flop in my car and sigh. I begin to map out going to the hospital ER. Which one? One of our faculty mentioned her husband is a cardiac electrophysiologist, I look on my phone to find which at hospital he is on staff. Might as well start there. I plan when to call Gerda and say I might not be in today. Can I get a cell signal from the ER? I hate to wake her up now. I hate this, plus I've missed two nights sleep. For about the 30th time I give one last hopeless check of my pulse... It is normal! Elation floods through me. Saved!! I get out of the car and celebrate by going back to bed for two more hours. Later in the day I track down the faculty member and ask about her husband. I must be finally becoming an adult, as I've decided to get evaluated and face this like a grown up and see what we can do. I schedule the earliest appointment I can which is still a few weeks down the road.

Gerda and I are back out roaring down the highways and byways of River City nursing homes again. I spent the last two days with the nurse practitioners who help manage hospice patient's in the various skilled nursing facilities. While Gerda does the palliative care, they manage the final days and weeks in hospice. There are two NP's, they are both thoughtful and committed to their care and they also have a wild sense of humor that helps re-awaken mine that had been stunned to sleep on my birthday.

Now Gerda and I are headed out to a very nice nursing home, well out from the north side of town when we run into a roadblock. Officials come out to our car and tell us that the road is closed except for people coming to the tournament.

"Tournament?" we ask.

The guard looks dumbfounded. "Golf...The Ryder Cup," he tells us sarcastically "Maybe you've heard of it?"

Gerda looks unimpressed. "I'm a hospice doctor," she states, biting off the words. "I have dying patients at the nursing home down this road, and you are keeping me from them." This sets the guard back a bit, and without another word, he waves us through from a safe distance as if we were the ones with something catching. Gerda grins over at me, "hospice and dying patients will get you through almost any roadblock."

The next day we are back in territory closer to home. As we go from room to room, we glance at the patients' TVs; All the channels seem to be tuned by the nurses to the same news. The economy has been rocky for a while, but now the market is beginning a plunge. As we go from room to room, we watch the Dow as numbers keep dropping. 300, then 400 then 500. Most of the patients lie oblivious as I shake my head, and Gerda becomes more and more agitated. "My 401K is tied up in the market," she blurts out. "I'm never gonna be able to retire if this keeps up." Unhelpfully I point out that I'm training to start a new career and I think I'm probably older than she is. We bicker a few minutes about age before Gerda coughs up a number. Indeed, I'm two years older. The market continues to plunge, passing 700. The silence between Gerda and I is glacial the rest of the day.

At church Wednesday morning, we have a newish minister for the cathedral's service. I think he is just another in a series of priests filling in, in this our tiny mid-week service. I do notice a certain drop in the usual informality of the group, but being new and slow on the pickup, it takes three Wednesdays before I figure out the identity of our newest Wednesdays pastor. He's been eschewing the purple shirt of his office for plain black as I eventually work out our guest is the Episcopal Bishop for River City. I figure it out only after his homily, when he begins talking about his retirement process and how it will take two or more years. Between him and Gerda, I'm beginning to feel like I missed an impending retirement memo.

Still, I progress on to the next nursing home to meet our NP's who are in their usual jovial mood as they introduce me to an older seminary student learning chaplain duty. During our rounds one of the nurse practitioners, Colleen slips and calls the chaplain student 'doctor' which confuses me. She tries to backpedal as she has clearly let something slip. Intrigued and undeterred, I ask him a "Ph. D, or D. Min student?" He grins, abashed and says no he's a retired neurologist 'incognito' coming back to start another career. Suddenly I feel better, as we leave him praying with a patient. We head into the room of yet another patient, Mr. Zock's, and find an angry daughter who feels hospice has taken her dad's side about letting him die with his cancer.

Colleen and I pull up chairs to make the situation less formal and intimidating. It doesn't help. When I reasonably point out that it is his life and he does have the capacity to make his decision, I run into a verbal tornado. It takes an hour or so to get us back to some semblance of family comity. Finally, Mr. Zock loudly declares "It is my decision and they've finally got me comfortable, end of discussion." Mr. Zock's daughter glares, she can't decide who she's maddest at. Grabbing her purse, she flounces out. Mr. Zock spreads his hands apologetically. "Sorry, she's always been that way when she doesn't get her way... Even as a five-year-old. "He shakes his head ruefully, "Somethings never change. She's still my daughter no matter how old I get, or she gets." We say goodbyes to Mr. Zock. In the hallway, I salute to the nurse practitioners and I'm off again. I'm running late for meeting Bev for dinner and attending Spanish lessons.

The next day, I find that talking my way past the golf tournament guards is getting easier, and I meet Gerda for more rounds at the nursing home and then make a hurried run across town to the VA clinic where only two patients suck up an entire afternoon. One is a lung cancer patient who has taken a very sharp decline and just barely made it into the clinic. I send him, still protesting that he's 'really fine, just fine' (with a blood pressure of "not much, over even less") to be admitted to the hospital. Part of the problem is the VA electronic medical record is glacially slow, and everything must be typed in by the doctor.

Only a government agency with slave labor could think this is a good idea. Years later, when the VA has a series of very public crises about hidden and missing appointments, I'm not at all surprised. I'm still learning the computer system and after a few minutes, knowing the next patient is waiting, I make some notes to myself and resolve to come back tonight and finish the input.

The next patient has bladder cancer. He looks almost as bad as the last guy. He's painfully thin and walks with a hitch in his step that wasn't there two weeks ago. He must see my expression because he gets up and spontaneously dances around the tiny exam room to show me how healthy he is. He falters when he looks at me and sees my sustained grim expression. I sit him down, and we have a heart to heart. Even then I'm a wuss. I'm telling him time is limited. I'm speaking in weeks to months, but even then, I'm thinking more days to weeks. Ever a good soldier, he thanks me. We agree to meet again and see how he's doing next week. He declines anything else for pain reiterating he's 'fine, just fine.' I wonder to myself if that's a phrase they teach in boot camp.

More nursing home visits. I'm waiting for Gerda at one nursing home parking lot, when Colleen calls me from another nursing home asking me to come do an emergency family meeting. As Gerda arrives, I make quick excuses and hurry back over to meet the family and plunge in. My notes show that I made it to five nursing homes that day. I celebrate by taking a long bike ride that afternoon. My weight at the YMCA the next day is under 300 pounds for the first time in over a year.

The next day, another skilled nursing facility, this one church affiliated. I meet with a young pastor who is supposed to be leading a pilgrimage to Europe with family and church members. Dad, a retired pastor, has had Alzheimer's and hasn't known anyone for a year or so, which is why he's in the nursing home. Now, he looks like he's got less than a week to live. Do they stay or go? I don't have an answer. I help them tease apart the guilt of going versus staying and what does dad know or understand. I try for substituted judgement, what would dad want for the son, the group and himself?

Are there other family members who can be with dad? We go around and round for a while. Finally, the young pastor thanks me and says he'll have to spend some time praying for guidance. I never hear what they decide, and dad dies a few days later. Meanwhile, Mr. Zock's family is haranguing anyone who'll listen, that we're letting him die. I go back over to try again to talk the ring-leader daughter into coming to grips with his very fatal illness. The nursing home staff thank me profusely for helping with the daughter and family. Mr. Zock, stoically hangs in, watching the play like an experienced tennis spectator. He doesn't change his mind and she's still angry. What a miserable way for him to spend his final weeks.

I have a follow-up meeting with the faculty about my "improvement plan." I had written a brief memo stating in bullet points "fellow will do the following: keep individual cards with each patient and clinical information, review cards daily, fellow will review -plan of care on each patient daily. Labs will be recorded each morning for access. A place on each card will be available for notes and requests.

I meet with the lead faculty member on this project, she flips through my typed plan and then tells me she's not happy. I'm a bit surprised. I have researched 'improvement plans in books and on the internet. I then I had put a good amount of time, thought and self-reflection into what I could and would do better or differently. I had taken the observation for self-improvement seriously. So, I ask how I can do it over to Marci's satisfaction.

Marci's reply sheds new light on our increasingly testy relationship, "You didn't use the definite article at the beginning of each of your bullet points," she declares pedantically.

I scrub my face with my hand in confusion. "I'm sorry I was a biology major in college. In my time it was that or chemistry to get into medical school. It's been a long, long time since freshman English." I say asking her to explain.

"The!!...a grammatically called a definite article" She replies impatiently, "You didn't use the word 'the' as in the fellow will…"

"But the content, the plan itself?" I start.

"Oh yes, yes, that part is fine," she says. But you have to observe proper grammar."

Now I'm a little irritated. I've been doing bullet point presentations without "THE" for years. I feel like I came to learn Shakespeare and I'm getting graded instead on my handwriting. All this unsaid but, she sees my darkening expression. "Oh, you don't know?"

"Know what?"

"We're all English majors, all the faculty, even Howard." So, when you miss the definite article, you're already in trouble. We assume you don't know what you're talking about because we're judging your grammar." I grimly nod, I re-write the action improvement plan adding in 'the' everywhere I think it'll fit.

It is accepted.

The next day, I hit three more nursing homes. In one commons room a demented patient stares off into space as I try to talk with her and engage her. Gerda is at the chart rack hunting some labs. I should probably be helping but instead, I'm squatting down beside this patient trying to talk to her. Suddenly, I'm mortified as I lose my balance and slowly topple over. (Remember I'm about 300 pounds, so it is not a graceful tumble.) For the first time, as I lay sprawled on the floor, the patient makes eye contact with me and begins to laugh, a slow rumble, blooming into a full belly laugh. I grin sheepishly in response. The staff is so excited about her laughing they almost trip over me to get to her while she's still hee-hawing. Crawling to a nearby chair, I hoist myself to my feet and shuffle back to the chart rack. Gerda grins at me without comment. She's found the lab work. We're done. I shuffle out of the facility to the knowing smiles of the staff. I'm back at the Y that evening for a workout with renewed energy. That night I have another bout of atrial fibrillation to keep me up. After a few hours it ends, and I can sleep. The cardiology appointment is coming up I head home for the weekend.

The news from our son at college is bad. He says his car's been stolen and he needs a ride to get back home to see his brother for fall break. He says someone can bring him halfway, so I drive two hundred miles to the slightly more than the halfway point. Son calls again announcing the ride from his end has fizzled. I drive the next 150 miles to get him and bring him home. The weekend is shot, and I'm seething. Next week it turns out the car is not stolen. He forgot where he left it when he went bar hopping. His mother and I find it the next weekend when we take him back. There is some heated conversation with his mother trying to buffer the two of us. When that fails, Gayle goes into full "protecting my baby" mode. The mood on the six-hour ride home is frigid and quiet.

Back in River City, I take a quick break from rounds and go to see the cardiologist about the atrial fibrillation. It is a short visit. He takes one look at me. I can see his thoughts on his face- 'over fifty, overweight, hypertensive and out of shape...heart attack looking for a place to happen". He quickly schedules me for a stress test next month, to see just how bad things are. Nearing the end of the month, Gerda and I are at yet another nursing home when we see on the TV that the House of Representatives has rejected a bailout, and the stock market again drops 777 points. Gerda and I now grimly agree we're both going to 'work until we die'. Thus, ends the month. Good riddance!

CHAPTER THREE

October

After going to the VA clinic for months, this would be my first time of the Veteran's Administration hospital service. I begin with (another!) orientation. At least no one threatens to blow us up this time. The nexus for most of the action for our hospice and palliative medicine service is a four-bed inpatient unit for veterans who are dying and need symptoms controlled. After rounds there, we do palliative care consults around the hospital. We meet with Janice, the IPU attending this month. Janice is yet another young and recent graduate of our program. Our team includes a chaplain, a social worker, a physician's assistant, a resident, me and two medical students. Janice and I share another connection to me. Her husband is the cardiologist I saw for the recurring atrial fibrillation a few days ago. I'm waiting for my stress test.

Our first visit, an African American veteran who is getting close to the end. Surrounded by weeping family members he breathes in stertorous and irregular gasps, marked by substantial pauses. Janice comforts his weeping wife, a hand on her shoulder, and says it won't be a lot longer.

Afterwards, standing in the hall we explain to the student we don't give people firm numeric parameters, a set number like three days or four months but talk in orders of magnitude: Hours to days, days to weeks, weeks to months etc. Cogent to this patient, one of the students asks: "Do you ever talk in terms of minutes? "Janice has just enough time to shake her head, before a low moan erupts behind us, followed by shrill keening of the family which billows from of the room we just left. The patient has just expired. Janice makes a grimace, as we all troop back in. I hear the student mutter to himself. "Well maybe you need to think minutes sometimes."

We continue rounding and encounter a Mr. Watson who is clearly dying of lung cancer- a common ailment among the heavy smoking veteran population. I introduce the beginnings of a goals of care discussion to get to the obvious (to us) imminence of his demise. He's having none of it. Grunting with pain, he insists- "I'm a Christian, God won't let me die." His logic renders me mute. When Janice tactfully suggests he'd be more comfortable in hospice and he needn't to die in pain, he's having none of that either. "Hospice!" he sputters, "They just give you morphine and kill you."

This veteran's response typifies one we hear repeatedly from both patients and even some doctors. Morphine has been around a long time. Opium, the sap of the poppy flower, was used by the Sumerians and Egyptians for millennia. But it wasn't until 1804, when a German scientist isolated the chemical, we call morphine and naming it for Morpheus, god of sleep. Inexpensive, ubiquitous and predictable, and almost synonymous with hospice, morphine strikes fear into patients and many doctors.

After my fellowship, I had a neurologist ask me to see a patient clearly nearing his end. The family asked him to consider morphine for the patient's on-going pain. "I've been doing what I can" the neurologist explained on the phone, "but morphine well ...that stuff is ...well that's just out of my league." Ironically, when I visited the patient, I was bemused to find him on 200 micrograms of fentanyl, a far, far more potent medication! But, oh Lord no, it wasn't 'morphine.'

This "morpho-phobia first showed itself in the fellowship at University ICU when our team entered the ICU. Reading my name badge, one of the critical care doctors mockingly hold up his fingers in the form of the cross, like confronting a vampire and then, smirking he edged around me. I couldn't resist holding my white coat like a cape across my face and responding "blah, blah blah!" in my best Transylvanian accent.

In another case, I was called to see a woman I'll call Suellen, in hospice who was within an hour or so of death. She was gasping and struggling for breath. We accessed her hospice emergency kit and gave her a tiny dose of morphine to help her difficult breathing. She died peacefully an hour or so later.

A few months after that, I was visiting a palliative care patient in a nearby home. I'd seen her several times. Her pain was mounting daily, and I suggested adding some long acting...you guessed it, morphine.

Her husband reared back shocked. "Oh, Hell no! Some doctor from hospice saw our friend Ms. Suellen down the road a few months ago, gave her morphine, and killed her on the spot!"

"I did not kill her," I snapped. "She was dying, she had no blood pressure, and I kept her comfortable as she passed."

Then we both looked surprised. Him, because he didn't know it was me, he was talking about and, me because I blurted out confidential patient fact. I shouldn't have admitted I treated Ms. Suellen, or even admit I even knew her. While he continued to refuse long acting morphine, we continued to visit his wife for months using stronger and more expensive medications but never morphine, ever.

Back at the VA the following day, I discover that Walter, our long-term patient with abdominal catastrophes, has returned septic again. We are brought back in to help with his pain, confusion and to provide support to his wife-Amanda. Amanda is a veteran of many hospitalizations with Walter and welcomes us back with hugs. She takes a compassionate, but hard-headed, approach to Walter's illness. She is fond of us palliative care fellows and is happy to have us back on board.

After seeing Walter, towards the end of the afternoon I see a small huddle of our staff clustered at the end of the hall, several weeping. A nurse practitioner who had been in the palliative care team had been diagnosed with colon cancer some months before my fellowship. She had only worked there a short time, but she was always pale. It wasn't until she was diagnosed with a bleeding tumor and transfused, that her color returned to 'normal.' Today we learned she had just died at the age of 30. Despite what we all do for a living, we are all a little shaken by this death of one our own.

After the arduous week, the weekend brings a welcome change. The weather is finally cooling and there is a party scheduled for the fellows and the faculty. Gayle has not been to visit in months, and I encourage her to come. She wants to see some of the city. As an additional draw, I tell her there is some sort of art fair this weekend in the old city that we can cruise the day prior to the party. The art fair turns out to be such a premier event that even the city schools shut down for so everyone can attend. It is a pleasant interlude to my pending cardiac stress workup. Traffic is diverted away, as blocks of booths and stalls line an area of historic Romanesque homes, shaded by trees in blazing fall foliage.

I'm a little worried about the party. First Gayle was mad at me for leaving for the fellowship. Now she's still angry for me about the critical feedback debacle on my birthday. She is still fuming and wanting to give someone a piece of her mind for 'picking' on her husband.

A strange part of our thirty plus year marriage: she can be mad at family members, but God help the person who speaks ill of us. The party is a small gathering, only two fellows and to my relief Gayle is charmed by the faculty. We have a better time that I think either of us anticipated. By party's end Gayle and Bev have bonded.

After Gayle leaves Sunday afternoon, I give into my anxieties, go over to the YMCA to do my own stress test on a treadmill in advance of the pending cardiology visit. I have downplayed the whole thing to Gayle saying they just wanted a test or two to make sure there are no other complicating issues. At the YMCA, I place myself on the treadmill, hands on the pulse readouts, and run my heart rate up to the hundred and thirties to see if I have any chest pain. I also want to make sure I don't humiliate myself by giving out before reaching a decent heart rate during the test. Nada, I'm good, ego intact.

October eighth brings a role reversal, I used to do stress tests years ago in rural practice now I'm the patient. At the cardiac lab, I'm wired and harnessed six ways from Sunday as I begin by slowly trudging along the belt. Then the pace and the incline pick up, and then again, and yet again, On the monitor, I see my heart rate accelerate. I breath harder as I struggle to look over the tech's shoulder to read the EKG strips, but she's obliviously in the way. We finally reach a target rate, I'm sweating and gasping for breath, but I succeeded in not collapsing. I still haven't seen the strips. I ask if I can see them. To my surprise, the tech crisply declines, "No, the doctor needs to review them. You'll meet with him tomorrow."

"But it was okay, right?" I ask, toweling sweat off. She smiles at me and said, "Honey if it was terrible you wouldn't be leaving this room." That...wasn't quite the whole truth. I had failed, as I learn the next day at the cardiologist's office. The stress test suggests probable coronary artery disease. The cardiologist reviews the strips and images with me. The echo looks okay, but the EKG strips are 'discouraging.' We both know that more testing will be needed.

He schedules me for a cardiac catheterization for a few weeks hence. A few weeks! I'm wandering around with a potentially fatal illness. Should I avoid any activities? "Well, no mountain climbing" he jokes. "For that matter don't exert yourself too much, avoid stairs and stuff." His words leave me a little nonplussed. As I leave the office, I'm reminded the world looks a lot different from the patient's side of the desk.

Dejected, I head back to my apartment. Once parked in the dingy garage next door, I walk into the tiny apartment building lobby in a funk to find, for the first and only time, that the elevator is 'out of order'. I can only believe this is some sort of cosmic karma. I look at the six flights of stairs and decide it'll serve the universe right if I collapse ascending the stairs. The joke will be on them when they find the body halfway up. No such luck, I make it to my apartment just fine. First, I call Bev. She is usually good for some clinical reflection, and she's a friendly voice. A good and trusted colleague, I value her opinion. We discuss the test. She thinks I should call back and insist the catheterization be moved up. I grumble but agree. Then I ask if she'd consider being my ride to the cardiac procedure.

There is a long chilly pause. "Why won't you get Gayle to come up and drive you?"

"Well I didn't want to freak her out. Health issues upset her, and she's still angry that I'm here doing the fellowship. This will just make thing worse."

Bev's voice goes up an octave and few decibels. "Are you out of your f*#king mind? How could you not tell your wife? And what am I supposed to say if you have to go for surgery or even die in the cardiac catheterization?" Her voice swells in volume and indignation—"ARE YOU F*#KING NUTS? Now either you call her, or I will."

The gentle reader may be seeing a pattern here. Doctors make terrible patients, but I may be in a class by myself. Permit me a true anecdote: I submitted a story about an incident I endured to a widely read physician's magazine- Medical Economics. It was story about a laughable injury in front of a large crowd, what a bad patient I was, and how ridiculously non-compliant I was. Medical Economics agreed I'd set a new low, and paid me to publish the story under the title: I'm Glad My Patients Aren't as Bad as I Am." It maybe that my own person foibles allow me to see other patients 'medical non-compliance' in a more forgiving light.

Beverly forces me to agree that it is a bad idea not to include Gayle in the up-coming cardiac procedure, and I grudgingly call Gayle and tell her the grim news. She echoes Bev's concerns about the delay and insists that I call immediately and have the test moved up. Of course, she'll be there with me on the day of the procedure. I make the call and manage to have the test rescheduled to the upcoming week. I head back to Knoxville for the weekend and immerse myself in a frenzy of chores. Quietly, I fear that if the news is bad, I may not be doing yardwork for a while, if ever.

The following week, finds me getting ready for the cardiac cath. I tell work I need have a few tests done, but I should be back the next day. Gayle, my daughter Tiffany and newborn Abby, all come up and camp out in my apartment. Gayle and I are at the hospital at 6 am. We shuffle through the interminable paperwork. I present my living will/advance care directive naming Gayle as my surrogate in case things go badly. My clothes (and dignity) are shuffled off for the usual hospital gown that fails to cover my substantial posterior.

The invasive cardiologist, not the same one who did the stress test, arrives. He reviews my tests and looks me over. He too doesn't like what he sees. Overweight, over 50 and hypertensive. He scribbles a few more few things to the procedure permit and hands it back to me to read. So, in addition to agreeing to a heart catheterization, I find myself giving permission for possible cardiac stents and/or emergency by-pass surgery. The cardiologist nonchalantly shrugs.

"You're overweight, you failed a stress test and I won't be able wake you up and quiz you." Chastened, I agreed to it all. I find myself a little relieved that Gayle will be here if all this is going to happen. Despite my usual cheery demeanor, I'm a clandestine pessimist, so Gayle gives me a kiss for luck, I hope it's not my last, and I'm wheeled out of the holding room to the lab.

An hour or so later I wake to Gayle grinning at me. When my head clears, she says "Nothing. They didn't find a thing."

The cardiologist, concurs, disbelieving, he is shaking his head. "I thought sure with all that against you and all those risk factors, I was sure we'd find something. You are one lucky guy. Go home, take better care of yourself."

The strange part in all this was the cardiac catheterization essentially ends my evaluation for atrial fibrillation. Everyone lost interest. I'm to stay on the medications with periodic bouts of a fib, and we collectively agree to wait and see, an arrangement, I was complicit with.

Next day, Gayle and family depart to Knoxville, I return to VA rounding. Janice nods knowingly to me and says nothing. Two vets together in a room are each being slowly worked up for a similar lung mass. I mentally tag them as Smith and Jones. The VA isn't in a hurry. A test a day seems to be the typical speed here. As we round through the hospital, I find I really love the vets. For the WW II Navy vets, in their stories of combat on the seas, I can see my father in a more forgiving light.

I am drawn to ask for the stories Dad never would or could give us kids. The veteran's laconic matter-of- factness about life and death and dying never fails to impress me. For them the VA is like old home week, and they seem to really enjoy the time they spend together sharing wartime experiences that leave me as an outsider looking in.

The biopsy for the veteran closest to the door, 'Mr. Smith,' come back the news is bad--cancer as expected. I'm assigned to go break the bad news to him. 'Mr. Jones' is out for tests. I peer around the around the doorframe looking to see if any family members are there. We usually like to get all the family together and share the news. Smith knows who I am and what I might be there to say. When I ask about family, he shakes his head and says, "my wife's gone for the day why don't you just go ahead and tell me what you know." I offer to call his wife's cellphone; Mr. Smith shakes his head, as he levers himself up to a sitting position on the bed.

"Get on with it, I know you guys are not good news. It'll just upset her anyway, better that I tell her my way." That brings me up short for a moment's personal reflection, then I pull up a chair and sit facing him, almost knee to knee.

His body is slightly bent forward with the stoop of an older man, he is breathing a little hard from emphysema. I too lean in. Incongruously, I am reminded by the pose of priest and penitent and I wonder which I am. I start down the prescribed method of sharing bad news. He holds up a hand and stops me. "Doc" he says, "I've learned when a doctor sits down it is always bad. Just tell me what it is." I tell him it's lung cancer that has spread to his adrenal glands and liver. He looks at me unshaken and asks "so, how long are we talking here?"

I start again. "Well, I'm not God, but I'm guessing were probably talking months." I pause and look at him for reaction. He sits back on the bed, leaning on the wall.

He takes a reflective breath in and lets it out with a sigh, "Months, I can do something with that." He sticks out a hand to shake mine and thanks me for telling him the news. I apologize that his wife is not there to hear the news. He says, "Naw, I asked, you told- thanks."

I return to the rest of our rounds and patients in a bit of a hurry. It is Spanish night, and I'm waiting at the restaurant for Bev before we go to our lesson. This once a week meeting has become an important part of my life, we both blow off steam and compare notes. The Spanish part has become more secondary to the encounter but still an interesting challenge. Bev is late, then later. I call, concerned. She hems and haws a little bit.

"Well Greg, I've learned something in the last few weeks. I've learned that I want to be able to speak Spanish, I just don't want to learn Spanish. I'm quitting." I finish my dinner and go to class and mutter an apology for Bev. More than half the fun of the class was an opportunity to share. A few weeks later, I drop out too.

It's the next day and Mrs. Smith has gotten the news of husband's cancer. She is livid that she wasn't there when I broke the news. I don't disagree with her anger, but he did ask, and asked me not to wait for her or call. All of which I try to explain, but she's not hearing it. She now sees it as her duty to protect him from me and flies into a snit any time I come near. This makes it a bit of a hide and seek game with me dodging her to talk to him. I continue to round on him for the following week adjusting pain medications and planning for hospice care.

Her fury and my efforts to avoid her becomes a matter of some hilarity for Mr. Smith's roommate, Mr. Jones. He giggles every time I walk quickly by and glance to see if Smith's wife is there. If she's not, I circle back and enter to talk with Mr. Smith. Mr. Jones knows that the wife will have tantrum if she's there and he finds this charade the peak of hilarity.

After a few days, the biopsies and scans for Mr. Jones come back. Again, it is my job to share bad news. I wander down the hall and reflexively look in the room at the first bed. Stifling a laugh, Jones indicates that Smith is downstairs for more tests I look him in the eyes with as much compassion as I can muster and explain, " I wasn't here to talk to him, I need to talk with you."

"Aw f*#k", he grimaces, "'I've been waiting for you to come by and tell me. Our coughs are the same, our symptoms are the same, we even served in some of the same places in 'Nam." We talk over the details and tests that will be forthcoming to stage the cancer and treatment options. Again, the handshake, the thanks, and resignation as he settles back into the bed with a sigh. This time there is no wife to rage, to protect or to comfort.

Parking at the VA is at a premium, and late arrivals like me today must park far out in a field. I make the long trek from the parking lot at the VA. Accompanying me is Greta, our team's physician assistant, who's been at the VA for years. She is a vet and protective of "her people." We get off the elevator and, as usual, head for the break room just outside the four-bed hospice unit. As we come down the hallway, towards the doors of the unit, we can hear shouting and screaming. Then more screaming. Greta, who has never been seen to move faster than a leisurely meander, breaks into a run towards the doors, as I struggle to keep up. She is muttering, "oh f*#k, oh f*#k, oh f*#k, not again."

Helen, a Vietnam era nurse, had come in early yesterday afternoon writhing in excruciating back pain from cancer metastasizing into her back. We'd spent all the afternoon and part of the evening working to get her pain under control. It took some hefty doses, but we finally got there. When we left, she was awake, but finally resting comfortably. Most of the nurses on the unit are experienced hospice and palliative care nurses. However, occasionally, when they are short staffed, a floor nurse is pulled in to help. To the floor nurses unaccustomed to our protocols, the doses, the medications and algorithms to control pain are out of their experience.

As we reach the swinging door opening into the hospice unit, an elderly nurse, one of the few still wearing a nursing school cap, erupts from the doors. Fixing Greta with a glare, she says "You people are crazy; I can't use those doses. You're putting my nursing license at risk. What you are doing is euthanasia! You people should be ashamed!" That said, she stomps off down the hall. Greta spares her not even a second glance, but charges into the patient's room to assess the patient and spews orders. It takes several hours but again the patient is resting comfortably and thanking Greta profusely for helping her.

Surprisingly, even years later, this is not an uncommon phenomenon. I have had to ask for the medication syringes to be handed to me when the hospital nurse refused to give the patient the pain medication. Said more than one nurse, 'but the patient could get comfortable, drop their blood pressure and die.' To which I wryly reply, that 'a hospice doctor standing at bedside is probably the single worst prognostic sign in medicine.' I often indicate that death is expected, the question is not if, but how. I also tell the staff our mantra that 'pain is not a pressor agent.' Meaning we do not make the patient suffer to keep their blood pressure up in the fact of expected death. Still a survey of hospice and palliative medicine specialists once showed more than half have been accused of murdering patients.

Amazingly, the next morning, the same resistance to our orders by inexperienced staff greets us again. This time the patient is hysterical. "That was horrible. Doing it again and knowing there was no hope from the nurses until morning. I was praying I would die" she sobs. "The pain was so bad." I am stunned, Greta is apoplectic! This repeated disaster prompts a call to the night shift supervisor and a heated meeting punctuated by shouts and threats between nursing and the hospice unit staff. Fortunately, whatever was said in the meeting puts Finis to these episodes.

A new veteran we see the following morning insists that he is on 200 milligrams of methadone, which is a pretty hefty dose-even for us. The team has concerns that he may be exaggerating in order to get more drugs. I'm assigned track down and to call a pharmacy in Indiana and confirm the accuracy of dose. The dose is correct, but we still pare it down a little, to insure we don't overdose him. We can always give more, but an overdose can be fatal and depressingly permanent. Our two new medical students are wide eyed at the size of the doses of medication we seem to casually prescribe. "Our motto," We tell them, "whatever it takes to get them comfortable."

Rounding the next day, I meet an African American Korean War Vet. He seems comfortable, arms linked behind his head, and his body stretched out in a bed almost too short for him. We chat a minute more as the group moves on. He then turns and fixes me with a piercing look. "Nobody ever asks a black man how it feels to by dying!"

I fumble in surprise for a second and then turn back to him. "OK I'll bite, how does it feel?"

"Feels good!"

"I'm sorry, I know my hearing's not great, but it sounded like you said 'Good'?"

"That's right," he nods expansively, "I'm 85, my kids are grown and turned out good. I'm in this VA hospital, being respected for my service. The pain from my cancer is controlled, my family visits, but doesn't stay so long it gets obnoxious. Like I said, feels good."

I shake his hand and wish out loud in heartfelt fashion, "I hope when my time comes, I can say the same."

It is now time to re-introduce the key player in my saga—my mother: Cynthia Phelps. Mom was a housewife and full-time mom for my brother, sister and I until my father succumbed to alcoholism. Then they divorced. At that point, my grandmother, tiny but fearsome, an independent and well-to-do woman, moved in to support the family while my mother went back to graduate school. Grandma's husband had been an internist who died youngish but left her well off. She was most proud of being a physician's wife and even years after grandpa's death, a copy of MD's Wife was always on her front table. Grandma was a southern belle from Chattanooga, Tennessee who had only two years of college from the Martha Washington Girls College, but she was a ruthless businesswoman. She parlayed a small inheritance into a substantial fortune.

Mom finished her master's in library science and moved to the small town of Marion, South Carolina, to act as the head (only)librarian for the county library. I was starting my first year of college, and my grandmother drove me to start school while mom got settled in Marion. Mom was a heavy smoker. My recurring vision of her is curled up in her chair, nose in a book, cigarette smoke curling up above her head. It is from her that I inherited my love of learning and books.

Years later she too developed alcoholism that cost her, her beloved job. She endured several rounds of rehab and landed another job in another library. After another relapse, that job ended similarly. Eventually she retired and became sober. Her alcoholism may have had something to do with her mother, who had been a merciless critic of every woman in our family. Becoming a doctor like her beloved husband, meant I could do no wrong. My sister, however, could do no right. Grandma supporting the family came at high personal cost to Mom and Kathy. In the end Grandma succumbed to dementia and finally died in a nursing home some miles from Mom's home.

With Grandma gone, Mom was finally free of daily critiques on her many failings and sobered up. Her experiences and education left her one of those rare women who as she got older, became more liberal and less religious as she aged. On several occasions, she questioned my extensive church involvement, but admitted she liked going to Christmas Eve services with our family. Her politics likewise ranged further left as the years progressed. I recall her reading the paper muttering about "that f*#king moron Bush." She suffered fools poorly.

Her mother's passing had left a substantial inheritance, and mom was finally able to do what she always wanted, which was to travel. Grandma talked in lofty tones about the educating experience of travel, including her trip around the world. Mom was determined to beat Grandma's mileage. Several trips to places in Europe including England and Switzerland had already occurred. Now she's embarked on the big one- a tour of China. It is on a Memorial Day weekend when the phone rings at six AM. It is Mom. "Greg, oh thank God," she wheezes. "I'm in the hospital!"

Having been freshly woken on a holiday weekend, I groggily respond: "No you're not, you're in China."

If she hadn't been in pain, she probably would've been a snarled as she responded, "I'm in the hospital.... in China." Long story short, Mom had managed to fall off the Great Wall of China.

In rapid conversation, it turned out the she'd been with her tour group seeing the Great Wall of China. A film crew was making a commercial near the steps leading off the wall. Mom was watching the filming as she descended. When the steps turned, she didn't, and over she went.

The accident had happened over a week ago. She'd been having a horrible time trying to reach me. As it so happened, the area code for Knoxville had been changed just a few weeks earlier. Mom had been trying to call me without success for a week. The tour group having brought her to the hospital, had moved on long ago. It wasn't until a rare English-speaking staff member at the Beijing hospital came by to talk to her, that she was able to get someone to ascertain and dial the correct number. Hence the six am phone call.

I tried to have a conversation with the Chinese orthopedist. Unfortunately, his English was marginally better than my (non-existent) Chinese, but not by much. I hastily contacted an orthopedist friend of mine at the hospital where I was the medical director. Outlining the situation in terse detail, I asked him if he would let his mother have a hip replacement in China, "Absolutely not. Get her back here as quick as you can."

As it turned out, Mom, in her thoroughness, had purchased travel insurance that included medical transportation. Nevertheless, it was a brutal, time-consuming process to get her back to the US. The travel insurance company was in England, the travel evacuation company was in China, and I was in the US working logistics in parallel with my brother who had much more travel experience. The insurance company agreed that major hip surgery in China was far from optimal but refused to fly her all the way to the US. They offered Hong Kong or Singapore. The evacuation company in Beijing would start planning flights then quit, without telling us, when the insurers vetoed flying their proposed itinerary. I wanted her in the America, preferably my hospital where our major specialty was orthopedic surgery. There were many false starts and days of arguing with evacuation and insurance companies. I am acutely aware that everyday delaying surgery is producing a rapid decline in Mom's already precarious health. After a full two weeks of this nonsense, I had final chilly conversation with the London based travel insurance company, as they tried to veto yet another travel proposal to bring her to the US.

"Listen," I snapped, "My mother is a wealthy woman, she can write a check for the expense. Put her on a goddamn plane, get her back here. Do it now. We can sue you and your company later."

There was a moment's pause with the adjuster, before in very stiff British diction, he gravely responded, "Sir, I don't know that that will be completely necessary, but we will do as you ask."

Mom wrote the check. They flew her home. (Eventually the insurance company did pay most of the bill.)

The Learjet taxied up to the runway in Knoxville and unloaded mom its sole passenger. She was accompanied by a nurse provided by the evacuation company. Mom looked like death warmed over, as she weakly hugged us. It had been almost three weeks, and she was in terrible shape. Her sodium was low, her blood count was low, and her lungs were worse than usual. It took over a week to get her healthy enough to risk surgery.

Recovery was worse. Due to various complications she eventually accumulated nine different doctors. (I don't count, I was more referee and traffic director) She almost died twice. From each doctor, I'd get a different story, every report in isolation from the other, and the patient in general. Thus, the orthopedist came in a few days after the surgery and admired her well healing hip wound. Patting the gauze back down over the incision, he smiled, jammed his thumb skyward and exclaimed, "My part is looking great." Then he gave mom one more affectionate pat on the back side. Unfortunately, at the time, mom was nearly comatose. Had she been up to speed, she probably would've decked him.

She suffered multiple setbacks while in the hospital. A week after the orthopedist visit, I was driving to one of our affiliate hospitals in a neighboring state. My good friend and her gastroenterologist called me to say that my mother was unconscious, and they suspected a stroke. "I'm sending her for a CT scan ASAP, then I'll get a neurologist. Where are you and when can you get here?" he asked wanting me there immediately. When I told him where I was, he urged me to turn around and come back quickly. I drove back sobbing most of the way.

In the end, it wasn't a stroke. Ironically, it was overmedication from multiple doctors. Mom finally recovered enough to move briefly to a nursing facility for rehab and then spent several months at my house getting physical therapy. Therapy was slow as Mom was sometimes resistant. Apparently, it had been worse in China when the nurses tried to move her to keep from getting bedsores. "Those nurses in China," mom announced grimly, "know at least three words of English…DON'T touch me!"

Finally, however, almost six months after her Chinese odyssey began, she finally limped out to her well used Toyota Camry to go back home to South Carolina. As she slipped into her seat, she grinned cheekily saying, "I guess I'll have to be a bit more careful traveling."

Ever the dutiful son, I strode over to the car, leaned into the window and only semi-teasingly said," If you go out of the country again, I'll break your other leg." Mom smiled, patted me on the cheek and totally ignored me. She actually did break the other leg, well, ankle, in a trip to Belize two years later. She hid the injury from me for years until my sister spilled the beans.

On the hospital side, if nothing else, I had gotten a ringside seat to what our patients endure day in and day out in our very broken healthcare system. It was the beginning push that eventually propelled me to looking for a better way to comfort and communicate with patients and eventually led me to palliative care.

So now I'm back at the VA as the month is winding down. Wednesdays are "Popcorn Day." I am a long-time popcorn fanatic. Retired vets come to sell large bags of popcorn in the lobby for a dollar. The perfume of popcorn wafts into every corner of the hospital calling me. To me, the smell is heavenly. My order keeps increasing as I haul more and more back to the break room for staff, residents and nurses and myself.

Wednesday is also time for early morning church service. Many Episcopalians are notoriously liberal and several of our tiny Wednesday morning prayer group are sporting "Another Momma for Obama" buttons as we head into the last days before the election.

Later in the morning at the VA, Rolling Thunder, a long parade of vets on motorcycles comes through on their way to Washington DC to make a statement about the poor state of veterans' care. All the residents, medical students and many nurses duck out to watch the seemingly endless parade thrum past. Two new medical students have joined us enthralled: popcorn and a parade on the first day. They might like the VA after all.

I leave the students watching the seemingly endless line of motorcycles. I step onto the elevator, and a younger woman gets on with me and glances at my lab coat. Then she tries to pronounce the palliative in Palliative Care. She mangles it the word. I help her out suggesting she think 'pal' like a friend in the hospital. She concedes having a doctor as a friend would be an asset in a place like a hospital. She asks what I do, I stumble a little trying to think of a quick, concise answer as the elevator heads upward. Palliative care helps people who are in pain or suffering."

"That sounds great!" she responds. "Can you come see my dad?"

This becomes a little awkward as professional etiquette says as we are only supposed to see a patient when consulted by a physician on staff to help with life threatening or very serious illness. We've not been asked, and I have no idea what her dad is there for. "Well there's a bit of a downside." I push my hospital ID, clipped to my lapel and she sees the whole title "palliative care and hospice."

Her smile fades, it is her turn to hesitate as the elevator dings her floor. With a brisk shake of her head, she quickly steps off and walks away. In business, I'd often heard the term "elevator speech" as a shorthand to describe your pitch in the time on the elevator. I realize that I need to come up with a better one.

After considerable thought, I come up with this: the three 'C's of caring.

--The first C is comfort: we treat suffering-pain, shortness of breath, constipation, (small smirk) and even spiritual angst.

--The second "C" is communication: We engage the patient and family in two-way communication, listening and talking with patients about what is important to them, providing information about diagnosis, possible treatments and prognosis and likely outcomes. Thus informed, we listen, about how they want to live their life.

--The final "C" is coordination: Once we understand the informed patient's goals and wishes, we try to get everyone including the patient's family, care givers, doctors, nurses, etc., all on the same page.

If I have more floors on this metaphorical elevator, I explain that while palliative care grew out of the same philosophic underpinning as hospice, palliative care can be different. Patients may be supported in serious illness and yet recover. They may seek aggressive treatment or live well beyond the six months often associated with hospice. Doing my fellowship in the bourbon capital, I explain that just like not all whiskey is fine bourbon, not all palliative care is hospice!

Late that afternoon, while riding my bike, I get a long-awaited phone call. My younger son has been 'missing' at college for several weeks now. I've called and called as has his mother. Nada. We don't know the numbers of any of his friends to call. His sister suggested I try Facebook.

"Facebook? What is that?" I had no idea what she was talking about. She explains this new internet sensation to me. I registered on Facebook and then tried to friend my son. Today, finally, he calls. I see the area code for his college town and hit the curb almost toppling trying to answer.

"Hi Dad," he cheerily calls out. "Why are you trying to friend me on Facebook?"

"Because I'd like to know why you're not returning our phone calls," I answer trying hard not to sound both relieved and angry.

"Ohhhhh, my phone. We were getting out of a friend's jeep, I dropped it and he backed over it. I've been trying to get a new one..." He trails off clearly hoping I'll offer up money for a replacement. The last phone got dropped in the ocean.

Instead, that weekend I go to the phone store and grimly ask for a phone "so well protected you can drive a jeep over it or drop it the ocean." I leave the store with essentially an armored phone to pass to my youngest. "This or nothing" I explain proffering the sizable, armored phone to his disappointed gaze.

The month is almost over. We've been trying to manage the pain for Mr. Ray in the VA hospice inpatient unit. Now we've got him comfortable, it is late afternoon when I write prescriptions and chart the information to send him back to his wife for home hospice to take over. He shakes my hand heartily. The change in him with his cancer pain controlled now, is astonishing. His color is back, his pained hunch has been transformed into the ramrod posture of the Marine he was. Though thinner, he still gives me a bone crushing handshake as he thanks me for all our efforts. He tries to hide his pleased glow announcing that his whole dispersed family is coming together for the first time in years to spend time with him. Healings like this is what makes my time away from family invaluable and I smile as I wave him out the door.

The word for healing comes from an Old English word for wholeness. It is not the same as curing which implies resolving or eradicating illness, avoiding impending death. However, at some point, everyone, will eventually die. Healing is more about restoration of self, relationships and community. In this sense, despite the cancer, Mr. Ray is healing. This parting encounter with Mr. Ray has buoyed my mood and I am up for the festivities of Halloween. I'm hoping there might still be a few trick or treaters to terrorize when I get home.

November: The Hospice Inpatient Unit.

The area hospice has a large inpatient unit (IPU) of 12 beds, compared to four in the VA medical Center. The hospice unit is in a wing of a partially decommissioned hospital. Like the VA unit, patients come here to have uncontrolled symptoms managed. It is often also where people die. I arrive on the floor, and the nurses nicely point out I lack an ID badge and decline my entry. I walk back to the elevators to grab my badge from my car. The elevator dings, the doors open and disgorges EMTs arguing over the contents of their gurney. They are arguing as to whether the patient has died in route. The gurney rolls out to stop in front of me.

I may have forgotten my badge, but I have my stethoscope and a white coat that says Dr. Phelps. I pull the stethoscope out and plunk it down on the traveler. No pulse. The nurse comes around the desk and does likewise. Same result. There is no frantic effort at CPR. Death was expected, perhaps just not this quickly. The family has yet to arrive, so we park the patient in an empty room. When they come in a few minutes later, desperately seeking 'Dad,' we usher them gravely into the family room. Seeing our expressions, they understand, and tears begin to flow.

The chaplain steps in as we step out. After a suitable interval, we ask if there is anyone else, we need to contact and which funeral home they wish us to notify. The death was expected, and they have a funeral home name and number for us. The pattern is begun my first day, patients coming to the hospice unit rarely leave still breathing. Death everyday soon becomes the norm.

The next day is Election day. Bev and I both voted early by absentee ballots We take off our Obama pins before going to work. River City is an island of red in the southern blue sea of the surrounding rural countryside. In hospice though, given the nature of our caring, it is hard to find people who aren't trending liberal. Bev and I get together at her place to watch the results and share a beer. It looks close, the results might go late into the night. At 10:30 we're both drooping with fatigue. We finally we agree to go our separate ways. I walk down the block to my building. As I enter the apartment, my phone rings. It's Bev. "Oh my God!" she shrieks. "Two minutes after the polls closed on the west coast, the whole west end of the country went blue!! We won!" Surrounded in River City by a conservative media and press, we've forgotten there is a whole country out there. We bask in the glow only a few moments before we realize tomorrow is going to be another long day in health care, and we go our respective ways to bed.

The IPU is a constant shuffle of patients arriving with terrible symptoms, often dying. I spend much of my time rounding on new patients, writing admission histories and crafting orders to make them more comfortable. I also continually shuttle up and down the long hallway among the patients to check for signs of progress in relief or decline with the patients. In between all this, I run over to my VA clinic experience and see more veterans, or I go to different departments lectures for exposure to fields not related to palliative care. The cornucopia of potential topics is wonderfully intoxicating. For a perpetual student like me, this is heaven

Today, in the IPU, we have a tough one; A 36-year-old with terrible, widespread pancreatic cancer. He is exceptionally young for this virulent and largely untreatable cancer. He previously had a Whipple procedure, a surgery so extensive, physicians call it the 'walking autopsy,' followed by chemotherapy and radiation to no avail. He went all in; at his age, I probably would have tried too. He is moaning in pain and terminally restless. The family is tortured by his pain despite our best efforts involving eye popping amounts of pain medication they ask, hesitantly, but repeatedly, if we can 'help him along.'

Reluctantly, our team begins the discussion about 'palliative sedation,' in which being asleep is the best thing we can do for the patient until they die. It used to be called the less politically correct- terminal sedation. There are strict protocols and rules that involve informed consent and a life expectancy estimated to be less than 2 weeks. These protocols involve using near anesthesia levels of medication to put the patient into a coma, usually until they die. It is not euthanasia however, as we do not intend lethal doses and the patient is regularly monitored at intervals, to ensure that the dying process in not inadvertently hurried.

The patient moans but is awake enough to hear us describe palliative sedation. "Anything," he hoarsely whispers, "is better than this. "Just give me some relief." The family crowds in offering individual goodbyes and 'I love yous'. I too, am misty eyed, as we prepare to start a ketamine drip to render the patient insensate, along with a narcotic drip and another of sedation. An hour later, the patient is resting comfortably. The family settles in for their vigil. As he is otherwise young and healthy, it will be days.

The weekend comes. Gayle is sick with a cold. I can't say too much I probably gave it to her over Halloween. I make myself scarce and go out to do work at our cabin on Douglas Lake. We love the locale, the lake and the mountains it is however, a never-ending set of chores, but I enjoy the work and relish the solitude.

The road next to our cabin is named Pappy Van Winkle which, I've soon learned is the name of a bourbon, and our street address is on Pot Still. Looking for a good way to extend the alcohol related puns we christen the cabin Stillwater both for the quiet of our cove and the liquid refreshments often consumed there.

Back Monday at the IPU, I encounter Sister Rita from the nearby Catholic hospital sitting with a patient holding his hand and letting him talk. Other patients, more obtunded can at least appreciate the presence of a warm hand holding theirs. Sister. Rita is a fixture in the IPU. Having come from a Catholic hospital myself, we bond. The patient on palliative sedation is still holding on with occasional boosts to his medication to keep him comfortable and insensate. The algorithm dictates we follow the protocol for a week and then rouse the patient and check for improvement. It is, admittedly rare that a patient lasts the week. The family and I develop a companionable relationship with Sister Rita joining in to help the family reminisce about happier times with the patient.

The belief among medical professionals, is that sometimes a patient may hear even when seeming comatose. To that end, we encourage families to include the patient in the conversation as the process seems healing for all. Frequently, I learn about the patients in a way that makes me wish I'd known them prior to our care. Despite the melancholy undertones, the conversations remind me to open myself to the joy other people can bring.

Veteran's Day, a huge deal for the VA where I'm attending clinic. There is a crowd of administrators and politicians reading proclamations on the front steps. Our palliative care team and most other care teams are invited over to join the scrum. All of us, in thin white coats, are huddling in the cold unable to exit until the last speech is read. Then we all hastily return to our units and the hospital warmth. Politicians make a big deal about veterans on Veteran's Day. I'm cynically reminded that despite lip service and empty promises, this often appears the only day they really seem to care.

Back at the IPU, a 50-year-old woman with breast cancer comes in. We'd been expecting her transfer the evening before, however, knowing the reputation of where she was coming, she was trying to postpone her arrival another day or so. Now she is barely conscious, cachectic, mottled and dying. Anna, our attending, runs down to the ER to see her to get her quickly admitted to the IPU. She dies three hours later. I review my patient cards and am stunned to see that in a third of the month I've had 24 deaths! Anna nods and gravely intones without apparent irony that it's been a 'slow month.' Forcing myself to leave this reality behind, Bev and I go to a lecture by the medical school dean entitled: Poverty as a Carcinogen. I'd never really thought about socio-economic status as a specific health risk and can see quickly how it applies to many of our hospice patients!

It's a Wednesday so I'm back at the church first thing in the morning. The campaign buttons are gone, but a generally celebratory mood persists about the election. Service over, I hurry out into the cold to get to work. When I get to the IPU, four more people have died during the night. One of those was our palliative sedation patient who only made it six days. I'm saddened. I was really hoping he'd make the seven days and get a chance to speak with his family again in better circumstances, before dying. But the harsh reality is the family is gone, the bed is empty with fresh sheets awaiting the next patient. Days like this it feels like we manage a mechanical factory for the end of life. I struggle to remind myself that our care is a blessing for people suffering. Admittedly, I often work hard to remind myself of this fact and block out the discouraging reality of day to day care.

Several patients are struggling with their pain and we initiate a floor wide crusade to start patients on methadone. It works well. The downside we've found, is the name methadone tends to create panic for patients and their families as they usually this associate this specific medication with addiction and the stigma of methadone clinics. Methadone, however, often works well where other opioids don't, as it also affects a different second set of pain receptors and works in patients for whom other pain medicines have been less effective. Our crusade this morning works well most of the patients show substantial improvement in their pain as we work through the day. I'm cheered to see patients now smiling and chatting with families where they had been groaning in pain this morning. My buoyed mood, the lasts almost to the evening when I'm pulled aside by Marcia to discuss my October faculty review.

They are still not happy with me or my performance. I push back a bit saying Anna has been complimentary of my work on several occasions. Marcia hints that Anna is not really one of the 'tribe,' so her comments don't really count. I asked for specifics that I can correct, and in return, I get general statements that don't help me address any specific problem. The most descriptive thing she can say, is she's not finding what she wants. To me it feels like guess what I'm thinking. I leave the meeting frustrated and confused.

I know that I need to put aside Marcia's criticism because the following day is a big one for me. I'm to give the palliative care lecture for the group at the noon conference. My topic is the interplay between addiction medicine and palliative care. Addiction medicine is specialty of mine that gives me on a firm and experienced footing. Aside from the material with which I have 20 years' practice and certification in, I am also a polished presenter. I've spoken at national conferences and written and published on the topic. This is my chance to shine. Despite yesterday's less than stellar review, I am excited for this new day to begin. I dash out the apartment building door to my car that morning, my anticipation evaporates, I find my windows smashed and my car robbed.

I stand stunned, looking around the otherwise empty garage for a moment. My car is literally the only one in the brick-lined cavernous expanse. Sweeping the crushed glass off my seat with a sigh and muttering foul curses, I go over to the IPU to round before heading to do my talk.

The talk goes extremely well. Howard grins when he shakes my hand and says, "Wow, you've got some speaking chops." I grin back and begin to reply but he rolls on. "Marcia and I would like to review a couple of chart notes with you. We think there are a few things you could improve." He gestures down the hall. Talk about a buzzkill! He could have given me at least a few seconds to enjoy the moment!

Marcia is already there waiting in a conference room with a small stack of records. We quickly find part of the problem is that the records we're reviewing, are handwritten and my handwriting has been execrable since at least the fourth grade. Handwriting has interfered with my notes, papers and records since elementary school when my mother was called in to meet with my teacher. "Mrs. Phelps if your son doesn't become a doctor..." she warned ominously, "he's doomed." Mom put an optimistic spin on her conversation when she came home saying "Your teacher says you are going to have to be a doctor!" Still,

I was forced to practice penmanship for weeks but years later it is obvious the practice never took root.

So, almost fifty years later, when Howard and Marcia say I didn't address the patient's pain, I point to a section in the handwritten notes and read back "Patient complains of 7/10 pain that radiates down the right leg and feels like 'electricity'. Pain is aggravated by standing and bending and relieved with rest." I lean back with a slightly smug smile.

"Is THAT what it says?" they ask incredulously. After some discussion, we agree to set aside the handwriting issue to look at some typed notes. I will be responsible for pulling some of my VA notes which are typed on a computer. Still, I'm dejected that evening.

"It just constantly seems to be one thing after another. If I cured cancer, they'd probably complain about me causing unemployment for oncologists," I grump to Bev over our weekly dinner.

Bev commiserates. "I don't get it," she says. "I read your notes, I think they're great, and then they come along and snipe at you. I look at my notes compared to yours and keep waiting for the shoe to drop." By now we've both dropped out of Spanish but still gather for a weekly dinner. Our relationship has evolved into one of two struggling students just trying to get through. Bev is a supporter, colleague and a friendly ear for commiseration I worry to myself that Bev seems to be doing most of the supporting.

My sister Katherine is beginning to worry about me too. A professor of finance at a Missouri University, she picks up my thinly veiled depression as I unload my trials and challenges.

Like Bev, she commiserates and gets defensive for her baby brother. Springing into action she mails me DVDs of a BBC series called Coupling. She bills this as the funniest TV series ever. She follows up with an email where she worries, I might be getting depressed. This is sound advice that I cannot bring myself to acknowledge. The TV series, however, is hilarious, and I watch an episode or two a week finding it really does lift my spirits. The author Norman Cousins wrote in <u>Anatomy of an Illness</u>, how he set out a program of humor and laughter to relieve his illness. I find his therapy as proposed by my sister as a helpful anodyne. I subsequently buy seasons 2-4 and spend occasional evenings through the rest of the fellowship using it for comedic relief. Lifting my spirits becomes an apt phrase when later I hear a chaplain referring to his work, say: "It is not about God or religion; it is whether I've raised your spirits during my visit....If I did, then my job for spiritual care has been done." God was placing answers in front of me that only in retrospect, could I appreciate

I'm still a little whipsawed from yesterday's ups and downs and Katherine's email and to top it off, I need to go to meet a guy to get my car window fixed. The garage says they have a video disk of the thieves robbing my car. They offer me the disc, but I realize I know almost no one in River City to recognize and it would be too much to impotently watch people I didn't know rob my car. To their surprise, I tell the garage owners that it wasn't that much to steal, I'm over it. I go home for the weekend, I burrow into a recliner, mope and read.

The following week we have a new guest in the IPU. I glance through the door at a 24-year-old girl with stunning curly red hair. She is made up, her hair arranged and comatose. Even in slack repose in the bed, sheets neatly tucked around her, she is beautiful. At her bedside, clutching her limp hand, is her younger clone, maybe four, also red headed and destined for her mother's looks. The family looks on weeping as the child perseverates," Mommy, mommy, mommy, wake up, wake up, pick me up. Mommy mommy...."

Quickly returning to the nurse's desk, I hastily scan the chart, which reveals a first try at crack cocaine and an unknown and unsuspected brain aneurism. A drug induced surge in blood pressure blew out the aneurism resulting in a catastrophic brain bleed. The neurosurgeons reportedly took one look at the CT Scan of her brain and resignedly issued a referral to hospice saying our least favorite phrase— "There's nothing we can do."

Digesting the chart, I grimly compose myself, enter the room and introduce myself to her family. Many families look at a new doctor as a new hope. This family just nods with mute expression and sheds occasional tears as they steal glances at their daughter. I find myself flashing to the possibility that, but for the grace of God, this could be my daughter and my new granddaughter. Young, beautiful, vivacious one moment, and suddenly an empty shell no longer holding any possibilities for the future.

Companion tears, to match the parents' form in edges of my eyes. Ducking my head to so no one sees my own sorrow, I make a show of pulling out my stethoscope and bending over the patient for a brief exam while I compose myself. The exam will tell me nothing that I didn't see from the door. The only thing I can do at this point is be a decent human being offering all I can in terms of empathy and support.

Nodding to the chairs, I gesture to the family to let me sit with them and share their grief. I encourage them to tell me stories about her and talk with their granddaughter who continues to orbit her mother. Cocaine does not come up. Once everyone is relatively collected, I offer information. "Would you like me to discuss the next steps, what goes on from here?" There are a series of mute nods. I talk about how death approaches. Sometimes it comes with sudden decline and seizures; more commonly it comes as a slow stealing away of breath with longer and longer pauses in between until the next breath just doesn't happen.

I discuss time frames cautioning them that their daughter is otherwise young and healthy. I warn them that this is likely to be a marathon, not a sprint. I make suggestions that they take time to rest and spell each other, hold her hand, and talk to her, include her in the conversation. I repeat my mantra to this family that sometimes hearing is the last sense to fold down, and she may at some deep level know that they're here and love her. They nod, and again as so many patient's families incongruously do, they thank me. Levering myself up, I invoke a little of my preventive health background.

"Has anyone else in your family ever had a brain aneurism?" I ask. They recall an uncle who had a brain bleed a decade ago and an aunt who died of a stroke. "These things sometimes run in families," I ruminate. "It might be a good idea to see your family doctor and get tested." Again, they nod and thank me.

I check in with them over several days, and I always sit to chat. Compassion- (Latin for to suffer with), is the only therapy I have to offer. By Thursday, her breathing slows, she begins to have episodes of breath holding- apneic spells. When I come in Friday, she's gone, the bed made up. I feel not just the loss of a patient, but of her whole family and their dashed hopes. The empty bed in some way again mocks my own sentiments toward closure. I pause inside the empty room for a few moments to offer a prayer for both patient and her family. I have some glimmer of their pain, as early in my practice years our small town went through the initial cocaine epidemic and I lost several friends. When my kids were teens, I told them I'd put up with a lot, but if they did cocaine and it killed them, that by golly I'd dig them up and kill them all over again! So far, the message has stuck.

That afternoon at the VA clinic, the first patient is late, so I pull up a of couple patient charts on the computer and print my notes for Howard and Marcia to review later. By then, my patient has arrived from oncology. I walk in the room to introduce to myself, but he is already reading my name tag and department. Unlike the substantial majority of patients, he knows what palliative care might imply and comes apart! "Oh my God," he moans clutching himself. "I'm dying, and no one told me!"

I try to reassure him that I'm there to help with his pain, and he eventually unclutches. He has stage IV cancer, and he IS dying but I'm going to give it another week before introducing that topic again. I review and adjust his medications, and I schedule him for follow up in a week where we may resume exploring his prognosis. His reaction was such a stark contrast to the family with the redheaded daughter, that I must remind myself, yet again, that every patient, and every family comes to this point from a different place.

The day continues, as I hurry back to the IPU across town. A few days earlier, a pancreatic cancer patient in severe pain had made it out of the unit to go home- pain controlled. Her elation though was short lived. Over the night, her symptoms recurred with a rush. She waves weakly with a grimace and in a voice purloined from the movie Poltergeist…says" I'm heeeere." I smile at her humor and bravery. An hour later she is fading, obtunded and dies late that afternoon. Our consolation is she was comfortable and surrounded by family as she breathed her last.

We've had another patient with agitation and dementia in the unit. She arrived from a nursing home no longer able to cope. Spitting, clawing and shouting for someone to help her she was a handful on arrival. We've had for a few days of medication adjustments and compassionate work to keep her engaged and oriented. She is finally calm enough to return to her nursing home. She triumphantly waves goodbye and blows me a kiss as she is rolled out by the EMTs. That puts a slightly better coda to a day of exhausting and incessant downs and ups. Finally, snug in my tiny apartment, I park myself with a copy of Final Gifts by a hospice nurse, pour myself some of Kentucky's most famous export and sink into a chair.

That weekend brings a few snowflakes. I worry about getting over the mountains to Knoxville, but the ride is easy. Gayle, my daughter and grandchild have all gone to South Carolina to see Gayle's 91-year-old mother Sally, in the nursing home. It is Sally's first time to see her great grandchild. Gayle tells me they were all overcome with the sense of connection and continuity which they memorialized in a four generations photo that still sits in our den. Left alone for Saturday, I'm out at the lake cutting trees and moving rock. The physical work is a welcome respite for work frustrations. Gayle gets back Saturday night. While my spirits have been low from the medical work, she too is down a little after seeing her mother continue decline. Since she has been regularly hearing stories of dying patients (blinded of identifying details of course) from me, she can't help but apply some of my observations closer to home. She also worries that her mom has been hanging on to see the great grandchild and wonders what will happen now. We share our fears and provide what support we can to each other. It is a welcome interlude to our recently testy relationship engendered by the fellowship.

I return from the weekend to find three new patients in the hospice IPU. Anna has not yet made an appearance. Patient census is a little light, so when I finish rounds, I pull out my omnipresent book and begin to read. The nurses joke about how I read whenever I'm sitting-probably even in the bathroom.

I look up from my book, another hospice text, smile and nod. "In my family we call it the oculo-rectal reflex. The need to read while pooping. And yes, I do have a bookshelf within reach of the toilet."

The head nurse nods smugly and says, "I knew it, my husband does that too."

That evening I'm working on an abstract for the American Academy of Hospice and Palliative Medicine. As fellows, we are "strongly encouraged" to come up with a short, interesting topic to submit. Walter, our recurring abdominal catastrophe, who has returned several more times, presents unique challenges in getting pain medications. I've researched and learned of a variety of ways including inhaled, skin preparations, rectal, subcutaneously, intravenously, sublingual (under the tongue and others.)

I've been working on a few paragraphs on our experience with Walter, humorously titled "There May be Fifty Ways to Leave Your Lover, But I give You Opioids in Fifty-one!" (This does call for some creative accounting) I've sent the abstract to Howard and others to review. Howard says he likes it, but he is still reviewing it... for weeks. It is only a few paragraphs! Given that we've established that all faculty were English majors in college, I'm assuming I'm having my English heavily corrected in an unfathomable fashion. With time to the deadline running out, I've resorted to almost daily emails to get my abstract back.

On the final day, Howard returns the draft with surprisingly minimal corrections. Now I must figure out how to upload it to the AAHPM website. I struggle with this new and unfamiliar format of computerized transmission, but I'm eventually rewarded with a button asking- "Do you wish to submit," at the bottom of the flickering screen. I highlight yes and press the button which blinks, then close the computer. Whew... Done with three hours to spare. Little do I know that I have unknowingly sown yet another seed of doubt that will come back to bite me months later.

The next day brings an African American family whose 85-year-old matriarch has suffered a massive brain bleed. She is unconscious with stertorous breathing with apneic pauses that herald impending demise. Her family are angry and resentful that the diagnosis was made in the emergency room, and that the patient was immediately sent to the hospice care unit for her final hours. They had wanted surgery that the neurosurgeon said wouldn't help. They wanted ICU to keep her alive, but also wanted to be with her if the end was coming. More than once, I hear variations on the surreptitious comment, I suspect I'm meant to hear. "I bet if she was white, we'd all be in ICU, unnnh- hunh."

Looking at the patient, I think the neurosurgeon made the right call, but probably didn't deliver the news in the best way. I sit and explain, drawing pictures of the damage and consequences of this bleed. I bend over backwards to explain the devastating neurological sequelae. We talk about the kind of life she would have in the unlikely event she'd had surgery and survived. Then, we talk about ICUs and what would have happened there with ventilators, tubes and how little time they would have to be with her as the end approached. The anger slowly transmutes to resignation as I point out how they can spend all the time they want with her in the spacious Hospice IPU rooms instead of being stranded in the ICU waiting room. The hostility level drops substantially but still lurks. Working with this family and hearing their concerns forces me to reflect on race in health care.

I grew up in Bloomfield Hills, a wealthy, almost totally white neighborhood outside Detroit. At that time Detroit was riding high as the fourth largest city in the US. In my high school of 1600, there was one black student. The only African American I knew reasonably well was Alberta, the maid that my parents and grandparents shared. I never heard her last name. She was just always there as Alberta. I remember as a child, Alberta being the person who was most upset when my grandmother died. When my mother, father and we children received the news, Alberta was the one who was hysterical, as she slumped over the kitchen table sobbing and wailing uncontrollably. She shed more tears than the rest of us put together. My family, progeny of New England Puritans and stiff upper lips, looked on with astonishment and stoicism. The unspoken message to me was 'those people' just don't know how to comport themselves. To say I was oblivious to the underlying issues of race, cultural norms and the privilege of being white would be a gross understatement. I was embarrassingly ignorant. When the Detroit riots of 1967 occurred, we were all stunned as we watched the grainy television images from the safe remove of our summer beach vacation.

So, it was this naïve innocent who moved to Marion, South Carolina in the early 1970s. As liberal, hippie wannabes, my brother, sister and

I all felt more kinship with African Americans trying to assert their basic humanity, than with the rednecks driving around with trucks flying the Confederate flag. Desegregation just a few years earlier had resulted in a white flight emptying the public schools in favor of "Segregation Academies." My sister Katherine was briefly placed in one of these academies- "where all the white kids went". But a liberal Northerner and several fights later, our well-intentioned mother quickly transferred her to the less elitist public high school. My wife Gayle was one of only four students who remained behind when this white flight phenomena occurred in her hometown of Denmark.

We did discover that most doctors' and dentists' offices had segregated waiting rooms. They were no longer marked as such, but "everyone knew," except the new people" like us. By happy first-time accident we placed ourselves in the "colored" waiting room. We noticed that the room was a little rundown and empty but thought nothing of it. Shortly thereafter, a nurse peeked into the room to check for patients and was horrified to find my brother and I sitting there awaiting our appointments. She quickly yanked out of turn and placed us in the dentist chairs. We caught a glimpse of the crowded "whites only" waiting room on our way out and figured we were on to a way to beat the system. We wisely played dumb Yankees and went into in the wrong room for several years thereafter, never waiting long.

One person who refused to segregate was Ira Barth MD (his real name), a mentor to me. Ira was a profane, heavy smoking, heavy drinking Jew from New York who built the first the single integrated doctor's waiting room in the county. "They burned a cross in my yard the year I did it," he said, "but I didn't give a f*#k. They needed doctors too badly, and eventually they got over it." Over the following several years of medical school, I spent my summers shadowing him in the office and hospital. Ira treated everyone we saw equally with a mixture of bemused, ironic contempt and compassion. From outside the door, one could never detect the race of the patients within.

A few years later I was in practice in another small town in South Carolina. I tried hard to carry on Ira's legacy. This led to one of my earliest and profound lessons on death and dying and one I carry still today.

The chart on the door said Ida Blackwell. When I opened the door, there was "Aunt Ida" as I would learn to call her and George. Aunt Ida was African American and pushing 90, and I came to know her and her nephew extremely well. Oddly enough though, George is the focus of the story although he began as a minor character. "Miss Blackwell," I opened, "I'm Greg Phelps the doctor." (I always dislike the asymmetry of introducing myself to the patient as 'doctor' while addressing the patient by their first name as was common practice. However, I was so young, many people did not realize that I was the doctor when I introduced myself as just "Greg Phelps." Most memorably, I finished a pelvic exam on an elderly woman, telling her everything looked fine. She smiled as she sat up and said, "Oh good, when will the doctor be in here." Hence my formulation "Greg Phelps, the doctor." In later years, my mother would look up any doctor she was to visit on the internet, If he came in saying "Cynthia, I'm doctor--- She'd respond with "Bob, my name is Mrs. Phelps, when you get to be my age, you may call me Cynthia."

Back in my office though, Miss Blackwell looked slightly addled by my question of what brought her in and said, "I'm here because I hurt."

"Well, where do you hurt Miss Blackwell," I asked gently. Apparently unaware I'd be playing twenty questions with her; she shrugged and waved a hand from top to toe. Then she pointed behind her.

"Ask him, my nephew George," she said, "he knows." Meanwhile, George seated behind her, made a shrugging gesture and tapped his head to indicate that Miss Blackwell may not be entirely with us.

"Can you shed some light?" I asked. George was dressed as were most blacks in poor rural South Carolina- ragged T-shirt, worn overalls and tennis shoes. When he opened his mouth to respond, I saw extensive dental decay, but I was totally unprepared for what came out. In a middle country accent, carefully enunciated, well-modulated and educated radio announcers voice, he first introduced himself "I'm George Blackwell. This is my aunt Ida, I came down from Ohio, because I was worried about her medical care. I wanted her to change to a newer, more recently educated doctor," he explained. He then proceeded to review her medical history in full, well-constructed paragraphs while I frantically took notes. I needed to ask only a few clarifying questions.

Then followed a very extensive physical exam with George and my nurse supplying practiced verbal distraction for Aunt Ida, as I worked. I recommended several medication changes. George announced himself as satisfied, and we parted as friends. Every month or so thereafter, Aunt Ida and George visited with most of the time being a review and exam of Aunt Ida's medical status. I also found time however, to try to slowly sate my curiosity about the dichotomy between the image George put forward and the disconnect to his apparent education and diction. George was a bit of a mystery to me. At one point, he gestured to his teeth and said that he had serious heart problems that precluded dental work

On another visit, George explained how after college he worked in radio as an announcer and later took up the purchase and resale of radio stations. He told me that he had a system to learn all there was about their talent, format, finances and structure. He could study sales figures, station issues and problems before they even knew there was a possibility of being sold. He explained his system for scouting out a target station, as he gestured to his clothing and his teeth. "I'd walk into the radio station, head straight for the janitor's closet, get a mop and bucket, and as a black man dressed in ratty clothes like this, I' be invisible. I could walk anywhere in the station, listen to any conversation and no one would notice." Then he laughed lightly, punched my shoulder and said, "keep an eye out for us."

My wife Gayle filled in at my office when staff were sick. George came to be one of her favorite patients. They would often chat and share when I was done with Aunt Ida's visit. During one visit, George stopped Gayle as I worked my way down the hall to the next room. "Mrs. Phelps, your husband doesn't dress well. He chubby and tends to walk on the back hem of his pants and sometimes he looks like something the cat dragged in, but he's a good doctor so don't hold all that other stuff against him…" The two of them stared down the hall at me appraisingly.

Gayle drawled out, "yeah, guess you're right. I'll have to hang on to him… for now." Then the two of them burst out laughing as she walked George and Aunt Ida towards the checkout desk.

A few months later, George came in alone, no Aunt Ida, for an urgent visit. Breathing a heavy sigh, he opened the conversation straight to the point. "I've mentioned I've got a bad heart. I was hoping to outlast Aunt Ida now I'm not so sure. I'm having more angina and shortness of breath." I quickly listened to his heart and lungs, neither of which sounded that bad. "Do a chest x-ray" he urged. "You don't know how bad it really is, the chest X-ray will convince you."

I shrugged, and nodded, ordered the X-ray and went to my office to wait for the results. The X-ray tech's eyes were wide, as she gestured me urgently to the X-ray boxes. "You gotta see this!" George's heart was enormous, the size of a volleyball, it occupied almost the entirety of his chest. I returned to George visibly shaken.

Despite his condition, he grinned, as he wheezed and in his deep announcer's voice intoned, "NOW, I think you comprehend the gravity of the problem."

George went straight to ICU. His trips became a recurring, almost monthly, ritual. One time a rental house of his caught fire as he was in the ambulance en route to the ER. He heard the address on the EMS scanner, and promptly went into cardiogenic shock. I tried to ship him to Columbia our nearest major heart center, but he had no insurance and refused to go. Likewise, entreaties to send him to a cardiologist went unheeded. In a later episode, in desperation in the ICU, I urged him to consider a heart transplant. "Still no insurance doc, I guess I can't afford to live." Those were some of the last words that he spoke to me as we put him in the ICU and then on a ventilator and pressors trying to support him and buy a little more time.

The next day, an ex-wife and two sons I didn't know about showed up at bedside. His ex-wife Sharon was beautiful and cultured, his sons both handsome and accomplished. Even though they'd been estranged, their love for him was obvious. I thought I might be berated for not doing more, but Sharon, and his sons told me that George had mentioned frequently that he'd admired how hard I had tried to care for him. George continued to decline and could only minimally respond to them through the sedation that we gave to keep him comfortable on the ventilator.

As his family looked on helplessly, neither they nor George could appropriately say goodbye. That weekend, George lapsed into a coma, and when his heart beats began to stretch out into longer and longer pauses, with a nod from the Sharon who was holding his hand, I shut off the ventilator. As the remaining family and I hugged in the ICU room, beside George's body, I knew there must be a better way for people to experience their final days. Gayle cried when I told her. I cried with her.

In today's current context, minorities are an underrepresented population in utilization of care towards the end of life. Some of this is a partially justified fear of hospice emerges from what the mostly white health care's institutional motivations might be. Many African American communities have long memories and can recount stories about health care refusals which resulted in injury or death of a loved one. They recall the misappropriation of tissue from Henrietta Lacks, detailed in the book about her- The Immortal Life of Henrietta Lacks. They recall the Tuskegee syphilis experiments and other examples of medical racism. Black Lives Matter applies in contemporary health care as well. It is often a matter of building or restoring trust and that is usually between individuals and less so institutions.

A few years ago, I was visiting an African American family in their home to discuss the family patriarch's advanced lung cancer. The wife, sons and daughters looked on with skeptical eyes as I explained his grim prognosis. Looking up at their disbelieving eyes, I took a small risk and said: "let's discuss the elephant in the room. Are you wondering why a white doctor is coming to your home to explain why the time is nearly up for your African American dad?"

 Brief glances skittered around the room. One of the daughters burst out laughing. "You must be some kind of mind reader; we are all thinking that." Various heads around the room nodded and the atmosphere in the room lightened considerably. Trust was raised a little in my question, and the conversation flowed more freely after that. We were then able to come to some consensus as to how to best to proceed to make the patient comfortable. I have spent a good bit of time trying to reduce my earlier naiveite about ethnicity, race and healthcare but it still often looms in the background to be recognized for what history and experience hides behind it.

Back in the hospice IPU, we're getting close to the Thanksgiving weekend, but we have two surprises in the unit. The first is Mr. Bohannon who is HIV-positive and was diagnosed with lung cancer two years earlier. He'd been lethargic when I saw him a few days earlier. We were pretty sure he'd be comatose today. Instead he is wide awake, walking around the room asking if he can go home. Another patient who was brought in comatose, a Miss Partridge, with pancreatic cancer is sitting up smiling, wondering why she's here.

Four months ago, I would have been thrilled to see a patient so close to death improve like this. But I have learned about the phenomena of "Rally Day." None of us in hospice has a physiologically useful explanation for why a moribund patient suddenly, briefly improves and can talk with family and look suddenly and inexplicable better. I hear the word 'miracle' often at this moment and have learned to educate families about it and the rally's ephemeral nature. While we can't explain it medically, I tell patients that theologically, it is a brief interlude of grace, for patient and loved ones to share with each other. In most cases, the moment is over in hours to a day or so, then patient reverts to the earlier obtunded state, and usually dies soon thereafter.

Rounds done, I go to meet Marcia and Howard to have the long-postponed discussion about my typed, not hand-written VA charts. Howard desultorily flips through them. "Standard stuff, boiler plate, more boiler plate, physical and assessment, it's all there," he grudges. Then then as he flips the final chart on the desk behind him, he and Marcia lean forward, they want to discuss my occasional lapses about specific patient details. After they belabor the topic, I rebut that everybody forgets something sometimes, and point out one or two of each of their own lapses I've noticed. They seem concerned that I don't' keep all patient details in my head. I remind them of my 'action plan' and pull out the patient minder cards I've been faithfully keeping of those details that I do write down to have available to me. This mild belligerence only seems worsens my case.

This time they want a "personal improvement plan." They point out they can't 'demand' such a plan of me. I'm not sure why they feel it is important to make the distinction that it is not mandatory, when it seems a career limiting choice to blow it off. These critical conversations and endless badgering have occurred so many times now, that I'm not overtly upset, as much as pissed off as I promise to consider a new personal improvement plan. I'm really not sure exactly what they expect I can do differently, and worse they seem unable to articulate exactly what they'd like.

Beverly's husband, Jay, has moved to River City to join her, and the three of us go out for dinner. It is probably worth noting how I spend most of my evenings. I live only a few blocks from River City's entertainment district and dozens of excellent restaurants. I am however, under a temporary vow of poverty and weekday celibacy. In current circumstances, I'm effectively single, but still married, so no bar hopping, parties or nights out. Bev and Jay are my once a week social outlet.

Each night I call Gayle. I used to make a similar call to my mother each evening after the Great Wall incident. We called it the "Not Dead Yet" call. Most nights with Mom, we'd chat a few minutes. Other nights, I'd call mom, and she'd answer the phone with "not dead yet". Then, if she was reading a good book or watching a show, she'd just hang up. Now, post heart procedure, with cardiac arrythmias and living alone, it is for myself I make the nightly 'not dead yet' call to Gayle. Occasionally I go to a movie or the bookstore, but most nights I microwave a frozen dish, then I read, some novels, but mostly book after book on various aspects of end of life, hospice and palliative care. Such is the exciting life of a medical fellow.

Thanksgiving break is cold and rainy. Weather and traffic are terrible, and everybody arrives late to our home for the massive yearly feast. Gayle grumbles every year about all her cooking, but God help anyone who gets in her way to help. Over the weekend, we do the usual things, eat leftovers, watch movies, eat more leftovers, socialize and read. Monday brings a new month, IPU is done, and I return to University Hospital.

December

Howard is the attending. It is a light day with only three patients. I've done the meet and greet with this month's crop of medical students and one resident. The next day brings a new patient from the gastrointestinal (GI) service. When I come in to visit, his wife starts out with a bare bone's assessment delivered in a flat voice. "His liver is fried. He did it to hisself." She sounds more resigned than angry about his years of alcoholism. The GI staff have worked up his prognosticating MELD (Modeling End Stage Liver Disease) score; it is abysmal. The number suggests that he has a 15% chance of living three months. The patient is the classic end stage alcoholic. Tiny wasted limbs hang off an enormous belly of fluid, covered in bruises from lack of clotting factors no longer supplied by his failing liver. The patient is obtunded, only moaning occasionally. I sit next to his wife and explain the disease process and prognosis. She listens grimly, nods, and asks if they can go home with hospice today. I agree and go out to make the calls.

The picture of this patient provokes a flashback to the very first patient I ever saw die. I was an orderly at Marion County Hospital in South Carolina the year between college and medical school. I was the only white orderly, and everyone knows I start medical school in the fall. My fellow orderlies were middle aged African American men for whom this was their full-time job. To them, I resemble a transient dilettante. They did, however, appreciate my eagerness to experience hospital life. For them, it meant I was the first to jump up and answer a call. Several of the physicians on the tiny medical staff have taken an interest in forwarding my medical education. We were in the orderly's holding room awaiting our next call when Dr. Jameson stuck his head in.

"Ah, Phelps, just the man I need. Come here, I've got something interesting to show you. You need to see this to help you learn about liver failure." Ike, the other orderly that day, who had been holding forth on his tobacco farm, nodded to me and waved me out of the room.

Dr. Jameson took me down the hall and into a darkened room where a youngish woman was in the final stages of liver failure. She was bright yellow and covered with bruises, a massive belly full of ascitic fluid almost obscured her head from which incoherent moans issued. I looked up in askance. "She's dying," he says in a clipped accent. "Shouldn't be long pay attention and look at these signs." Then he with gestures to the patient he quickly sketches out the stigmata of liver failure to me: the bruises, the wasting, the ascites, the jaundice that make her eyes look like something from a zombie movie, the encephalopathy that leaves her confused.

Then bids me good day.

I have no idea what to do, so I sit and hold her hand and repeating- "It's Ok, I'm here."

A few minutes later, she rolls to the side, vomits up a prodigious amount of black and bloody material on me and the floor and then flops back in the bed. She lays still a few moments. It takes a few beats for me to realize she is not moaning and then another few to realize she is not breathing. We are not to try to resuscitate her, death was expected, but I spend a few more minutes peeking at her hoping to see her start breathing again. Finally, I wash my hands in the sink, still looking over my shoulder at her, hoping to see some sign of life, but nothing. I wipe her mouth and face, I fold her hands on her chest, and pull up the sheet up to cover her face like I've seen on TV. I go out and tell the nurses. It is the first patient I've seen die.

Back at University Hospital the next day, I hear from hospice that our liver patient made a similar and equally expeditious exit. Our team has been following, Mr. Langerham, (again, not his real name) who has had a major abdominal surgery. I've inherited him from the November team. Palliative care has been working with his family to provide support as he's been touch and go. I have been slowly developing my own slightly tongue in cheek- prognostic tool the "Phelps Tube to Illness Severity Index." The "PTISI" level is relationship between the number of tubes, lines, drains and apparatuses inserted into the patient and likely prognosis, the more tubes, the poorer the prognosis. Given my run ins over my sense of humor, I keep the index to myself. As best I can tell this gentleman has set an all- time record with ten, including a rectal tube. Still, he is slowly improving and over the next few days, and the number of tubes slowly declines to five. We have some hopes he might make it out after all. That day we give him and his family an encouraging smile and thumbs up as another tube is removed. (Years later, I have surgery of my own, and wake up to find myself applying the index to myself. I'm dismayed to find I have five.)

Leaving Mr. Langerham, we exit the ICU to enter a floor room where another patient blithely announces he has stage four lung cancer. I pause a moment trying to match his emotional affect to his grim prognosis. Then I query, "And what does that mean to you?"

 He looks a little puzzled. "I'm not sure, just that I got a number four cancer?" Howard gestures for me to stay and explain to the patient as the team presses on to the next consult. I sigh inwardly as I seat myself. I begin as I often do, by prepping him with the familiar phrase of wishing I had something better to say but…Then I carefully explain the cancer stages from one (not so bad) up to four. I take my time and add in some details to draw out the conversation and let the implications sink in. When he sits up with jerk, I know that his likely prognosis just registered.

"Holy shit!" he expostulates, "You're tellin' me I got the worst kind of lung cancer there is?" I slowly nod sympathetically. "But the doctors just told me I had stage four cancer like they were telling me the weather," he protests.

He mulls this news over in silence as I wait. Sometimes silence and presence is the best response I have. Then he surprises me by jumping straight into resuscitation or code status, but with a twist. "I don't want to be on them machines or nuthin" he says nodding emphatically, "but I need you to code me until I can see the light on the other side. Can you do that?" I gently explain that I would have no way to know when he sees that light and he'd be in no condition to tell me if it came to that. He nods glumly and says, "Ok then, no machines, no code."

Back after the weekend, we find that Mr. Langerham took a turn for the worst Friday night and died early Sunday morning. As I had gotten to know and like his family, I am disappointed to find some validation for my nascent PTIS index. There's little time for reflection though, as we are quickly consulted for the next patient who now occupies Mr. Langerham' s bed.

Mrs. Tyrell (please remember none of the names are those of actual patients) has come in with breast cancer with tumor spread to the brain. She began having intractable seizures from the brain metastases and has ended up on the ventilator in the ICU. I spend much of the day at the bedside with Mr. Tyrell and the neurologists trying to control the seizures. I find myself acting as sort of a medical interpreter and part-time chaplain for Mr. Tyrell. I find that he and Mrs. Tyrell were very spiritual in a deep way that allows him to see life as finite and set in a larger context of spirit and God. Feeling a little out of my depth, not being ordained, theologically educated about 'do's and don'ts about religion and end of life, or any exposure to chaplain education, I offer on several occasions to get a "real" chaplain, but he declines, and at his request we pray together. It is worth mentioning that years later, feeling this lack, I have worked extensively with a local chaplain education group- the Chattanooga Association of Clinical Pastoral Care.

The following day, we have another protracted conversation about her life and the meaning she found in it. I am deeply moved as he assures me that the two of them know there is a better world coming, and that she would not want to stay in this world like this. It is just the two of them, so I proceed with the removal of ventilator.

Later that day, I receive my November review and discuss the results with Marcia. It is a very good review from Anna. Marcia seems a little surprised, but hopeful that perhaps I've turned a corner. I'm cynically wondering if it is more a change in reviewer instead of the reviewee. Still Marci leaves me some lingering doubts though in her tone of voice.

Her lingering doubts are propagated a few days later in a mentoring session with Howard at a local restaurant. Howard is always kind, but as I tell my daughter Tiffany later, our meeting went downhill quickly. Howard expressed concern about my memory, my attention to detail and 'thinking." I admit to succumbing to stress with all the external scrutiny.

"I know you were a high functioning physician, educator and executive before coming here," he commiserates. "But it is hard to reconcile that person with the guy presently sitting across the table from me."

Ignoring my surprised look, he plows doggedly on in his determination to get his concerns out. "Did you have a secretary that did a lot of your work, corrected your spelling and grammar? (Ah, we're back to the English major thing again)

"No," I respond a little tartly, "I did all my work then as now, by myself, and seemed to do just fine.

"Anything wrong at home?" he asks.

"Well, I'm managing between three households over two hundred miles apart. My wife is furious with me for taking this position and is angry most weekends. I'm making a sixth of what I used to make, and I am spending my savings to stay here. Other than that, things are going pretty good." My sarcasm seems to slip by

"So how did the people you worked with in Knoxville feel about your mental functioning?"

"Honestly, seriously!?" I asked nonplussed. He nods earnestly. So, I try to give an honest answer. "I don't know how this will sound, but I'm usually the 'smart one." We had a consultant meet with our hospital management team a few years ago. Out of the blue the consultant asked, 'who is the smartest person in the room?' Half the team pointed at our VP of government relations; the other half pointed at me."

Distracted he nods again, "I'm just worried about your memory. You know as people get older, stuff happens, sometimes sooner than later.

"You mean like dementia, like Alzheimer's?" I ask my voice rising a bit.

"I'm just worried there might be something wrong with your brain," he kindly opines.

"Wow," my daughter Tiffany breathes as I finish relating the story. "What happened after you hit him?"

To be clear, I didn't hit him. I sat there in stunned silence and then after the moment passed, we went onto other small talk. I was shocked at his comments-devastated really. I spend the next day or so in hard reflection wondering if I've really slipped that far? It doesn't feel like it to me. In my family we've always seen both intelligence and education as assets to be prized. Both my siblings have PhDs. We grew up engaged in "paper warfare," as a competition as to who could get the most certificates and pieces of paper from school. The unkindest thing you could say to my dad was to remind him he never finished high school because he was drafted into World War II. I'm in a funk; these comments accelerate my emotional tailspin. Maybe, just maybe, I was never as good as I hoped I was. I ruminate at length on Howard's comments and concerns. I desperately need some affirmation to remind myself that I'm not as stupid as they seemed to think I am.

I'm not particularly proud of dredging up old records, but what I did next shows some of the depths of my apprehension for something I valued highly, my brains and ability to learn. Some years earlier, I had applied to get my master's in theology while working at St. Mary's I was told I'd have to take the Miller Analogy Test. This was a graduate school requirement for this program. I quick checked the University of Tennessee graduate school website and found out the next test was offered two days hence, and the application deadline would pass before the next opportunity. Grad school said they didn't care about the score but had to have it on record. If I wanted in the program that year, I'd need to take the test un-prepared. I didn't even know what the test was about. With zero study time, I took the test cold. I went back a few days later to get my test score to send on to the seminary. As they passed me the sheet, someone at the University of Tennessee, admiringly said that score might be high enough to qualify for Mensa, the high IQ society. Focused on getting the score off to grad school time, I nodded and brushed it off.

After my conversation with Howard, I was so depressed and upset over this attack upon something that mattered so much to me, that I went back and researched the score. I needed some external validation to regain some sense of my self-esteem, that I wasn't as dim a bulb as he seemingly thought I was. To redeem my self-respect, I called the school where I'd had the score sent and confirmed the result. I'd crushed it, I was well over the required Mensa score. I held that fact in grim humor for the next several weeks. It was vain and prideful, but I had to do something to restore some semblance of my self-image.

The month continued toward Christmas. I had another patient dying of liver failure. His blue bruises and yellow eyes serve as a color contrast to the holiday decorations going up on the nurses' station counters. For good reason, the holiday cheer has not touched this patient. Another bitter wife's acerbic comment," all he ever loved was cigarettes and booze…never me." As he moaned and tossed, her comment served as a coda; she seemed to take an unusually vengeful satisfaction in for his final hours.

With a few days before Christmas break, the residents and student become a little silly. Back in the team meeting room, one of the residents comments on how all the other medical disciplines have an image of their specialty on their lab coats. Cardiology has miniature hearts, pulmonary a set of lungs. GI- a stylized stomach and intestine. We don't really have an organ to portray. Speculation then ensues as to the ideal logo for hospice and palliative medicine. "What would ours be," a resident asks.

"Tombstones" one suggests.

Another student jumps in with bat's wings. Another, chimes in with little miniature figures of death with sickles. A med student jumps in and suggests a pair of fangs dripping blood on the pocket.

Before I can intervene, another resident corrects the med student, saying "no vampires, that'd be hematology'

I extend cautionary hands, I've been down this path, "Guys, guys," a little respect for our patients and our work." Then with a half smirk, "Clearly we need angel wings."

"Like we're making angels??" They ask

"No," I say dryly dismissing that interpretation, "Like we are angels of mercy, relieving symptoms." They are still debating the logo matter when I leave. I'm sure I'll get dragged in and smacked around again, but this minor sin escapes notice.

Along from our pre-holiday levity, we get a little snow to get us in the mood for the holiday. The snow comes in time for a Christmas party in the break room for residents and students. I leave the party to do a ventilator withdrawal. The contrast is not lost on me- joy and loss. We celebrate a birth, while on the same floors we live with illness and death. Right now, I am emotionally exhausted, numb. The holidays could not get here soon enough, and the day comes I bid all goodbye for the year. The fellowship is half over, the question for me is can I hang on to finish.

CHAPTER FOUR

January

One of the forgotten pleasures of being a student is vacation. I am off for two weeks at Christmas. I hadn't been away from work that long in over thirty years! The break restores some of my relationship with Gayle as we spend time with family and friends over the holidays. It also helps give me a new perspective on the fellowship. I spend time with my children and getting to know my new granddaughter. I'd seen how important family was to so many patients, and I make a conscious effort to cultivate and renew my relationships with my own family. The time away allows me to pull my head out of the rut I've been sinking into with the all-consuming focus on fellowship. As Gayle reminds me, several times, there will be life after fellowship in six short months. Returning from Christmas vacation to the second half of the program, I have a mission, something previously approached only in a desultorily fashion; I need to get a job when this is done.

When I left St. Mary's, I had been convinced that there was a strong need for the service that I could offer. My position as medical director, and the struggles with families, treatment conflicts and communication in the hospital had engendered in me a new certainty for improved and effective communication via palliative care. The fellowship experience reinforced this view daily. Palliative care not only helps patients suffer less and live a little longer, but also improves hospital quality scores and patient satisfaction. and yes, even the hospital bottom line. The shock, as I began my job search, was that due to the newness of the specialty, hospitals did not yet understand the benefits.

As part of our fellowship training, the faculty offers advice on job hunting. For her fellowship project, Bev reports she is working on a presentation about evaluating and processing potential jobs. Howard throws some cold water on the selection process for hospice and palliative care jobs, a wrinkle that had not occurred to me. Howard speaks ominously of the need for total commitment and support from the very top of hospital administrators. "Every new palliative care program runs into resistance from doctors and/or patients who object that palliative care is the equivalent of euthanasia. If you're in a new position, starting a program, you need a strong administrator to watch your back. Every new program needs unyielding support and protection until you're able to demonstrate your value, and the objections and resistance die down."

Some years later I run into this conundrum myself. I have a new position as a hospice medical director. I've been working almost a week when I go to one of the local hospitals. I get on the elevator and notice that my fellow passenger is a white coated physician in administration. (I now have a good elevator speech, so I'm ready.) I stick out my hand and say: "Hi, I'm Greg Phelps the new hospice medical director." His reaction would be comical if not for the implications; he folds his arms and steps away from me to the back of the elevator."

"Hospice," he almost hisses at me, "I sent you a patient twenty years ago and you took away his meds and killed him!"

"Well I've only been here a week," was my rejoinder, "so I'm pretty sure it wasn't me." Since he seemed certain that justice argument- that I would go to jail for killing people had already been preempted in his mind, I tried a practical argument. You don't understand, it makes no sense for me to kill people, as hospice only gets paid for every day, they are alive! It is not like there's not like a bonus for doing them in. He just glared at me the rest of the ride up.

I had long planned to return to St. Mary's to start the palliative care program which I believed was so urgently needed there and at every hospital during my earlier tenure. I had tried to educate our CEO and senior leaders on the value of palliative care before starting the fellowship. Despite vague words of support, I didn't get much traction with the CEO. When I left for the fellowship, she became too busy to take my calls. I then talked to the Chief Financial Officer, Ed (not his real name) whose office had been across the hall from mine for years. He was sympathetic but lobbying by himself and others not helped.

"Greg, I hear what you're saying about better and cheaper care. We all want you to come back, but right now all our talking on your behalf is getting you…and us, nowhere. There's just too much else going on right now."

"Well" I muttered, "I guess I'll just wait and talk to the CEO's successor." I meant it as a vague, but unsubstantiated closing comment. To my surprise, a few weeks later, during both national and local hospital financial crises, the newspaper announced our CEO would be taking a sabbatical, it became permanent.

With the change in leadership, I made an appointment with the new interim CEO from the national corporate office whom I had known for years. He at least gave me an audience to discuss the virtues of starting a palliative care program. "Greg, I hear all your former colleagues in the C suite talk about you and your project. I understand that palliative care can result in better quality of care, improves patient satisfaction and helps the bottom line, as Ed has reminded me repeatedly. Really, I do, there is just too much else going on here, too many fires to put out. Give me a year or so…"

Now after the new year, I only have six months, and I try again to advance my palliative care agenda. This time, the highest I can climb in the corporate organizational chart is the head of physician's services who is polite and kind but discourages me from any further pursuit palliative care at the institution. This time, I finally I take the hint: it just isn't going to happen.

I begin to look elsewhere. I interview in a city two hours away from Knoxville and on arrival prospects look promising. After a tour and introductions, I am quickly led to an interview with the whole board. There are a few opening questions and then the kicker. "Can you explain what led you out of the 'C Suite/corporate' path and back into care of the sick and dying?" I talked some about mission, meaning and purpose in life. As I am expounding on this theme, near and dear to me, I mention my faith heritage as an Episcopalian leading me to this ministry. To my surprise, there was a sudden, collective whoop- an exclamation of enthusiasm amongst the interview committee. It turned out more than half of the committee were also Episcopalian. My prospects for the job, already warm, improved substantially.

Jubilant, I returned to Knoxville with the beginnings a job offer. My enthusiasm was quickly dampened on my return with Gayle's less than warm reception. She hemmed and hawed. Something's not right. I urge and prompt her to clarify finally, she admitted she'd probably stay in Knoxville to help with the grandchild. "We could see each other on the weekends and get together at the lake house in between the two cities," she tentatively, but hopefully suggested. The next day, dejected, I called the interview committee chair with whom I'd so recently bonded and shared the news- I was dropping my application. A year apart was already too much.

My daughter Tiffany works for another hospital system in Knoxville, which years earlier, had brought me to Knoxville from my teaching position. Tiffany mentions to her boss in hospital administration that I'm doing a palliative care fellowship and job hunting. They are express an interest in meeting with me. Ironically, it was also the health system that fired me, and all my co-workers, only eleven months after I'd begun a new job there years ago, so there is some history that makes me a little tentative. I make a hesitant phone call and I'm warmly invited to an interview a few weeks hence.

Once again, I am back in River City, a new year, a new six months to go, and back at the VA, and we begin with a bang. We have a new resident and two new students to initiate. I'd admitted three patients in the short week of the first of the year... they are already gone. And we have no time to mourn. we have ten new consults that Monday. Anna divides our team up, and I work from 7 am to 7:30 pm trying hard to devote to each patient time for me to listen, show attention, and give compassion while at the same time, feeling the pressure of knowing that many more await my visit. I am also aware of the learners in our train. I remind myself they learn more by what I demonstrate than what I say. To quote St. Francis- "Preach the gospel always, use words if necessary."

The following day, someone had come to the ER the night before just feeling 'poorly'. In an impressive speed for the VA, he is quickly diagnosed with end stage lung cancer, and he is in our VA inpatient unit that next morning! This veteran says his pain is better, and he's feeling rejuvenated having gotten his first decent night's sleep in months. But he still doesn't understand the clinical implications of why he is there. With students watching, I pull up a chair, sit down and begin with "Well I wish there was something better I could say but..." He quickly tumbles to the understanding of his prognosis. In usual veteran style, he adapts in moments, with stoicism.

Wednesday morning begins at church with a sermon to our tiny group that begins by predicating, "there are no outsiders here." The topic is most apropos, as the church during the winter opens its doors to the homeless for shelter. As I'd come in that morning, I picked my way through the homeless in sleeping bags in the entry vestibule. The dreary morning and our tiny group of worshippers remind me again that although it can be a cruel world, there is hope in people and community. Just opening the doors to cold people can be an act of outstanding humanity. Mother Teresa, we're reminded said, "Not all of us can do great things, but we can do small things with great love."

Walter is back at the VA. I greet him warmly as we try to get through his pain problems and stomach issues. He seems even thinner than before which I wasn't sure was possible. He smiles wanly, but he is happy to see a familiar face. Despite his discomfort, Walter and Amanda ask about me and Bev. They joke about us as Batman and Robin. I tell them Bev is at the University hospital and that having Jay her husband around has been an improvement in her life. Walter is beginning to think a little about a future for his wife without him. "Say doc," "he asks, "are you married?"

I'm a little puzzled. I've been asked a few times by women, but never a man, I hold up my beringed ring finger in response.

Walter persists: "But are you happily married?" He cuts his eyes to Amanda, his long-suffering wife. I'm about to give a flip answer, when both his wife and I realize the implications of his question.

My mouth drops open, as Amanda smacks him on the shoulder and says lovingly to him, "he doesn't want some used up old lady like me. You're the only husband I ever want...sorry doc."

It makes for a very awkward, but touching moment. I leave them cuddling in his hospital bed.

That afternoon I pick up Bev at the airport, after her trip to Washington state for job interviews. Bev meets me in the luggage area lugubriously dragging a heavy bag. "I almost didn't come back." She declares," being outside this place, back in Washington, talking to real people who weren't dying! I saw happy healthy people living their lives. I swear I'm about over it, I really don't want to be here anymore!" The interviews, however, went well, job is almost secured, a few details to work out and husband Jay is staying behind to house hunt. Still she perseverates on how miserable returning has become.

I try to cheer her up on the way to a dinner meeting with the area hospice physicians. I'm doing the evening presentation on how systems fail. Drawing on my experience as a preventive medicine physician and hospital administrator, I paint analogies to holes in Swiss cheese, airplane crashes and fishbone skeletons, to illuminate how things can go wrong. The talk is surprisingly well received. Howard leads the group in thanking me. This time after laudatory comments, there is no deflating private aside. Still, I've learned to enjoy the moment and run. I grab Bev and we exit quickly.

Back at home, I have family issues to deal with. My older son is in his first year of business school at Duke. He calls -traumatized. He has not gotten an internship for the summer. In business school, he insists, a missed milestone like this is often seen as a harbinger of a failing career. I'm perhaps not as sympathetic as I should be, although I try hard. Surrounded by people who are on our unit, dying earlier than they should, I struggle to find sympathetic words. Still, I realize this is a significant setback in his nascent ambitions. So, I find the fatherly reassuring words, and we promise to talk more. Despite his sad news, at some level, I'm warmed that he still reaches out to 'Daddy' for support.

A medical student named Bill is rounding with me the next few days. The VA team is more dispersed than the University team, so it is just the two of us. The nurses call me about Mr. Fitzsimmons whom we just finished admitting two hours earlier. They say, "He doesn't look so good." On our service this phrase has ominous implications and I quickly send Bill who had helped with the family meeting, ahead to scout out the problem. I follow in a couple minutes arriving to find that Mr. Fitzsimmons has already died. Bill is comforting Mrs. Fitzsimmons and sitting beside her, talking softly, holding one hand while she continues to hold the hand of Mr. Fitzsimmons with her other hand. Once we walk out of the room, Bill looks at me and asks, "Is it okay if I cry a little?" I assure him it would be fine and send him to find privacy. I tell him that knowing his feelings and acknowledging them is part of staying sane here. This is an professional survival process I failed to learn for years.

Bill's question about mourning a patient pulls me back to my final year as a family medicine resident. I was working pediatrics in the emergency room when a child, a beautiful blonde cherub, comes in convulsing non-stop from an outside hospital. As we work frantically, we get a jumbled story from the EMT's and chart notes. He had come in for a routine tonsillectomy. There was carelessness involving the IV fluid rate, and the tiny child was given volumes of fluid appropriate for a 200-pound adult. This huge bolus of fluid drastically diluted the child's blood, lowered his sodium to fatal levels and caused his brain to swell and die. Despite over an hour of our best efforts between me, the intern Eddie, the ER doctor and the pediatrician we called in, the child died. The pediatrician elected himself to be the one to deliver the news to the parents. Outside the ER doors, one look at the pediatrician told the family of the outcome. Their anguished cries and wails drifted off as the pediatrician led them into a private conference room. I was relieved not to have to do that duty.

After a moment of brief reflection, I turned back to the chart rack of incoming patients. The flow into the ER had not stopped while we labored in vain. As residents, we'd had been given several lectures professional boundaries, therapeutic distance, avoiding emotional engagement which potentially cloud therapeutic judgement. This particular education had dovetailed nicely with my personal history and experience of avoiding family dysfunction and avoiding feelings. So, stuffing down the child's death, I turned to the next case. Two patients later, I felt the call of nature and headed to the lavatory, where I found Eddie my intern, sobbing. I was so emotionally divorced, so distant from my feelings that I honestly had no idea what was wrong. "Eddie! oh, my god, what is it. Are you hurt?" I asked.

"I'm not sure I can do this," he sobbed. "How do you turn away and go on to the next patient? He was someone's child!" All at once, the enormous gulf between me and patient and family dissolves as I think of my own children. I am at once almost consumed in a blast furnace of and grief, feeling what Eddie is feeling at the hospital that doomed this child, and grief for the family. I realized at that moment how terribly far my feelings had become separated from my work. Holding up an emotional wall had required so much more effort once I had children of my own.

Guys back in the eighties didn't hug much, but I patted Eddie on the back, commiserated with him for a while and then told him skip the rest of the shift and go home. I sat alone in the call suite a few minutes, wiped a few tears and went back to work. Since then for decades, I've never discouraged anyone from tears or grief or anger. I recently heard a psychologist talking about physician burnout. His comment was- "Physicians eat grief for a living." Later that day at the VA, Bill reappears and thanks me for the time to reflect.

I'm back in Knoxville for the weekend and a late birthday celebration for Gayle. On Sunday, we gather for a family baptism for granddaughter-Abby. Seeing a whole new generation of my family baptized means the world to me. This was the church we'd gone to for decades. Our priest Father Cal, (his real name) married my daughter and her husband and baptized my nephews. Still it wouldn't be the Phelps family without a little twisted humor. As the Father Cal pours baptismal water over Abby (Episcopalians are dippers, not bobbers), my daughter hisses- *sotto voce*, "it burns, it burns," as if Satan himself is being driven out. Cal glances over his shoulder, hinting a smile while trying hard to frown, the rest us, gathered around the font, all giggle and snort. That's the kind of family I have.

The following Monday, I have another job interview at the hospital in the Knoxville area. It quickly becomes obvious the hospital uncertain how to incorporate palliative care in on-going patient care but have heard they should be offering this service. I'm pleased that they want me in some capacity. They also want me to talk to the head of their hospitalist group- Dr. James. My face falls a little. Dr. James group had also been the hospitalists at St. Mary's,

Dr. James is a gentleman I've known, worked with, and butted heads with over the years. I had a lot of respect for him and his group, but my job as hospital medical director was to hold his doctors accountable. Our clashes had at times gotten heated enough for him to go to my boss as our CEO told me later, "He told me he doesn't want you in any more meetings with them. He says you're pushy and demanding," a grin grew on her face. "I told him that was what I wanted." Eventually, Dr. James and I reached a limited, wary detente. Now my future job hung on how that détente might hold.

I meet with Dr. James a few weeks later. We discussed our history. To my relief, he says" Hey you were doing your job, I was doing mine. We're good." He sees a real need for palliative care in helping patient's make the transition from curative care to end of life care. He's excited to have someone who has specialty training to take on that responsibility. I leave very encouraged.

There is one last bit of business at home. When my daughter Tiffany was 16, the only thing she wanted was a dog- specifically a Shi Tzu. Not a car, not clothes just the dog. Gayle was not a dog person. The one dog we had was mine, a mutt I loved but who lived mostly in the back yard.

However, after much begging and pleading, Tiffany got her dog and named her Tribble after the creatures in Star Trek that are hairy mops with a reputation for breeding quickly. Tribble soon found a way into Gayle's heart as well. Teenage girls grow up though and go off to college where dogs can't go. Tribble became Gayle's dog, and although she grumped about it, she was delighted. Eventually Tiffany came home from college and wanted her dog back. There was a loving, but loud tug of war that as all expected, Tiffany won. Tribble, however, also changed Gayle who became a small dog fanatic even taking an active role in Small Breed Rescue of East Tennessee, but Tribble was still first in her heart.

Now Tribble was old and suffering from semi-paralysis from a debilitating neurologic condition. After some weeks of literally holding the dog in a towel to pee, we reluctantly decided it Tribble's time, and we made an appointment at the vet's office for a Saturday when I'm home. Tiffany gathered Tribble in a blanket. I turn to Gayle who is still sitting and patting Tribble in Tiffany's arms. "Are you coming?" I asked a little irritably. I don't want to do this anymore than you do, but it is obvious the dog is suffering.

Gayle looks at me then Tiffany and finally Tribble and sighs, "No, I guess not."

I'm a little surprised. "Why not?

Gayle tears up a little and says, "I'm afraid when the vet comes in with the syringe to put Tribble down, that I'll grab the dog and run screaming out of the office." Tiffany and I agree the Gayle should probably say her goodbye at home and the rest of us leave.

The next weekend, I show Tiffany my new updated advance care plan now naming her as my surrogate decision maker. I point out that her mom couldn't find the wherewithal to put down the dog. If I had continued heart problems, I might need someone who could make the hard decision to pull my plug if necessary.

Tiffany snorts in disbelief, "Dad, there is a huge difference between your dog and your dad!"

"Yes," I reply acerbically, "and your mother didn't make it past the dog."

The following week brings more challenges. I've been slacking off from working out at the gym promising myself I will do better later. Since I have not yet kept the promise, I'm home that evening when I get a phone call from Gayle. The nursing home has called, and Gayle's mother Sally has fallen, and she is in the emergency room. Just to round things out, Sally's sister is also being admitted to the same hospital, from the same facility at the same time for worsening confusion. It turns out both have urinary tract infection UTIs. Both sisters are in their 90s and progressing further along that long slow decline I've come to recognize too well.

Back in River City, I arrive at the VA just in time find Mr. Jones, a lung cancer patient we've hospitalized several times, not looking so good. He is pale and sweaty, and his blood pressure is not much over even less. I quickly call Mr. Jones's daughter, whom I've talked with previously, and say he doesn't look so good and she should probably come in as soon as possible.

Apparently, it was a bit of a drive. Several hours pass and Mr. Jones succumbs to his lung cancer before she arrives. We break the news; it was expected, and I comfort her, but she is distraught not to have been there when he breathed his last. I wonder aloud later to the team, if I had been more direct about the imminence of his demise, would she have made it. Back in the team room, we have a spirited debate as to whether it's fair to tell a family member that the patient has died or is immediately dying before they arrive. We all concur that this is a conundrum. We hate to do deliver this news on the phone: it is hard enough in person. Still, we don't want someone to have an accident by speeding, trying to reach loved one before they die.

I tell the team a story of a time from when I was chief of staff at a small hospital many years ago. We had a newly minted physician taking flying lessons for a new plane he'd proudly and recently bought. A hospital in another state called him to say that his dad was dying. In his urgency to get back, he took his plane and flew in a manner he wasn't yet cleared for. He left so quickly that he forgot his wallet. The plane crashed and the doctor was killed. The only information he had was a business card in his pocket for our hospital administrator. So, the fire and rescue workers called that number and after some confusion, we discovered that we'd just lost our new doctor. No one told the father who died the next day that this son preceded him in death. This incident is always in the back of my mind when I'm calling family.

Another VA patient, Mr. Traxler is struggling with end-stage COPD a side effect from a two pack a day 40-year smoking history that he began when he was only ten! He comes in obtunded and gasping. He's only fifty, and we debate whether we should try ventilator support or just keep him comfortable with morphine. We try to imagine the patient's wishes because in this case there's no family and no indicated wish. He is clearly is dying. The question is, in the face of inevitable death, how hard should we try to prolong his life, as opposed focus on comfort. Working with the critical care physicians who want to be more aggressive, we negotiate a middle route. We won't intubate him but instead put him on what is called BiPap or non-invasive ventilation with a mask and machine. The flip side is he won't get as much morphine as we would like to keep him comfortable. The following morning, we learn that he has died and not terribly comfortably.

Beverly and I have dinner that night with our new VA chaplain Charles. Charles came from the Navy as a chaplain and is now working at the VA. He brings in an irreverent sense of humor to what is often seen as an isolated position. At dinner, Bev continues to be a bit melancholy about her progress in the fellowship. Her review is tomorrow. She brightens some after I explain to Charles, with Bev chiming in, on how the review process can be so stressful, when so many reviews are not that favorable. There is comfort in shared misery! Charles helps us with some perspective and encouragement.

Surprisingly, the next morning Bev comes back to our team buoyed by a better than expected review. Charles smiles "See I told you." We continue rounding. There's a new patient on the team I don't know well yet. In my response to my question as to how this patient is doing, Charles makes a familiar circling gesture with his finger indicting that the patient is approaching the drain.

"Oh no!" I hiss, surprising him with my vehemence, "you never want to do that, ever. I've been brought in and slapped around for that gesture." Charles looks surprised as I relate the story to him of my first faculty intervention.

"Seriously?" he asks incredulously. I assure him that I am dead serious. "Wow that is just, just …weird!" Bev nods in grim accompaniment. Charles is thoughtful and a bit subdued as we continue rounding.

January continues. A few days after the 'circle the drain incident,' we have a massive snow and ice storm that shuts down the city. Having grown up in Michigan, I am determined that this inclement weather will not keep me from work. As I slip and slide on the hill up to the VA, I have cause to regret this decision, but I make it to the hospital person and car intact. I wander into the team room and find that I am a team of one. I shrug to myself and begin to make rounds alone. It feels a little weird as I encounter no one else from our team the whole day and the following day and the next, the same thing. We don't have a cell phone list, so I can't contact my colleagues, but the patients need care, so I just carry on. The hospital continues with a small but determined skeleton staff. On the fourth day, I encounter our department head who greets me with surprise. She asks me, somewhat accusingly, what I'm doing. I explain that I've been making rounds for three days by myself.

"Oh no," she exclaims, "you can't do that!" I counter that I'm a big boy with thirty years of physician experience and have an independent license in the state of Kentucky, so I think I can.

"Plus," I add pointedly, "I'm the only person who showed up."

She appreciatively thanks me, but says, "The rules say fellows can't work unsupervised."

She sighs dramatically, extending a hand, "Give me your list of the patients, I'm gonna have to spend all f*#king morning signing all your notes to make it look legal... But good job, thanks for showing up." I grin, and we carry on. On Friday, the rest of the crew shows up and life goes back to normal. One veteran with lung cancer clung to life on through the entire ice storm, waiting for his wife who could not reach him. She arrived Friday morning and he died only a few hours later. He was holding on, waiting for her to say goodbye. A final coda to the storm, a month later at the VA, the administration hands out commemorative T-shirts for those of us that came in. The shirts proclaim- "I Showed Up During the Great Ice Storm." They don't have shirts in 3XL, so I do without.

I've mentioned my reluctance to mention my illnesses until I've resolved them. I should mention this this is a family trait I get from my mother. After mom's hip fracture and recovery, we continued the nightly "I'm not dead" phone call for several years. One night, Mom happened to mention that she had a little bit of hoarseness and had gone to see her ear, nose and throat doctor. Mom reported that she had been sent for a CT scan of her neck, and that her doctor told her it looked fine, nothing to worry about. She told me she'd have the doctor's office fax a copy to me "I'm having the results faxed to your hospital office, just so you can have them on file."

A few days later the fax duly came through and I desultorily thumbed through the pages. Then I stopped and reread and then re-reread again, the body Mom's report comparing it with the conclusion of the report. The body of the report mentioned a mass in the pharynx with the dimensions listed, mentioning that it was suspicious for cancer. Paradoxically, the concluding impression at the end of the report, failed to mention the mass. It was clear that like a lot of hurried doctors, her ENT had only skimmed the extensive verbiage in the report skipping down to the to get to the important conclusion. I called Mom and reported the bad news and encouraged her to get back with her ENT.

Her doctor was duly chagrined, according to mom and acknowledged that he'd looked at the end of the report and missed the mention of the mass. He contacted the radiologist who was stunned at the error in his report. The radiologist was even more upset when he learned how the error was caught, and by whom. He did confirm there was indeed a mass in her pharynx. The ENT proceeded with an endoscopic biopsy under minimal sedation. The result was what we feared but expected: cancer of the pharynx. It was hardly a surprise though. Smoking and heavy alcohol consumption are risk factors. Mom's picture was probably in the textbook

The doctor started to plan radical neck surgery, but Mom had understandably lost confidence in the health care in her hometown. I was also concerned that such a radical surgery as proposed might be more than her emphysematous lungs could tolerate. Furthermore, we both knew there would be substantial recovery time, and she lived alone in South Carolina. It made more sense for her to pack up and come stay with us in Knoxville for the six or eight weeks expected duration.

As a physician, I'm often asked, 'what would you do if it was your mother?' Now it was. As medical director, I knew the oncologists at our hospital and chose the one I would want for my mother. Dr. Reinhardt (not his real name) was youngish, bright and very patient-centered. His academic and training credentials were impeccable. More importantly, the hospital staff loved him and thought he was excellent. We set up an appointment with him for the following week.

The oncologist's office was sleek glass, slate and chrome. "Oncology must pay well," Mom observed archly. The expensive decor served in marked contrast to many of the patients in the waiting room; people on oxygen, walkers, head scarves…debilitated and bald. The variety of ill patients was a depressing assortment, and I could see Mom assessing her future. Fortunately, they called us back with alacrity.

Dr. Reinhardt was everything I had hoped he'd be. He quickly put mom at her ease with a laudatory quip about her son. Nothing wins a mother over faster than saying nice things about her son! He soon demonstrated that he had extensively studied her records before our arrival. He also performed a physical exam that was thorough, but to the point.

Like me, he was concerned that her age and comorbid emphysema would make surgery extremely dicey. Therefore, he outlined an ambitious program of radiation to the neck and chemotherapy. As he was winding down, mom raised her first question as to the treatment. As usual it went straight to the point. "Dr. Reinhardt you seem like a nice guy," she began, "but I have a question. Will this treatment cure me? Put me back like I was? Look, I'm eighty years old. If I have the cancer for six months and it kills me without treatment, that's okay… if the other option is I have the treatment and vomit up my toenails for six months and I'm in no better, well, that doesn't seem like a great option. Agreed?"

Dr. Reinhardt sat back down on the wheeled stool and scooted forward into her personal space until he was almost knee-to-knee with Mom and made eyeball to eyeball contact. Sure, he now had her attention he said, "Mrs. Phelps, I honestly believe that we can cure your cancer and get you back home." Mom nodded once, stood up and turned toward the door. I paused to shake his hand, and we left.

A day later, radiation oncology fitted Mom for a mask that went over her face to precisely position her for the radiation. A bite bar, much like an ice cream stick projected down through the mask into her mouth to make sure it was centered directly. The treatment room where the radiation was delivered, had heavy concrete walls that made the room seem tomb-like. To counter the oppressive feeling, the walls had a large photo mural of an outdoor forest to reduce incipient claustrophobia. Chemotherapy began a few days later.

At first, treatment went well. I accompanied her to the first chemo and radiation sessions. After those, she insisted on driving herself. Since Gayle and I worked at the same hospital system, we would often meet her to keep her company.

Part of the therapy included a hefty dose of steroids the day before chemotherapy. These were intended to blunt some of the more toxic effects of the chemotherapy. Steroids, in this case dexamethasone or Decadron, had the additional side effect of extra energy and sense of wellbeing. This serendipitous side effect became known as "Decadron-shopping day." The radiation treatments were scattered in between.

As the treatments continued however, Mom began to flag. She spent more and more time in bed. Getting her to treatments became mounting effort. No one said anything, but Gayle and I quietly began taking turns driving her to treatments. Mom's appetite began to flag and eating became a chore. Being a gastrointestinal nurse who'd seen the damage the radiation could do to the patient's throat; Gayle had strongly encouraged Mom to consider early placement of a feeding tube to keep up her nutrition. But the oncologists and radiation therapists dismissively opined that a tube would not be necessary. As no one wants a feeding tube flapping in their belly, Mom listened to her doctors over her daughter-in-law. After month of chemo plus radiation to her neck, mom's weight failed, along with her appetite and her ability to swallow. Gayle's wisdom became more apparent.

As her face thinned and her belly softened, the oncology staff eventually, reluctantly, agreed, mom needed a feeding tube. This was placed during an outpatient procedure and Mom hated it from the beginning. Likewise, her energy continued to fail. She spent more time in the bed between treatments. Eventually "Decadron day" was the only day she felt like doing anything. It was heart-wrenching to watch this independent, well-educated woman slowly fail. As a librarian, a book or three was always at her side. It became my job to assure that she didn't run out, and the used bookstore, McKay's, became my best friend.

Mom had worsening and increasingly disturbing incidents as she grew weaker. One time, Gayle and I went to dinner and returned unable to find mom. She had collapsed between the coffee table and couch and although unhurt, was unable to get back up. Because of the radiation damage to her vocal cords, she was unable to respond when we called for her. After an unnerving search of the house, coming back into the den, I saw her feet sticking out past the couch. Running around the side of the couch, I looked down at her unhurt but stuck and stupidly exclaimed, "Mom what are you doing down there?" Her eyeroll spoke as loud as her sarcasm ever had.

The treatments continued with periodic trips to the hospital for pneumonia. She was on oxygen at home but would get confused and pull the oxygen off during the night. We would come to her room in the morning and find her hypoxic and obtunded. We repeatedly had to call the ambulance. Still, Mom resisted assistance or helpers with all her being for as long as she could.

I'm a doctor, my wife is a nurse. We both had full-time jobs, even spelling each other and sneaking early out of work, caring for Mom as her debilitation worsened eventually became too much for the two of us. Our kids were in college, so we reluctantly hired first a nighttime sitter and then soon after, 24-hour sitters. Mom was highly insulted, but when I pointed out the alternative was waking up in the hospital again, she acquiesced. She insisted though that it was her money that paid for the additional care.

She never did finish the full cycles of chemotherapy and radiation. She was just too weak. After yet another trip to the hospital for yet another bout of pneumonia on her weakened lungs. We would have to talk about rehab at a nursing home. To say mom was livid underplays the moment.

Some of Mom's strident refusal about nursing homes came from her experience with her own mother. My grandmother developed dementia, which in the end turned out to be a misdiagnosed metastatic cancer to the brain. Grandma, who was very sharp into her geriatric years, suddenly developed weight loss and worsening confusion and delusions. A medical work up didn't show the cause and eventually Mom had to place her in a nursing home for her own safety. Mom, her

146

only child, was the recipient of all her ensuing anger and vituperation. Mom received almost daily letters or calls arrived denouncing her as an ungrateful daughter. This hate mail ended only when grandma did. At that time, Mom had said to me, "When the time comes, if you need to put me in nursing home, remember what I say now, in my right mind- 'it is okay.' I opened my mouth to deny that it would ever be necessary, but she persisted. "Whatever you do, don't make that promise not put me in a nursing home."

Although we discuss it with some heat, the decision is postponed for a while by other clinical complications.

February

Back in River City, February is a month of electives for me. This means I can spend time on any rotations or services I think would be worthwhile for my fellowship experience. My first week is with the AIDS clinic. This was the free clinic where the poor and the underserved came for medications, counselling and treatment. AIDS, along with cancer, helped launch the modern hospice movement in the early 1980's, heralding an era where people often on healthcares' margins, looked for a counter-cultural way to experience the end of life. This kind of life's end- not being in the hospital, not in the ICU but at home surrounded by friends gained popularity quickly. The AIDS epidemic in the beginning in the early 80s and the nascent US hospice movement beginning in late 1970's overlapped.

Some of the patients at the HIV clinic are stereotypical, thin, young, and with a history of sharing needles. HIV is just one of their problems. Patients drop in and out, disappear for months and then wander back in when the illness progresses to desperation point. I speak with one patient's boyfriend telling him he needs to get himself tested, as his girlfriend has full blown AIDS and is down to 88 pounds. He smiles, nods and declines. I find such fatalism often.

Arnold offers a bit of a break in the pattern. He's 75 and affluent. He tells me that he contracted HIV in an assisted living facility. I cock a skeptical eyebrow at him. "Hell doc, almost all of us are single, and we have sex with anybody who's willing and able." A quick literature search later shows he's right. STD's are spreading faster in assisted living facilities and nursing homes than in many other populations! Having been living largely single during the fellowship, I grimly reassure myself there might still be hope yet.

It is only a week and it is flying by. The next day is eight patients. The clinic day takes on aspects of a slow death march toward quitting time. It's not so much the medical issues which are often protocol driven and straight forward as it is all the innumerable psycho-social issues that tie me up during the day and leave me tossing and turning at night. I'm getting a crash course in alternative lifestyles that contains routine drug use, LGBTQ relations, racial issues, domestic abuse and others. Our social workers are almost sprinting from room to room. I spend a week getting comfortable with the medications and philosophy for treating these patients over whom many doctors throw up their hands and dismiss. I work hard not to judge. My mantra is "We are all beloved children of God."

Abraham Verghese, an infectious disease doctor, began his career in Johnson City, Tennessee as the AIDs epidemic began. People told him there could be no HIV in this rural area and that HIV was a big city, bicoastal problem. He quickly found those gay young men that had left rural Tennessee and its prejudices would return home near the end to sicken and die. His experiences became his first book: My Own Country.

My few early experiences with HIV found an echo with his. I remember the first AIDS patient I saw in my rural South Carolina office when AIDS was new in the early 80s'. The young, gay, black man had returned home from San Francisco with the diagnosis. He had already been to two other physicians in the area and been summarily escorted out the door when he told them his presumptive diagnosis. I wanted to help, but he was my first patient. I suspected from what I read in the papers he would not be my last patient, but I needed to know more. My professional mantra has always included a preferential option for those who needed it, particularly the poor and marginalized. I called an infectious disease doctor in the nearest big city for advice. "Family doctors aren't competent to deal with these patients," he declared. At his demand, I dutifully send the patient to him. But of course, there were more.

My mantra about helping almost got me killed with the next AIDs patient. I needed a blood specimen to confirm the diagnosis, and my staff were all wary of his infectious potential. I wouldn't ask someone to do what I was unwilling to do myself, so I drew the blood. The patient fainted and then had and a small seizure as I was pulling the needle out. His hand slammed up into mine, sending the needle and tube arcing towards the ceiling. I reflexively stuck out my gloved hand to catch it. Catch it I did, needle first, into my gloved palm. There was a moment of stunned silence as I quickly yanked the deeply embedded needle out of my palm, and we lowered the unconscious patient to the floor. My nurse looked from the bloody syringe to me and burst into tears saying, "Oh my God, you're going to die."

At that early point in the HIV epidemic, there was no effective prophylactic treatment for exposure. Anti-retroviral treatment had not even been invented. A few minutes later, patient roused and dismissed, my partner and staff insisted on injecting the puncture site with betadine hoping to kill the virus. There were eight of them and one of me, so I stuck my hand out again. An hour later, I called the state health department to ask for advice. Even the health department suggested anonymous testing to avoid affecting my insurance. Subsequently, I spent an uncomfortable and celibate six months of testing before being declared all clear. The health department doc also told me injecting the site with betadine was not helpful and extremely painful to which I could heartily agree.

I also tried to engage our rural hospital in preparing for HIV patients by proposing protocols for diagnosing and treating patients. I thought it best we be prepared and thought it would be an easy sell. It was an open secret that several of our administrators and staff were gay, so I was dismayed that they too insisted it is a big city problem and we wouldn't have to deal with "those patients." The epidemic worsened over the next few years, and the number of patients began to rise. I tried to send another complicated HIV patient to the same infectious disease doctor, now clearly overwhelmed by the epidemic. "Why can't you treat the patient yourself?" he snaps. "The protocols are out there, look them up and don't send me any more patients!" Now I'm back in River City, HIV is more a challenging chronic illness than fatal disease. In this week, I'm trying to get my arms around the concepts that have evolved in 20 years of progress at the River City HIV clinic.

Halfway through an HIV clinic, the fellowship administrator calls to tell me that my VA office hours which had been cancelled, are back on. I make my excuses to the HIV clinic staff, and run from downtown out to the VA. The fellowship secretary also mentions the faculty want to look at more of my patient logs. The theme from Jaws plays momentarily in my head. I dig up the requested logs and run them over on the way to the VA clinic.

The end of the week happens to bring a Grand Rounds for palliative care and AIDS, which is a fitting conclusion for my AIDS clinic week. Entering the auditorium, I plop down beside Bev. She is in a foul mood. Whispering she tells me that she got yelled at by someone who wanted her on an ethics call when she wasn't on the call rotation that day. "They said they didn't care what I thought I should to be doing. I was supposed to be doing whatever they said I should be doing," she whispered angrily as the speaker started.

For me a moment of schadenfreude-a guilty relief not spoken aloud as I reflect-, oh good, I'm not the only one they are yelling at anymore. I commiserate with Bev. After grand rounds and our abbreviated pity party, we meet over dinner and drinks with Bev's husband, Charles, the chaplain from the VA, plus a couple of NPs from hospice. At the end, we're all feeling a little better. Camaraderie does help to share and thus lessen our stress.

Howard has been pestering me about the abstract I submitted a few months ago. I've heard nothing, and the meeting is in two months. I log back into the website where I had done the abstract submission. To my surprise I see my abstract come back up. I look at the text and the submit button I'd hit earlier. Exasperated, I shout, "what the hell?" at the flashing monitor and slam my hand on the desk. The mouse jumps, the bottom of the screen scrolls up. Just below the 'Submit' button a second button is now flashing- "Are you sure?" Stunned, I tentatively push it, only to be confronted by a new message that materializes on the screen- "Time for submission has passed." Gaaah! Recounting this to Howard later does nothing to assuage his concerns over my possible 'brain damage.'

The following weeks' elective, I pursue another new discipline. I must admit as a new grandfather, this one worries me. This week will be pediatric palliative care. I report to the children's hospital and meet my new attending physician for the week- Emily Taylor (Not her real name). Emily works long hours, and her passion is for her kids, but she is a bit of an Eeyore- Winnie-the-Pooh s' donkey friend. Following her directions, the first day, I find her outside the pediatric ICU. She greets me with a tired but warm smile and says, "Hi, I'm Emily. I'm the 'Pedibot,' (her word) I do both palliative care and I'm one of the hospitalists. I've been up all night, so forgive me if I yawn occasionally." She then demonstrates with a prodigious yawn. Nonetheless, she is relentless as she walks me through the hospital and the minefields of caring for dying children.

Most of the children fall into in two groups- The first is younger children with incurable genetic defects and malformations. Then, a slightly older group, suffering with cancers or life-threatening trauma that are now endangering their lives. Emily plows doggedly through the list each day offering hope to the often hopeless, a compassionate smile and generous dollops of her time for the parents.

In my fellowship so far, I've had many instances where doctors have clapped me on the shoulder and said, "Man I couldn't do what you do." I quickly feel that way about pediatric palliative care. I can deal with my own demise, but I have children and now grandchildren. Pediatric palliative care…this is too close to home, and I can't imagine what these parents are enduring. In fact, I speak to one parent whose teenage daughter is in a coma after an overdose. We sit together looking at the respirator in silence as I try to think of something helpful to say. What I blurt out is, "I'm not going to pretend to know what you are going through. I don't want to know what you are going through, but I want you to know I'm here to help however I can." The father nods in numb appreciation and Emily return nods, then we all tear up for a few minutes and then excusing ourselves- Emily and I move on.

A few more patients later, Emily glances at the chart and her affect transforms. A huge smile erupts on her face as she steps into a room for a teenager fighting an aggressive sarcoma. Candace, 14, wearing a biker style bandana hiding her chemo bald head with fashion flare, grins back and high fives Emily. It is obvious her fight has been going on for a quite a while, and Emily and Candace have bonded. I discreetly take a step back and give them their moment. Emily explains the situation in a few sentences. After a bantering conversation ensures Candace is not in pain and is here for more chemo, they exchange, smiles and more high fives and we exit.

In the hall, out of sight, another transformation, Emily slumps down in dejection. "The cancer is spreading," she grimly explains. "This is 'Hail Mary' chemo. Candace knows the score. It is my job to keep her spirits up and keep her comfortable."

On the fourth day, I meet a young mother from the Middle East. This mother's son of six months, the family's treasure, has an inoperable constellation of malformations that threaten him daily. Emily explained earlier that the treating doctors have done pretty much all they can. She notes that we can get a feeding tube placed to help with nutrition, but the outlook is dismal, and the end is not if, but when. Emily gets a page and wanders off. The child is in a crib, gasping for breath, even with ventilatory support, as he has ever since his birth. Part of our job for palliative care is to begin the long and difficult task of preparing the family to let go.

Sitting with the mother, I explain the procedure for the feeding tube, going slowly, to make sure she follows what I 'm telling her. The child's nurse hovers in the background, half in, half out the door. I follow the format "Ask, tell, ask again" as I work though the diagnosis and prognosis and proposed procedure. I also address the issue that this will only buy a little more time. I begin to lay the groundwork for impending death. I worry that there may be a language barrier, but her English is only lightly accented, and she understands me well…too well.

"This procedure, it is more surgery?" I nod. "The last surgeries have not made him better, how will this help him?"

"Well we hope it will help buy some time with his nourishment and nutritional intake…." I begin.

152

"But he still has the disease which will kill him, right?" She pointedly interrupts me. I glance at the nurse whose been caring for this child for months for suggestions, she shrugs. Mom continues, "He's not getting better."

"So," the mother continues, gesturing to her gasping child. "You offer me this tube thing, so he can continue like this a little longer until he dies? Buy some more time for this? "The thought that maybe she and the child, faced with suffering and inevitable death, might have had enough, begins to dawn to me.

The mother continues inexorably. "Can't we just focus on keeping him comfortable for a shorter time and stop all this?" She says gesturing to all the technology around her child.

"Yes ma'am, we can do that."

"When can you start? Can you start now?"

"Is there anyone you need or want to contact? Family who want to come visit?"

"No" she says with flatly, bitterness tinging her voice. "They've all given up. They've all left. There is only me." She takes a gulp that sounds a little like a sob.

I nod a little jerkily as I rise. "I'll see how quickly we can start."

The nurse follows me out and down the hallway a little before we stop. "Wow," she whispers *sotto voce*. "Usually we take days to weeks to get to this point, and you did the whole trip in under an hour!" I'm not sure if she's admiring or condemning.

I respond equally softly: "I wasn't driving this bus. Mom is, but if it was my son who is suffering and will die no matter what, I can understand where she is coming from."

I call Emily. She, too, is a little surprised that the mother so forcefully rejected the feeding tube and asked for comfort measures only. However, Emily, like the mother, ceding to the inevitable, is agreeable.

I quickly start some medications for the baby's gasping and discomfort. I'm not being too aggressive but giving enough morphine that the child can rest. Once he's resting better, we start withdrawing technology that has been helping sustain his life. The following day, he dies comfortably in his mother's arms. Again, I am, without a hint of irony, thanked for at least letting her child be comfortable.

It is the end of the week, and it has gone by fast. In parting, Emily shakes my hand, I pat her on the shoulder and say, "Man, I'm not sure I can do what you do, but thank God that you're doing it." She grins a little sadly and shoos me to the door.

Kharma, being what it is, however, years later, I am asked to do pediatric hospice by the local children's hospital. Three times, I and our hospice administration approached the topic with our staff. Three times, the staff rebelled and threatened to quit saying, like I had years earlier, that working with sick and dying children just too stressful. Many of our hospice staff were young mothers and the thought of caring for dying children like their own children was too much. However, on the third time, as the group starts to get a bit rowdy our newest social worker stands up and motioned for quiet.

"We take care of families at the worst time in their lives: when a family member is dying. Our nursing staff provides physical comfort. We the social workers, provide emotional comfort, and our chaplains provide spiritual comfort, all to help these patients and their families make the best of bad times." Heads nod, He proceeds a bit more forcefully. "This is our mission." Now what is the VERY WORST thing that can happen to a family? Wouldn't that be death of a child? Are you saying that we help people, except when the going gets too tough? Is that what I'm hearing? Because this is where the rubber really meets the road this is when we have the chance to really shine and do our very best for the neediest families!" Heads began to nod. "This is the time we need to show our strengths and not fall for our weaknesses. The tide begins to turn. He sits back down, and I shoot him a grateful look. He grins back. In the end, we did provide some pediatric home care.

Pediatrics is over too quickly but I can't help but breathe a sigh of relief to be done with this emotionally draining work. I still wonder how Emily goes back day after day. With the week ended, I return to

Knoxville for another job interview with the hospital group. Gayle is on call for her work in the GI lab and gets slammed. I hardly lay eyes on her before I turn back to River City. There are flurries of snow as I drive anxiously back over the mountain.

The next week's elective should be a little easier, a pain clinic. I had worked with our hospital's pain clinic in Knoxville part-time for years. We were at a medical staff meeting when I had happened to make a chance comment to one of our anesthesiologists at the pain clinic that I had addictionology credentials. Pain, as you might guess, also attracts addicts. The anesthesiologists were looking for a way to try to identify those with higher addiction potential. I wanted to learn about procedures, but they found I had more value in extensive interviews, surveys and counseling with at risk patients. I had done that for a few years but learned little about interventional pain procedures. So, here I was in again at a different pain clinic hoping to learn more about pain procedures and how they might help in hospice and palliative care.

Unfortunately, the pain clinic week was a bust, with minimal teaching. I spent most of the time with me standing at the outer edge of the sheet covered patient, while the anesthesiologist would push the needle into someone's spine snapping at the X-ray tech, "picture, take another picture. My notes comment mostly that during these five days, my feet were killing me. The other unhappy surprise is the anesthesiology resident with whom I am paired. To say he is unenthused about hospice is exceedingly generous.

"Hospice," he snarls, "you don't' treat pneumonia, you don't treat infections. You just push morphine and let people die. Why don't you just get a gun and shoot them?!" As I try to offer a rebuttal, he walks away, and we never speak again.

One patient from that pain clinic experience still haunts me he had Complex Regional Pain Syndrome formerly called Reflex Sympathetic Dystrophy. In these cases, an injury, often minor, sets off a cascade of nerve pain that torments patients for years. Pain injections, nerve blocks and medications can help a little, but the affected limb grows often shiny and weak and the slightest touch can be agony. We had seen Mr. Zorn at the VA in August and now he's at the pain clinic to try a lumbar sympathetic block. His face is a mask of desperation. He's tried several before. He tells me the blocks work for a little period of blessed relief and then wear off, all too soon. Nevertheless, he's desperate for any surcease from this pain that he describes as a black cloud surrounding him that smothers all life and enjoyment. Overall, my week with pain is the least fruitful of the electives.

Halfway through pain clinic week, Bev, Jay and I have our weekly beer and dinner. It is tough to say who is more down as we commiserate. A friend of Bev's back home in Washington state is dying of cancer. She wants to visit but lacks the money and time for another trip back. Closer to River City, it appears Walter, after cheating death so many times, may be truly dying. Still, he's cheated death so many times, and I've lost count of how many admissions he's had. Bev's husband silently sips his beer, his head pivoting back and forth between us as it would when watching a tennis match.

I start my final elective week at the wound care clinic, which involves patients who have developed chronic, non-healing wounds, often from diabetes, vascular difficulties or too little movement. Wound care has a striking familiarity for me as I and dress and care for the wounds and sores. When I was a kid, I was "all boy," which mostly meant getting scrapes and bruises from hard play, tree houses, forts and rope swings. The result of this boyishness was a never-ending supply of stitches, scabs and casts for me to pick at. My mother was constantly scolding me, "Don't pick at that!" Wound care clinic was heaven for me because it was an endless supply of patients with sores and scabs that patients would pay to have picked, cut and scraped. I learned about dressings and different wound types, but the fun part was the constant hand work of cleaning wounds. As my gloved hands worked carefully at a large diabetic wound, I snorted quietly to myself in amusement thinking, "I'm picking at this Mom"

It is Ash Wednesday in the middle of this final elective week, and I walk over early to the cathedral down the street in the grey early morning. I receive the ashes on my forehead and the grim reminder of my ever-present work- "Ashes thou wert and ashes you shall become." This remonstrance is particularly cogent as indeed, Walter did die indeed two days ago, a sad introduction to the Lenten season. From church I sprint to the wound clinic wiping the ashes off my forehead in my car mirror. Before I can enter the building, I'm called back to the University Hospital to an ethics consultation and then run to Walter's funeral visitation. This is a visit Bev and I are determined to make. Quickly after that it is back to the VA to talk about addictions for a class. I end the day feeling like an abused pinball.

That night Bev, her husband and I meet again for dinner. She made Walter's visitation but missed ethics consult and was later upbraided for her absence. She's tired and angry. "What are they going to do to me?" she asks plaintively. "One step forward, two back. I feel like I'm trying to tread water with an anchor tied to my legs." I offer companionable anger and consolation.

"Well" I riposte, "I just got threatened with 'academic review' for crimes yet specified. I'm not even sure what that is, but I think I'm currently winning the 'who's pissing them off the most- 'contest." Bev reciprocates with her own outrage. We hash out our grievances while her husband looks on bemused, sipping his beer. He's seen reruns of this show a few times now.

Late in the month, I get some welcome news. I call Gayle that evening. "Good news!" I crow, "Our program got accredited!" There is long, dead silence from the phone. I've been married long enough to know that this is the sound of an explosion about to occur.

She starts off slow, biting off each word, one at a time. "You. Mean. You. Quit. Your. Well-paying job. Leave me and go to a program that is not even accredited!!? Were you out of your mind?" She continues a while until when she pauses for breath, I manage to intervene.

"Whoa, whoa, whoa! There were no accredited hospice and palliative medicine programs until today when the national accrediting body issued accreditations for the first time. We're among the first! Gayle is not much mollified, but the steam begins to run down. I decide to get off the phone before I step in something else.

During my fellowship, Gayle's mom, Sally, who was ninety, was slowly declining. She had lived for years in a rural area of South Carolina on the Edisto River. After the death of her husband, Mallard, she continued to live there alone, mowing her lawn and tending her garden.

Her neighbors of over thirty years, kept an eye on her and called us when needed.

Sally, of course, never called to complain about health or other issues. But now she was beginning to visibly fail. Of course, despite being on the northern side of ninety, she was stubborn and refused to consider alternatives such as assisted living. "I don't want to have to stay with all those old people!" she exclaimed. When I reasonably pointed out she too was over ninety, she dismissed me with a brush of her hand. "That's just a number."

The summer just before my fellowship however, Sally came for a visit. Gayle and I had gone shopping while Sally was taking a nap. Sally got up and fell in her bedroom. She was unable to get up until we came home to find her. She was unhurt but shaken. It went unsaid, but we were all wondering what if this had happened at her home alone. It still took another few days during that visit before she casually mentioned she might allow us to arrange a visit with an assisted living/nursing home facility near her home. The visit went well. She recognized many residents in the assisted living facility. "Why I thought all these people had died!" she sputtered. "And here they all are!"

We moved her in a few weeks later. Even though she was walking unassisted and living in the independent living section, she insisted that we get her a fancy rolling walker with seat because "all the other residents had them."

However, in the ensuing months Sally weakened and began to depend more on the rollator in earnest. Then she began to have more falls, eventually she suffered a fall in January of my fellowship that resulted in a hip fracture. Coming back from the hospital and a hip replacement, Sally, reluctantly moved from the independent living side to assisted living. Gayle went back to South Carolina to help her change rooms at the facility. As there is a lot less of Sally's stuff to move, Gayle waves me off, and I spend the next two days back in wound clinic trimming nails, filing down calluses and cleaning out wounds.

In the afternoon, Bev leads a class discussion revolving about an article on caregiver fatigue. I wonder if she has a hidden message. The rest of class time, we do a long group debrief about Walter's two years with the palliative care service and share remembrances of his time with us, his humor: his love of life and his determination to hang on. Friday ends my electives rotation. I keep an eye on the weather and snow on the mountain, getting home for the weekend. Gayle is back from moving her mom. She's a bit depressed. We both know where this is headed. We meet up with our family friends and enjoy a rock concert.

It is late in the afternoon some weeks after Walter died that I get a request to call Walter's widow Sharon. She is trying to find out who is doing Walter's death certificate. He had so many doctor's in different hospitals that the funeral home is having trouble figuring out to whom to give the task. It has been a few weeks and she's getting desperate to start settling his affairs. She knows Bev and I best, and so has sought us out in desperation. As a fellow I'm not supposed to do the death certificate, but I can direct her to the medical records department at the hospital where he died.

It is probably worth exploring this grim bureaucratic detail for a few moments. I was only a week or so into my own internship when I got a late-night page to come to the medical floor in our hospital. At the time only a physician could 'pronounce' death. The nurse at the nurses' station was waiting for me to do that task on a patient who had died as expected. "What time did he die?" I asked sleepily as we entered the darkened room.

"Doctor," she said with some starch in her voice reserved for 'newbies' like me, "He's not dead until you say he is." I looked at the patient, looked at my watch and newly empowered, announced the time that would go on the death certificate.

Death certificates are a task that all doctors detest. I think it is partly more paperwork and partly fear that death implies failure and if litigation ensues, the likely first malpractice defendant will be the doctor's name on the death certificate. (Although state law actually provides immunity.) In complicated cases like Walters, with lots of doctor's, it can be hard to decide which physician bore final responsibility for the certification task and doctor after doctor would decline to be the signatory. As a hospital medical director, it became a bizarre and sort of pointless part of my job to adjudicate which doctor had to sign. I would go down to medical records and page through the chart for long periods of time and decide who I thought the appropriate signer should be. I would then write a tart note to that doctor saying I'd just spent an hour deciding who would have to do a task that took ten minutes or less to complete. The casual reader might think I must be exaggerating doctor's distaste for the task, so let me add that the problem is so bad that at least in Tennessee, there are penalties for doctors who fail or refuse to complete this task. The penalties can go up to loss of licensure for the physician who refuses.

This is because families can do nothing without this piece of paper including cremate the remains, file for insurance to get the money to bury the body, close bank accounts, sell cars or property. To do these things requires an original death certificate for each transaction. After my mother's death I requested twelve original death certificates and I used ten. As you might guess as a hospice doctor, I do a lot of death certificates. Until the state computerized the system, I was on a first name basis with many funeral home directors in the area who would often come by the office to expedite matters. One of them told me about a new employee whom he found looking at the large funeral home white board naming the deceased, planned funeral time, details and physician.

"Man!" he squawked, "I don't know who that Dr. Phelps is but don't let him anywhere near me!"

March

March begins blustery and cold. I'm back at University Hospital, and Howard, my mentor and patriarch of our attending faculty, is filling in for Marci. We grin at each other, two older farts, among a group of new medical students, who never age. Monday brings a backlog of weekend consults. Howard directs traffic, as we split up into two teams and hurry off, each with a trailing gaggle of med students and residents.

The cheery comradery of Monday is quickly extinguished Wednesday when Marci resumes supervision. While I'm running through a summary of the list of consults, Marci randomly asks for the vitals on a patient whom the other team saw. Logically, since I didn't see the patient, vitals are not in my notes. I get a short, but sharp lecture again, on not being "completely prepared." As she turns abruptly away to another resident, it is evident to all I've been demoted again in her mind. The following day, I hear a rumor that Marci is one of several in the running to be the next program director. I pray that I graduate before it happens. Meanwhile the consults continue to flow…

The next day the VA clinic looks light, only two patients. Then another patient is added, then two more come in 'off the street.' Finally, yet another veteran, Lester, comes up from the emergency room trailed by Anna, our sometimes attending. Lester has advanced pancreatic cancer and has shown up with a massive belly full of cancer fluid called ascites. The ascites is making it difficult for him to even breathe. Picture Lester as pregnant woman at nine months, then add three more months, then add spindly legs and arms as the cancer has eaten most of the protein from his muscles. He is panting and grunting in distress and Anna has decided then and there that we should drain his belly and relieve his fluid burden.

We hastily get the paracentesis kit and clean the belly, Anna inserts a large bore needle into the abdomen, then a plastic catheter through the needle that is attached to a bag. She opens the stopcock, and fluid gushes into the bag. The bag fills, then another, and yet another. Anna turns off the stopcock. Lester is breathing better but there is still a generous amount of ascites remains. "Take more," Lester implores her. Anna demurs. The fluid is rich in the very protein he needs. Too much fluid taken without supplemental IV protein can cause a vascular collapse.

"This will have to do for now," she says gruffly, returning to the emergency room, leaving me to explain." He reluctantly understands, and we make an appointment to see him next week. I measure his abdomen to get a number as a starting point for the evaluation next week. I know my other appointments are now seriously delayed and waiting. I stand to go see the next patient, but…

"Doc," he stops me, "tell me straight. How long have I got? I try not to sigh, as I turn back to Lester. It is an important question, for him, the most important question, one that deserves a full and honest response. It took courage to ask and needs my time, but, but, but…

I sit back down as if I have all the time in the world and commence the familiar (to me) conversation. "Well, I'm not God and we don't go by specific number of months, but by orders of magnitudes, hours, days, weeks…" Meanwhile I'm aware of time passing and patients piling up. It is not that we have that many patients at the VA. It is that their computers are old and clunky and completing a patient chart can take up to an hour per patient. So, when I finish the last patient that night, I run out for dinner and come back to get a fresh start on my pile of charts.

I'm fully aware that my charts will be scrutinized by Marci, howard and company for any flaws and that my charts need to be as close to perfect as possible both factually and grammatically. Still, the time with Lester is worth the late evening for me. Finally done, I snap out the lights in my VA alcove and step out of the hospital in the late-night chill, yawning. My car sits alone in the dark parking lot.

The next morning at University hospital brings me to Edna, a sweet grandmotherly lady with a cloud of white hair, delightful disposition, and a lifelong, but genteel alcoholic. Many alcoholics die from end-stage liver disease with ascites, bruising and confusion but Edna has acquired a virulent form of hepato-renal syndrome which will likely kill her in a few weeks. The medicine services' physician attending, Dr. Jennifer Ash, (neither Edna or Jennifer are their real names) has asked us to see Edna and family and explain the diagnosis and prognosis. Dr. Ash is another recent graduate of the medicine residency, now a faculty physician. Jennifer and I prepare to break the news and discuss to goals of care. We are outside the conference room where Edna and family wait when Dr. Ash abruptly asks if she can run the meeting and carry the conversation. "I need to get comfortable with this for myself," she explains a little plaintively.

Despite the gulf in age and experience between us, I acknowledge the situation, "You're the faculty attending, I'm just the fellow; you're in charge." Edna's family are clustered protectively around her wheelchair by the small table in the conference room. Edna, as usual, is smiling beatifically, and despite the circumstances, her smile is infectious for the group. Jennifer makes space for her chair beside

Edna at the prescribed 45° angle. The rest of our small team fill the remaining seats and a few of us line the wall. Jennifer begins explaining the condition slowly and carefully, making good eye contact with patient and family, and using terms and phrases they can understand. She gets to the clinical information and prognosis and smiles begin to turn to frowns and then visible distress. The family begins to tear up and to her horror, Jennifer's eyes also tear up. Then her nose fills and the tissues we always bring for family, are first handed to her and then the family for whom the tissue were intended. I can sympathize I've been there.

Jennifer bravely plows on as her tears continue to drip and she reaches over for more tissues. The whole room is tears and noses honking. The only one who seems unfazed is Edna. She's still smiling, albeit a little less so. I wonder to myself if maybe she's not understanding what's being said. She negates this idea, when she reaches over and generously hugs and pats Jennifer, comforting her and explaining, "It's OK honey, I've got good family, I've had a good life, I'm sure the next life will be good too. I'll be OK." The family nods in support and agrees. They take control of Edna's wheelchair and file out of the room. Each pause to hug Jennifer as the leave. The team follows.

Now it's just Jennifer and me. She dabs at her eyes and blows from her nose a final juicy blast. "I've never been so humiliated in my life," she sniffles.

"Oh no," I counter. "That was the finest gift you could have given. That patient and family know their doctor cared so much that she cried while delivering the news. They will never forget that, and they will never forget you." For a few seconds our roles are reversed as I reassure and comfort her. I find myself comfortable here. I also find that I am finally learning what I came to learn: a fruitful and genuine exchange. Jennifer gives me a tear-stained smile as I continue. "However, it's kind of hard on the doc. to cry like that. While it's a gift to this family I don't recommend it as a steady diet."

As we leave, I call to check in with the office they tell me Mr. Owens, another patient I'd seen a few weeks earlier, is back in the emergency room again with dementia and sepsis. The office clerk, skimming the notes, reminds me that our team had talked earlier with the family about withholding antibiotics on the next admission. I come down to the emergency room and find the patient and daughter in their cubical. Before I can say anything, the daughter admonishes me- "Remember, we agreed, no antibiotics this time." Mr. Owens dies before I can even leave the emergency room. The antibiotics would not have changed things.

Of course, it has to be Friday the 13th 'when I make my single biggest error of my fellowship. Edna, Mr. Owens and others are behind me; I'm hurrying, trying to get a lung cancer patient out of the hospital. I can't catch a break for the multiple phone pages, questions and diversions. I'm trying to calculate an opioid dosage converting from one drug to another and changing the delivery route from IV, to by mouth (PO). First a nurse interrupts me. Then a med student. Then a moment of peace.

So, according to my table, morphine IV at 10 milligrams would be equal to 1.5 mg of IV Dilaudid. I scrawl a hasty note- 1.5 mg. as a medicine resident slides around the nurses' station and engages me in a passionate discussion about another patient dying with pancreatic cancer. We figure out this new patient's pain medications. I return to my calculation where I'd written my standard dose equivalents and complete the calculation from my noted dose, not the patient's dose. My pager sounds yet again and the nurse steps in, hurriedly demanding the prescription. I glance at my number, and finish the calculation forgetting the 1.5 was a place holder in the conversion. I'm off again, thrusting the prescription at the nurse whose standing over me hand, hand out to get the patient out the door. At days end, I'm asked to run by Marci's office on my way out.

Night has fallen, Marci sits by the light of a desk lamp holding my prescription from this afternoon. It is shaking in her grasp, as she tears into me. "You miscalculated the dose. This would have been four times too much!" she hisses at me thrusting the prescription towards me.

"Fortunately, the nurse called me aside to ask about it." I look at the prescription, immediately recall the conversion and realize that she is right. Truly this time, it really is my mistake. Mortified, I abjectly apologize. I promise to do all calculations on paper to avoid a memory lapse. I resist pointing out that this is the very mistake her mentor had told me she'd committed months ago. I go home in a funk...again. This is different, I really deserved this chewing out. (Although, I do wonder why the nurse called my attending instead of me...) This is my fault this time. I can't direct my anger at anyone but myself.

One of my new weekend joys is going home and seeing Gayle and holding my new granddaughter. I have to admit though, as a guy, I don't find babies that enthralling. Babies mainly eat, sleep, cry, poop and pee. So, my time with my granddaughter is a few minutes cuddling and cooing over her and, then finding a welcoming mother or grandmother to hand her back and embrace her. This weekend, however, I am alone, as Gayle is going to South Carolina to check on her mother after the move from independent living to assisted living. I'm alone in River City so I spend the weekend touring the state visiting distilleries. A perfect guy's weekend of visiting famous bourbon landmarks. I miss the family time but have to admit I have a blast.

The rest of the month goes by quickly. We have a memorial service to remember patients who've died. I've been living it every day, but even I am astounded by how long the list of names, each read one by one. The memorial service over, we go back to the office for a job interview with a new applicant for a palliative care faculty position.

The candidate is another palliative care fellow that comes from the Boston program. I would have been in her class. I tell her about my interview experience in Boston and how they obsessed about my age and experience. She sighs and says she can believe it. "They are very hierarchical" she explains. "You would have upset all their models for who's up and who's down. "Her interview though, reminds me, yet again that, I don't have a job! I spend that evening at the YMCA, as I slowly grind my weight down some more. The month ends with yet another review with Marci. As usual, it's not laudatory.

"You're just not where I think you should be by now," she sighs with regret, reviewing another chart. She shakes her head in exasperation, holding a patient note of mine to the light of the setting sun. "It's all here, in the note, but it is just scattered. Where's the pain description?" I lean over and point to a detailed description of the patient's pain in the section 'review of systems."

"But why there?" she asks a tad plaintively, "is it not in the chief complaint or history of present illness? Pain is what we do. It should be front and center." I stubbornly point again to the detailed pain notation in the review of systems and say nothing.

At last she sighs and concedes the point, tossing the note on the desk between us. I push back a little." Do you have any reason to think I'm incompetent?" I ask point blank.

She looks a little surprised. "No, not that, it's just... just, disorganized. I thought you'd be better than this," she says pointing to the note.

The month ends early as we all head to the National American Academy of Hospice and Palliative Medicine Conference in Austin, Texas. The specialty is so small that we meet collaboratively with the Hospice and Palliative Nurses Association, this way, the combined group can put on one impressive and substantive conference. It is also a terrific way to accentuate the fact that our specialty is team-based and collaborative. Much of the conference is very encouraging as leaders speak about the growing numbers in our field and the changing medical culture that is just beginning to see "end of life care as part of healthcare, not a failure of healthcare." They talk about the aging population with ten thousand baby boomers hitting 65 each day. They talk about greater emphasis on holistic and patient-centered care focusing on the desires of the informed patient

In our off hours, Gayle and I wander and enjoy Austin. The highlight of the conference is when author Jeffrey Zaslow, shows tapes and talks about writing the book- "The Last Lecture" with Professor Randy Pausch. In the book Pausch, who died young of pancreatic cancer, talks about balancing his desire for a well lived life, and simultaneously acknowledging the end with clear eyes. Pausch first did a college talk that became an early viral internet sensation. Then with Zaslow, he turned that talk into a bestselling book to leave as a legacy for his children and students. The book was published mere days before Pausch died.

Later that week, back in Knoxville I am still interviewing with hospital systems and members of the hospitalist group. My daughter tells me that at an administration meeting she attended a few weeks earlier, her hospital CEO announced that "Tiffany's Dad, will be coming to work here in a few months," which had sounded really promising. Now, suddenly, my phone calls and emails to hospital administration about the status of my application are going unanswered. I'm puzzled and surprised. I finally use my doctor status to force a meeting with the hospital CEO who insists, "Oh no, everything is fine." Then of course, he goes back to not answering my phone calls. Both Tiffany and I are confused.

I wonder if the people in River City have somehow poisoned my well. It is plain they don't like me; however, since no one from Knoxville has requested references I don't know how they could have tainted my prospects. I try to reason through the lack of contact as I've been on the administration side. Sometimes finances or uncertainty about a position would emerge necessitating a re-review. Sometimes we were interviewing someone, and someone else more promising would come along. We'd have to try to placate both, while negotiating with both. However, from the hiring side, when the doctor goes silent, it often means they are interviewing elsewhere or waiting and hoping for a better offer. In my case, I'm left a bit baffled.

Meanwhile, the St. Mary's doctors at the pain clinic where I'd previously seen patients part-time see Gayle on a daily basis in the shared recovery area. They frequently ask her if I've found a job and if I might like to come back part-time. Simultaneously, the merger of St. Mary's and another hospital system have brought in a geriatric program, and I am to interview there for a position. My heart sinks a little I gently explain that while close, geriatrics and palliative care are different things. The interviewer however as an old friend is trying to do me a favor, asks me to stretch a little. "Isn't geriatrics just taking the long view of palliative care?" she asks. I'm grateful for the opportunity and I promise to think about it.

I call again to the Knoxville hospital who has resumed not returning my calls. At this point, I have little to lose. I get pushy and work my way up the chain of command, until I finally get the CEO's secretary. She promises to have him call me, but I refuse to hang up and long training on her part, will not let her hang up on a doctor, so she finally puts him on.

"Well," he says after meaningless pleasantries that imply, he'd been meaning to call me, but urgent business had kept that from happening. "The thing is the hospitalist group said they don't think they can work with you and didn't want us to hire you. We really wanted to hire you, but they would be your primary referral source and well…" I'm a bit surprised. I thought we had resolved that in my conversation with Dr. James, the lead hospitalist a month or so ago, but I let it go and politely thank him.

It is not until many months later that I run into Dr. James at a medical function and we get to chatting. I wasn't not going to bring up their refusal to work with me, but he pointblank asks but with a twist. "Why wouldn't you take the job to work with us," he asks with just a hint of belligerence. I tell him what I was told. "Huh, whadya know," he mutters drumming his fingers on the table, "that is exactly what he told us you said, that you didn't think could work with us. I think we both just learned something."

CHAPTER FIVE

April

April brings me back to the VA and the inpatient unit. The very first patient exposes me to not one but two seriously weird experiences. Both involve the afterlife, angels and the deceased. Jane is unusual, she is the rare older woman veteran amongst the hundreds of men. A Korean war nurse, now in her eighties, she is dying of pancreatic cancer. She is reputed to be slightly salty, but saintly, and is accompanied by a younger sister and niece. Jane has been nearing death, obtunded, sluggish and hard to arouse for several days in the unit. We work hard to ensure she kept comfortable.

Now, after a few days, she suddenly wakes up! It is another patient with a rally. After days of stertorous slumber, Jane is awake and chatty and her family is rejoicing, when I come in to check on her. The family credits me with her "recovery." I know enough to dodge their praise, saying quickly, "Well God works in mysterious ways." I have had the foresight this time to prepare the family for the possibility. I now tell families to think of a rally theologically, rather than medically, as offering a moment of grace, to provide a peaceful closure.

Jane greets me cheerfully and then begins to talk to someone to my immediate left. I'm at the foot of the bed, and her family are all clustered at the head of the bed. She is addressing empty space. Her family looks concerned. After a few comments and questions from Jane to this space, I can no longer curb my curiosity and ask who she's talking to.

"Oh, the angel standing next to you," she replies nonchalantly. I glance a little nervously to my left at the unseen space. Jane turns her head to look to more space at my right and nods approvingly.

"Another angel?" I ask tentatively.

"Oh no, that is my older sister Alma she says she'll see me again in a little bit. Alma, died a about five years ago." She says this last part calmly. I sneak a glance at the niece and sister who are almost as freaked out as I am, but they nod, that Jane is correct about Alma.

Jane chats casually with everyone, living and dead. She is calm and collected and seems totally rational. I am still trying to process her rapid change from obtunded to fully coherent, not to mention the participants in the conversation. I've read about such instances but hadn't seen one before. I decide that this experience with the otherworldly is surprisingly comforting. I don't have a theological or medical explanation but decide to file it as a moment of unexpected grace and reassurance at least for the patient if not myself. A little later out at the nurse's station, the nurse comes out to tell me that Jane has drifted off again. She does not awaken before she dies the next day.

Amazingly, I find myself amidst another paranormal event later the same week with another veteran. I'm asking about pain control and other symptoms. Out of the blue, he interrupts my questions addressing a spot above my head. "Just hold your horses I'll be there in a bit" he snaps to empty space.

"Let me guess," I try to joke, "an angel? "

"No" comes a slightly waspish reply. "My older brother Joe. He was pretty tall, 6'8" or 6'9". He is still bossy, even after being dead for ten years." I nod in uncertain agreement and move a step or two to the side to get out of Joe's way. Surprisingly, patients view this communication with angels and the afterlife as absolutely normal and seemed befuddled that we can't see these visitors. I was reassured by one patient who was talking to angels a few months later. Once again, the patient seemed totally at peace with the visit and totally normal. The patient explained the angel beside me was there to collect a soul.

"Not mine, I hope, I'm not quite done with it." The patient accepts my commentary as a friendly tease, treating my jest as a reasonable part of the conversation and relays my comment to the angel. Then she pauses for the reply. (I'm still having continued heart problems, so I gave her listening silence the time needed.)

The patient smiled at me at length and said, "She says not to worry. You've still got a good while to go here, but she'll be back for me soon."

I do not know why people see angels or dead family members. Perhaps the veil to the next side is thinner for them than for the rest of us. The patients are not confused, delirious or disoriented. They engage in normal conversation with others visibly present in the room, and yet include the unseen as well. I treat these exchanges with the awe and respect for mystery I think they deserve.

Later that week, Howard surprises me by asking me to mentor Marci on hiring issues. In looking at hiring another staffer, she is debating between yet another young nurse practitioner and older NP who is a little rough around the edges but has a lot more experience. I try to point out to Marci that almost her whole team is a homogenous collection of young, white women- "PLU's" (People Like Us). I propose that maybe she should look at someone with different life experiences and viewpoints. The advice falls on deaf ears and, "Candy" a young and overly exuberant, ex-cheerleader joins us a week later. Meanwhile, Marci sends me back to Howard for more 'mentoring.'

On Wednesday I'm back in church at 7 am. Because I frequently miss Sundays in Knoxville, I rely on these Wednesday morning intimate communions to help keep my sense of perspective and to help keep me sane. Like most services, I use the opportunity to pray for the patients and families I'll see. This morning the bishop is back. He spends his homily explaining how conservative and liberal forces are pulling apart factions of the church. He tells us he'd been planning to retire but is now being asked to shepherd a second diocese in Fort Worth that is seeking to break away from the national Episcopal church. The issues include gay marriage and women clergy. His homily is another reminder that even inside our tiny morning communion, there are larger forces and politics trying to change our church, our country and our way of treating others. For once, post communion, I'm not uplifted, but more depressed as I leave the service and trudge the few blocks to the medical center.

After a full day at the Medical Center, I'm asked to do a last minute "deathbed" consult in the evening. 'Sure, I have no life. I live alone, what the hell.' I go see the elderly gentleman who has been diagnosed with untreatable lung cancer. Maybe it is the residua from the church service that leaves me in a reflective mood. Mr. Ashin is aged, wizened and alone. He is wheezing some but is cognitively intact and a bit of a garrulous philosopher. As the medications I give relieve his pain and gasping, he opens up about his life. We sit and talk into the growing darkness. I'm struck again with the profundity of the opportunity I am provided to make a difference, to add some small measure of comfort in people's lives when they need it most.

After the day of intense highs and lows I get back to the apartment drained but fulfilled, to make my nightly call to Gayle. One more dip in the rollercoaster, her mother is back in the hospital. She is not heading back to South Carolina just yet though. This weekend is Easter, the theme of resurrection amidst my last nine months of death and dying holds special significance for me as we celebrate with children and baby granddaughter.

Aside from the lectures and patient learnings, both Bev and I are expected to produce a project tailored to our studies and positions. Bev has done a great job on presenting her project for fellowship which is bluntly titled How to Get a Job. She explores supply and demand, professional recruiters, on-line resources, evaluating a prospect, community and common contracting pitfalls. She concludes her presentation with a real-world example of her own job search and announces she will be taking her dream job in Washington state! Her topic is very timely for the graduating fellows and residents who crowd her afterwards with questions. I stand on the periphery of the group, still wondering what I'm going to do for employment. My fellowship project is coming due soon and I am spending most nights reading and researching and writing.

The weeks are slipping by. I'm pulled in for what is becoming monthly performance review. Per usual, I'm hammered again, Marci ratchets up the pressure adding a new threat," I just don't know, we may not be able to graduate you on time. We may need to keep you for additional training and observation." Marci and other faculty begin occasional hints that maybe I just should go ahead and quit. These not so subtle suggestions push all my 'stubborn' buttons. I attend another mentoring session with Howard who's really between a rock and a hard place, between myself and Marci and company. I'm a little pacified when Howard says he'll write a crucial letter of recommendation for me contingent on the condition that I spend more time with him.

It is a funny disconnect that as the pressure from the faculty mounts. I'm finding deeper and more profound satisfaction in my work. I'm doing better with the patients effectively relieving their symptoms, guiding family meetings and helping bring raucous family discord to consensus in support of the patient's choices. There is immense satisfaction when a patient was moaning in bed with pain and then seeing them relieved, sitting up smiling, pain or shortness of breath better. The most common question I get is, "Why didn't somebody do this for me/mom/my child a long time ago?" I am learning, growing and gaining confidence even with the continued discontent from some of the teaching staff.

In one hallway interaction, Marci she tells me that the residents don't find me 'user friendly.' I'm surprised, as I've seen my relationship with the residents and fellows as extremely amicable. They seem to find it somewhat ironic that I'm sharing their student life and yet old enough to be their parent. Early on, I'd told one set of residents not to think of me as an established physician but rather as intern like them, but with thirty years' experience! Just yesterday, I'd spent time with a few residents and students reviewing how to calculate opioid doses and pitfalls. Using my "Dare to be Stupid" pedagogy, I'd even used my recent prescribing fiasco as an example of how not to calculate. I told them not only the math and tables, but how to be aware of time and distraction pressures to avoid errors. They had seemed pleased to find an ally. Still Marci's criticism seems skewed as she continues to insist that I'm not seen as friendly or helpful. I wonder if maybe she's projecting her own insecurities.

That night I call my sister, the associate dean at a university in another state for advice. Sis is, as usual, emphatically on my side. "F*#k those assholes," she bellows through the phone. "They can't pick on my baby brother like that."

"I just need to back them off a little." I say. "I feel like I came to study great literature, and instead I'm getting graded on my penmanship."

"Here's what ya do" she continued. "Deans don't like problems. Remember, I 'R' one. You need to go to the dean and spell out your problems. You are only a few months from finishing. Keeping you over- beyond your fellowship or letting you go is messy and involves a lot of paperwork. Deans have enough paperwork, believe me. Paperwork often leads to lawsuits and publicity. We don't like all that. Your dean can probably get them to back off a little bit. Dean's like nice, non-messy graduations where we can preen and strut our stuff. We don't like paperwork, lawsuits and bad publicity. Curing cancer, solving poverty, that is the kind of publicity we like. Go have a chat." I promise to give her advice some heavy thought. But before I'm done thinking that through… a few days later I'm approached again.

I've had another miserable sleepless night. Atrial fibrillation, my nemesis, woke me up at 2 am and ran until about 6 am. After the cardiac catheterization and evaluation, the only recommendation for these bursts of arrhythmia had been take an aspirin. The arrhythmias had quieted down, but right now I'm groggy and feel hungover from lack of sleep. Marci confronts me on the floor with a posse of faculty members, apparently there to serve as witnesses. She says the usual phrase, almost apologetically, "We need to talk." Unsurprisingly, they are still not happy. And they've decided that desperate times call for desperate measures. I try to nail them down to what exactly it is they aren't happy with- have I made a mistake? I'm keeping cards on every patient to keep organized and I'm writing extensive notes. I'm even having Bev occasionally proofread and review the notes to see if I'm missing something. The patients and residents seem happy.

The posse struggles to explain, in the tiny conference room, something ineffable, indescribable about their discomfort with me. I ask the group to clarify or be specific about what their concern. They verbally grope around for definitive reply and fail. It's not patient care, it's not the notes, it is not 'the mistake.' Here Marci glowers at me clearly me to indicate that the prescription debacle last month has not left her mind. It's just, just … me.

They have "made a decision" Marci declares. They want me to have a physical and they are referring me to student health for an evaluation and recommendations. My job is to follow through with any recommendations. My continued fellowship depends on my cooperation. The school will pay for any testing and treatment. They say the process must include psychiatric evaluation. I could tell they still wondered if I had incipient Alzheimer's. Anytime needed away from the rounds, she continues, will be granted without question. At the end of the 'talk' during which I've said almost nothing, I'm handed a card. Apparently, I have an appointment with student health in the morning. I shrug and agree. They seem almost disappointed with my acquiescence.

I'm a standout in the waiting room at student health the following morning; I am one graying geriatric case in a small crowd of students my children's age. I get a few curious looks, but nothing else. My name is soon called, I'm ushered back to meet with the head of student health, a doctor only slightly younger appearing than myself. After professional pleasantries, he dives right in. "You're a doctor, I've been briefed in the referral request, so I know what 'they' want. What do YOU think might be wrong?" The doc is open and engaging. He says he has as much time as I need, but I've seen the waiting room. So, I try to be brief, dispassionate and fair, as I run quickly through the year, the problems and their concerns. I point out that I'm older than the other students, residents and fellows, and for that matter I quip, I'm probably even the medical school dean himself." This prompts his momentary consultation of the computer.

"Nope, he's got you by a couple of months." I'm not sure this helps me, since he's the dean of a medical school, and I'm a lowly fellow. I'm again reminded of my sister Katherine's advice that I hadn't had a chance to pursue.

"So, you're a doctor," he says, "you've obviously been ruminating on this for months. What would your diagnoses be?"

"Well, my wife wonders if I have sleep apnea and complains I don't seem to hear well, particularly when she's speaking. Personally, I think after over thirty years, she's just worn out her frequency," I joke. I tell him about the atrial fibrillation, and I explain the work up and unsatisfactory conclusion. He nods and sets that aside. He asks about smoking, and I say never. He asks about drinking, and I admit to sampling the variety of bourbons in the area but note that both my parents were alcoholics and I am careful around a substance that destroyed my family. Satisfied, he nods and moves on.

I fix him with a hard stare and address the elephant in the room head on. "I really don't believe there is anything 'wrong with my brain' that isn't an issue for any man on the north side of 55. I know I don't learn and retain information as fast as I did in my twenties, but from what I know that is pretty normal. I think that because my filing cabinet of a brain is full and messily organized, it takes a little while to push facts in and out. I have wondered if I might have ADD as one of my children does, but it seems a little late to make THAT diagnosis."

He smirks and says enigmatically, "You can never, say never." More history follows, followed by a physical in a cold exam room. He steps out for a couple minutes to chart and plan, leaving me to quickly dress. A few minutes later the nurse retrieves me to his office. He hands me a few notes and appointment cards. Nothing new has been found. Unlike a lot of physicians, I actually DO have a family doctor I've been seeing for 15 years. Notes will be routed to him as well. The treatment plan has what I expected. Hearing evaluation, sleep study and, of course the inevitable appointment with a psychiatrist.

The hearing evaluation was first and surprisingly thorough. After an examination of my ears, I'm sitting with headphones in the hearing booth not hearing a much. I begin to suspect things are not going well. The diagnosis: mild to moderate high frequency hearing loss, "presbycusis" the hearing loss of older age. "You probably do fine in one-on-one conversations but have difficulty in crowded rooms?" I nod." "It's not so much you can't hear, but the loss of higher pitches makes it hard to discriminate voices with background noise."

I express some surprise. I can still hear well with a stethoscope. They point out the earpieces mask outside noise and that heart sounds are usually of a lower register and still in my hearing range.

"Too many rock bands as a youth?" they query?

"Regrettably, no, I think it was power tools. So," I continue while holding up the hearing aid prescription," this will help me hear my wife better?"

The audiologist gives me a knowing smile, "I suspect that may not be so much your ears, as much as the material between them." The hearing aids are ordered and arrive. I don't notice much at first, but after a while, I notice I'm following conversations in on rounds a bit better and keeping up with conversations in crowded rooms. It is not a miraculous improvement, but my hearing is better. I still don't hear Gayle that well.

The psychiatrist is next. I'm escorted into her office and told she'd be along shortly. While waiting I spend my time doing what any doctor would do, look at her diplomas, years of graduation, calculate ages, credentials and academic firepower. I hear the door open but pause before turning. Based on graduation dates, she is mid-forties, slightly graying, glasses, a ready smile. She gestures to a chair, "Dr. Phelps? I believe?"

"Dr. Johannsson, (as always, not her real name) "I presume. Call me Greg, although, I answer to pretty much anything not too vulgar."

Still standing, Dr. Johannsson glances at the chart and the notes made both by me and staff. It is more for effect -she's obviously been briefed and read the information before. "So…. coming back to school again at 55? There's got to be a story in that." She gestures to the chairs again, and we both sit.

"What no couch?" I gently mock. She smirks and then turns to business starting the consult with a wide-open question:

"So how does a doctor who comes back to school at 55 find himself coming to see me?"

"Possible brain damage, incipient Alzheimer's, or maybe the world's oldest case of undiagnosed ADD." I respond with a sarcasm, tinged with a little heat. She gestures to continue.

What follows is a blessed catharsis. The story spills out: Mom's death, Gayle's anger, the problems and repeated "talks" since then. I try to be dispassionate and even handed acknowledging my problems, issues and the complaints from the faulty. My recitation of Howard's question: 'Do you think there is something wrong with your brain?' brings an open guffaw from her. "Seriously?"

Too quickly the hour is ending. She looks quizzically at me. "There's something I don't understand. While you're recounting this whole terrible experience, there was a smile, almost a grin almost the whole time. What you're telling me sounds anywhere from bad to awful, yet you present the situation with seeming pleasantries and smile. Why is that?"

"Well I'd like to say I am smiling in the face of adversity, but the truth is I tend to smile when I'm stressed. It drove my wife crazy for years. She'd be upset with me, and the smile made her think I was laughing at her. The madder she'd get, the bigger my smile. It took some marital counseling for both of us to learn that, although the smile still pisses her off."

Dr. J taps her pad thoughtfully, "I can see her point." Picking up her pad, she rises briskly. "I can see this will take some time to sort out."

"Uhhhhh doc, I've got less than three months to go here. "

A thoughtful, almost calculating look, "I think we can finish plumbing your psyche before then. See you next week." I'm not sure how to interpret that remark. Is she's reassuring me that the problem isn't that big or that there might not be that much psyche to plumb!

Meanwhile, back on the patient floors, Marci shakes her head. "I just don't know," she starts up with one of the usual tropes. "We may have to keep you longer just to make sure you've learned the essentials." Silently, I start to fume again. First, they want me to quit early, now they may try to force me to stay longer. It is obvious they are looking for whatever leverage they can. This is not the first time for this threat. I think they hope that I'll panic at the thought I might be running out of money. I just grimace and say nothing.

It takes two more weeks conversation before for Dr. J is ready to share her preliminary understanding of my problem. She starts with a validation- "Quite candidly I do not understand why you are not furious. You left a high paying job to come study here and, to you your analogy, you came to study Shakespeare and instead are getting graded on penmanship. I think you are justified in your anger and that in some regard they've lost sight of what it means to teach. Your age makes you a different kind of learner and they haven't really adapted their pedagogy. And no, I don't think you have Alzheimer's or any other dementing illness. You are attempting what many men your age would avoid, learning a new specialty at an age when many doctors are thinking to retire."

Briefly, blissfully, I do feel validated, affirmed, but then she goes on. "Of course, depression or the ADD thing is still a possibility. I'll have to think about that." Affirmed, but slightly deflated, I take my leave till next week.

This Thursday brings "Dawn at the Park" a long-standing tradition to celebrate the coming horse racing season where the men wear sear-sucker suits and the women dress in dresses and frilly hats to take breakfast at the park to inaugurate the spring racing season. The faculty are dressed to the nines in extravagant dresses and humongous hats. Bev and I give it our best effort but stand out as sartorially challenged by penury. Bev and I are also wearing down from the stress of the fellowship. We'd debated blowing off the excursion but are trying to be good sports. Due to heavy traffic, the horse park bus drops our group off a few blocks from the park itself, and we slog towards the entrance. As we look towards the grand entrance, I stumble on the curb and catch myself on a lighting pole just as a city bus whooshes by inches from my head.

"Oh my God," the group exclaims, "you could have been killed." I find, to my surprise, that I that my near demise doesn't particularly concern me, I'm feeling that numb. Breakfast is good, as the sun rises over the beautiful park but once done, Bev and I, having demonstrated out social graces, soon make excuses and depart.

The following week with Dr. Johannsson brings a sort of prescience to it. "I've been thinking" she opens as we take our chairs. "I think you might be depressed. In fact, you might even be 'passively' suicidal with what all has happened to you this year."

"I'm not sure I understand the 'passively suicidal' label?"

"Well, that means while you might not take your own life, you wouldn't be upset if you got killed." I stare at her open mouthed in surprise, feeling again the bus ruffling my hair as it blew past my forehead.

"Yeah, I can see that." I respond. I think she's waiting for an argument, so I explain the bus.

She wants to start an antidepressant. I'm agreeable. I'm a little surprised when she doesn't ask for an anti-suicide agreement that I might have insisted on for one of my own patients. But since I'm angrier about the position I'm in, than suicidal I don't mention it.

The next item on my list is the sleep study. I already knew I had some sleep apnea; Gayle had complained for years about my snoring. When I told her about the sleep study, she said, "Finally!! I've been poking you for years to 'breathe!'" The issue for me was that I had never had much in the way of daytime sleepiness, so I'd ignored the problem. Several sequential nights of testing confirmed Gayle's diagnosis of moderate sleep apnea. I am fitted with a CPAP machine to wear at night. I fret about losing a night's sleep.

Ironically, the mask's whistling as it is blowing forces Gayle to wake me up more than does the sleep apnea! I try to soldier on, but eventually, I join the 50+% who give up. Only years later with new "nasal pillow" technology do I finally get a handle of using the CPAP machine.

In my next session with Dr. J, she concedes that perhaps I might actually be the oldest ADD patient she's ever seen. She sees my career so far as an example of success in the face of daunting obstacles. I feel a bit bolstered that she views me as relentless and determined. She recommends we consider Ritalin.

"Uhm doc, I still have the atrial fibrillation at times. Might a stimulant like that make it worse?"

Her color pinkens. "Yes, it might possibly. Let's try Provigil instead, it has less cardiac excitatory properties." I carry the prescription to the pharmacy. It will be $277.00. I grimly write a check and take it for a month. Later on, as neither of us can see much difference, we stop.

May

Less than two months to go. I've been hoarding vacation against the possibility of a crisis of some sort at home. Now I'm in the final months and desperately need a break and take a week to head home. It is more of a 'staycation' as we have no money or plans for travel. It turns out that the break is incredibly well timed.

Early Sunday morning, we are sipping coffee with our friends who've come to visit for the week. We're debating about attending late church. The phone rings and Gayle wanders upstairs to answer it. We're still slurping coffee a few minutes later, when Gayle appears at the top of the stairs. Her slightly dazed look stops the conversation.

"I'll be damned. I never really, actually thought it'd happen--my mother just died." She announced with little fanfare. The rest of us clustered around her with expressions of concern, support and sympathy. She waved her hands in the air irritably, as if to dispel the concerns and pulled a pad of paper from a nearby counter. "I've got planning to do," she announced. Ignoring us she pulled up a chair in the kitchen, and she started a list of people to call and arrangements to make.

The rest of the week is consumed by drawing up and coordinating funeral plans, selecting a casket and other details. The casket Gayle selects come with a 50-year guarantee. I morbidly wonder to myself if anyone has ever dug one up at that point to check and see if they can get their money back. Burial will be back in South Carolina beside Sally's husband of over fifty years. We are also required to empty her room at the nursing home. There is little time for tears or grief. The effort consumes the week. We drag back to Knoxville Sunday in time for me to head back to River City. Where, of course we are starting a new month and a new rotation, and I'm cheerily greeted with "Did you have a great time on vacation?"

"No, my mother-in-law died, and we buried her." Talk about a conversation killer! Gayle was always her daddy's child and had a strained relationship with her mom. While I'm having a miserable time in the fellowship, Gayle's two main worries for the year, birth and death have both become reality.

The next week, I'm back with Dr. J. "I want to try something" she announces as I sink into my usual chair near her desk. She grabs a third chair out of a corner and pulls it up opposite me, and then parks herself in her usual chair nearby.

"Are we expecting company?" I josh.

"Of a sort," she responds briskly. I'm hoping to see the 'old Greg Phelps, the guy who was a Chief Medical Officer of a hospital system, the guy who is board certified in multiple specialties, the guy who took a risk and quit his job and left his family to embrace new course of study. I think I'm seeing a beat down semi-whipped student version of that guy, and I want to see the former professor/executive version. She gestures to the open chair. "That guy sits over there." I pause to stare for a moment.

"Seriously?" I query, not certain I am ready to be laughed at in some sort of game.

Imperiously, she gestures again to the open chair. "I'm still waiting for that version of Dr. Greg Phelps."

Uncertain, but game, I pull myself to my feet, stand, pivot and flop down in the new chair.

"I'm pretty sure the old version did not flop like an overloaded laundry bag," She snorts, then motions me to stand back up. I stand up again and sit myself primly and settle with shoulders back and meet her gaze with a challenging stare.

"Better," she says. "And now, here's the old executive/chief medical officer/ professor Dr. Phelps,", pointing to me in the new chair, "looking at Greg Phelps, the fellow," pointing to the empty chair, I just vacated. "What does he have to say?"

Indelicately, I blurt out the anger that's stained the last months, saying the first thing that comes to mind- "What the F*#K happened to you?"

She smirks in approval. "I've been wondering that too."

She gestures again for me to change chairs; 'Fellow Greg' unloads the burdens of the last months. He recalls the interviews suggesting he was too old, and the implications about going back to being 'just a fellow' not to mention that he might be perceived as a potential threat to younger and less experienced faculty. I spoke, I realized even to me, I sounded whiney! Still, with an encouraging gesture from Dr. J, I continue occasionally changing chairs to interrogate myself. I'm recognizing the value in this therapeutic modality and get enthusiastic about relating what has happened to me. As 'Fellow Greg,' I related how I'd tried to pull in, shrink down and be smaller so as not to seem threatening. I discussed about the constant "talks" I was dragged into and recent alternating threats about how I should either quit or be prepared to stay a lot longer.

"I notice a change now," Dr J observes, "You are not smiling. What are you feeling?"

"Anger," I reply, "maybe even rage."

She grins, almost a little relieved. "Finally, I notice you're sitting up straighter and seem to have 're-inflated some. Think about what else 'CMO Greg' has to say to 'Fellow Greg.' See you next week."

May also brings me back to the VA for geriatric home care. Unlike most health providers and insurers, the VA had figured out that comprehensive home care, which is inexpensive, can preempt expensive hospitalizations when pursued aggressively. The VA has staffed up geriatric and hospice care to the point where multiple doctors are crowded in shared cubicles. I'm sent out to make house calls with a variety of disciplines. I round with clergy, social workers, nurse practitioners and physicians as we visit patients in their River City homes to manage their care BEFORE it becomes a crisis needing hospitalization.

Thus, we meet Mr. Burrell who has diabetes and hypertension. Meeting in his home, we find that he is only occasionally taking his diabetic medicines, "when I think I need them," he reassures us. When we ask about his breathing treatments, we get the same answer. However, when we listen to his lungs, the wheezing makes it sound like he swallowed a harmonica! We discover his nebulizer has been broken for months and when we pulled from under a living room table it is coated in dust.

I am quickly relearning what I'd first seen in rural practice decades ago; that one home visit is worth a dozen office visits. The VA doctor makes plans to send out a new nebulizer and meds and warningly tells Mr. Burrell in an Arnold Schwarzenegger tone: "Ve' ll be back."

The month continues with visits like this. Time and again we find patients not following their plan of care. Old and new meds are jumbled in boxes. Equipment we've sent has never even been unpacked. The patient records are almost laughable in how disconnected they are from the patients' reality. On more than one occasion, I ask why the patients so often don't tell the truth.

The doctor with me that day hypothesizes - "They want us to feel better, that what we are doing is helping them, but the care is beyond them. Sometimes it's transportation, and other times not understanding the equipment, the medicines or the directions. Sometimes they don't want to look stupid by asking for help and other times they don't want to go to the trouble of actually doing all the work of trying to stay well. "As the days go by, I silently tally up the number of hospital visits avoided through intervention as the month wears on.

Meanwhile I'm getting mixed messages from the faculty. One faculty member says I'm a great teacher and should look at faculty positions when I finish. Another says I'm barely passing, and they continue to consider additional "tough love." I'm never sure what that means for me! My last conversation with the head of the department says my issues are "resolvable." The faculty plan to discuss my issues with the dean of graduate medical education. So much for my sister's idea of preempting them by going to the dean.

Meanwhile Bev seethes both for me and for some of her own seemingly unjust criticism.

"It just seems like they nitpick 'something' everyday she groans. We commiserate and then separate, each going our different ways. For me, after patient hours, I'm either reading hospice and palliative medicine books, or working on my fellowship project on addictions and palliative care. It has become a constant grind towards the finish.

A few days later Bev and I are at the palliative department rounds where we have a lively discussion around cultural issues and how underutilized hospice and palliative medicine services are by minorities. Given the history of persecution and prejudicial experimentation that I've mentioned earlier, such as the Tuskegee syphilis experiments on black men in Alabama, we discuss strategies to address the issue. The discussion, heated at times, goes well past the allotted hour.

The next day the faculty member to supervise my home visits is indisposed, so I take advantage of the time to catch up on notes at the VA. I'm still waiting to hear back on the dean's thoughts about my position. The faculty suggest obliquely that he's not being that helpful for them. (Confirming what my sister has postulated about deans not liking problems.) Meanwhile, the threats that I may have to stay another month or month alternate between that, "or you could just leave." Hint, hint and, "We just aren't sure we can confidently give you a letter allowing you to take your boards. "

That night, I sit down to order and diagram all the issues on paper. In a series of columns, I sketch out my alleged failures, my personal estimates on my failures, the faculty failures and program failures. I list all the missed opportunities for timely feedback that instead became after-the-fact disheartening surprises. I review the requests for improvement and my efforts to honor them. I sketch out feedback loops and dead ends, as I try to logically decipher this tumultuous year. I again feel the rage that has been slowly building. It gets harder to make visits, going through the motions, not knowing which land mine awaits me next. Frustrated, I turn out the lights and go to bed. My heart has been behaving, but I still find it hard to sleep. Ambulances wail as they carom past my window toward the nearby medical complexes.

Next day is geriatrics again, and the social worker Jennie and I visit an aging vet, Danny, whose wife of 51 years died a few months ago. He is slowly declining, as many men do after losing a wife. The mechanics of caring for himself, cooking, cleaning and housework had always been her role. Now he misses her companionship, and every day is another example of his inadequacy in the face of her loss. His predicament supports studies that find loneliness as significant a risk factor as smoking for the elderly!

"I just can't seem to get past it," he mumbles in a low voice during our second visit. "It's like that is all there is, her ...gone. I look at cooking and think of her, I look at cleaning or the laundry, and there she is. I'm a veteran, I fought in combat and witnessed so many deaths, but all I can think about is her." He sighs heavily, "I can't get over her, and I'm pretty sure I don't want to."

I'm thinking of prescribing antidepressants, when the social worker says something that I adopted and carry to this day. She steps over to a bookcase and selects a book at random opens it and shoves the text up into his face.

"What do you see, Danny?" she demands, but a hint of her tone shows compassion as well

A little startled, he responds in a querulous tone from behind the book, "Nothing, you've got this damn book shoved up in my face." She nods to herself.

"So true." She says with contrition. She eases the book back a few feet. "What do you see now?

Danny responds in a forthright manner. "I still see the book!"

"What else?"

"Well I can see the edges of the room and about half of Dr. Phelps."

She stands and steps back a few steps. "How about now?"

He gamely responds, "I can still see the book, more of the room and all of Dr. Phelps." He smirks a little. "He's really not much to look at."

"We can both agree on that," Jennie grins at me and takes a few more steps back "Now what?"

"I can see all of the room, and still see the book and you and Dr. Phelps and his looks haven't improved any." I'm happy to be the butt of the joke and make him smile, so I grimace and make a face at him. Jennie steps back to her chair and takes Danny's hand.

"Danny," she says earnestly. The book is the grief you feel for you wife. Right now, it is ALL you can see, but the world is still there. As a little time goes on, the book is still there. It doesn't change, but it doesn't consume your total view. The book, your loss, your wife will always be there. You wife won't be forgotten but you'll be able, eventually, to navigate the world and still remember your wife and her life at the same time. Don't let your happiness of your love for her be destroyed by her death."

Danny nods. "People say, 'you'll get over this' and I don't want to 'get over' my wife. She was my love, my life and my wife."

Jennie hands him the book. "You'll learn you can carry the book and still live your life remembering her." Danny nods and wipes tears. So, do I. Another visit two weeks later, shows his weight loss is reversed and he is talking and more animated. While some sadness lingers, it is becoming apparent he's improving. Jennie then provided Danny with material on grief support and pushes him to attend grief support meetings.

"These meetings are people who've been where you are now. It helps you see you're not alone. Promise me you'll come just once."

Donny takes the material and nods. "OK, just once to see." A follow up visit at the end of the rotation shows that Donny keeping his promise. He went once, then weekly. He is looking a little better.

Near the end of the VA Home Geriatrics, I took a long weekend to go see my sister Katherine the associate dean in Missouri. I still had quite a few vacation days left and the fellowship had only a month remaining. (Theoretically!?) Since she'd moved to Missouri a year earlier, I've not seen her house. Before new role as associate dean, she had taught business and finance at Marist College in Poughkeepsie, NY, and I'd never made it there. In the couple of years, it'd taken for me to learn to spell "Poughkeepsie," she'd moved on. River City was not a horribly long drive to Katherine's house, so this a manageable trip for a long weekend. She has a large beautiful home on a small lake out in the country. Her husband Keith, whom I've always adored both for his sense of humor and loving treatment of my sister, meets me in the driveway accompanied by their several large Rottweilers.

As he leads me through the second of two garages in a series he quips, "We call this architectural style 'Baroque Ranch Conglomeration.' The previous owners just kept adding, but somehow ...it works." My sister meets me at the door and following hugs and cocktails gives me the grand tour of the sprawling ranch house and its view of the lake.

Late in the tour, she is showing off multiple bedrooms. This seems a bit superfluous as my sister only has one child who is away at college. But Katherine comes to the last door and pauses. "This is Mom's room" she says quietly. I must've looked puzzled as Mom had died well before Katherine bought the house. My sister opens the door by way of explanation showing me a small room with what appeared to be an altar with some candles, artifacts from Mom's life and several photographs of my mother. They'd had an intense but complex relationship prior to mom's death. "This is where I come to cry," she says sadly, plopping down on a small stool in front of the altar.

"How often do you do this?" I ask shyly.

"Oh, pretty much every day, "she answers slightly more cheerful.

"Doesn't that seem a little over-the-top, or even pathological?" I ask doubtfully.

"Says the guy who quit his job, left his family and went to learn about hospice where his mother died" she responds sarcastically. I shrug and concede the point. We then spend several intense hours with the two of us talking about her new life in a new state and about my challenges and frustrations with the fellowship: The encouragements that I quit threats to keep me longer, or not graduate, and the insinuations that I am too old to learn this stuff. Katherine, ever my ally and advocate urged me to find a new way to fight back, however we could. Since going to the dean had been taken off the table, she had a new strategy. "Sue the bastards!" she said. I said something to the effect that I wasn't sure that the topic open for litigation.

"I'm an associate dean of a University. You wouldn't believe the shit I've seen. Trust me, everything is open for litigation! Her counsel seems a seemed a bit over the top, but I was heartened again by her strenuous advocacy and belief in me, her younger brother. The rest of the weekend was a wonderful blur- tours of northern Missouri, time out by the lake and then, regretfully but enheartened, heading back to River City.

I come back for the last week on VA geriatrics. The patients seem to meld into one another as stories of aging, loss and decline seem to slide into each other. Tuesday afternoon, yet another casual repeat of: "We may have to keep you into another year. Otherwise I'm not sure we can forward a recommendation to the board to allow you to sit for the specialty exam." A little bit later, another conversation with my attending. She doesn't like the math done for converting diuretics and starts in on me. I counter by saying I didn't do the calculation but rather the nephrologist had and asked me to write the order. The conversation grinds to a sudden awkward stop. I silently turn a corner. I decide to take my sister's advice, and later that afternoon, I call a lawyer and make an appointment. It is a move of desperation

The lawyer's appointment is downtown, a converted warehouse on Main Street. The lawyer is youngish (compared to me!), and she takes notes as I awkwardly lay out my grievance with the University and the program, the threats and my performance. I detail the required evaluations and the psychiatrist I've been mandated to see. I end my now well-rehearsed recitation. "I just want to finish on time. I want to join the specialty and do what I feel called to do. You know," I continue somewhat plaintively, "in baseball they have what they call the 'brush back' where the pitcher heaves a ball near the batter's face to force him back, intimidate him a little. That is what I'm looking for. I just want to give a warning that I've had enough, and I just want to finish next month, on time, and get back to my life." I've spilled my soul and 11 months of frustration. I look over at the lawyer for her reaction

She looks at me, looks down at her notes, and sets down her pen on the table beside her and meets my gaze and blushes slightly. (Who knew lawyers could blush??!) "Well this is awkward." She seems to be struggling for words. "I'm not quite sure what to say. I had no idea what you were coming to discuss with me..."

I think the issue might be money, so I jump in, "If the issue is money, I have adequate supplies for what I'm asking for and subsequent litigation if needed. My mother died and left me an inheritance that allowed me to take this time off....." She shakes her head in agitation as she interrupts me.

"No, money is not the issue. Or should I say YOUR money. You see my firm usually DEFENDS the University in cases like this. So, as you might guess, although I hear what you are saying and think you have a reasonable grievance, I cannot commit the firm to prosecute for you against a client that sends us hundreds of thousands of dollars in business. She shook her head apologetically. She seems embarrassed to have wasted both our times. I'm chagrinned but take the refusal gracefully.

"The good news," I point out as a saving grace, "Is that now you cannot defend the University against any claims I might make as I already came to you beforehand, and it would be a conflict of interest." She smiles and concedes the point while briskly rising to her feet. Clearly, we're done.

"I will ask one favor; can you suggest another lawyer without this conflict whom you might recommend as a potential "worthy opponent?" She seems perversely cheered by this idea and quickly gives me a name. I write it down, we shake hands, and I leave her nicely appointed conference room.

Although I've just been turned down, I'm somehow, strangely cheered to have begun the process of pushing back. The next day, I place a call to the lawyer she recommended. Mr. Hall is not in right now I'm told. But he'll be happy to call me back 'soon.'

The call comes during my several hours drive from River City to Knoxville on a Friday evening. Mr. Hall (not his real name) asks if I have few minutes to speak and I tell him cheerily that I have hours to drive so let's 'have at it.'

Having already done rendition of my tale of woe once, I find I'm able to give a much more succinct version this time around. So, I give him the 'Reader's Digest 'version. He asks a few pointed questions then admits this is a first for him. He asks again about the Dr. Johannsson, I go to expand on her commentary saying, "my psychiatrist says…"

"Whoa, whoa doc!" he interrupts, "Let me give you a piece of free legal advice. Never lead a legal argument with 'My psychiatrist says'…." We both laugh. I acknowledge the point and we continue talking as the miles fly by. I explain the 'brush back' concept again. "I just want to get out on time with no penalty flags. I'm not really interested in a lawsuit. Just something to push back and make it easier to get me out than try to 'fix' me." I realize a moment later that he can't see the air quotes I just signed in the air in my car, but he gets the message. "I was thinking just a letter from a lawyer like you might be enough to make them reconsider their strategy."

The pause is so long I wonder if my cell has dropped the connection. But then he comes back. "Doc, I can see what you're saying, it might even work but will you give me a chance to tell you what I think will work better, with less pain?" He continues, "once you have them contacted by a lawyer, EVERYBODY starts to 'lawyer up." Positions harden, people stop talking, and things can get nasty."

"Honestly, I think your sister is right. Hang in there. They are trying to get you out early and go away. They want you to solve their problem. All this is to drive you out, get you to quit. Don't. Instead tell them you are committed to staying until hell freezes over to get this done. Admit no weakness, show no distress. Don't talk about needing money or your wife missing you. Say you'll stay for however long it takes. They often decide it is better to just get graduate you with the less stink the better. If not, I'm still here with plan B."

Now is my turn. I pause so long that he asks if I'm still there. I affirm I am. I'm thinking what he is saying is good advice. We make a deal. We'll try his way until the end of June when the fellowship is ending. If things go south at that point, we'll 'lawyer up' and have at them. Even though he has pulled me away from open confrontation, I again feel buoyed that there is a strategy, a plan, and I'm not just drifting. I meet with Dr. Johannsson the following week and she agrees with the plan. She says she's glad I stopped playing patsy. I tell her how the lawyer said never lead an argument with the words 'my psychiatrist says.' She laughs and agrees that is sound legal advice.

Mr. Hall and I never discussed fees and he didn't ask for information to bill me. However, I felt the advice and time were worthwhile. I Googled average hourly fees for lawyers and wrote him a check including a note saying it was well worth it and thanks. We finish the month with a final visit to the cardiologist who wants to avoid any more interventions and see how the CPAP and sleep apnea treatment work.

One final detail for the month, in yet another mentoring session with Howard I'm pointedly asked how my fellowship project is progressing. Beverly has already done her project presenting on employment evaluation and getting a job. Howard wonders when my project will see the light of day. I tell Howard I've finished my research and I'm well over half-way through and on page twenty of my report. Somewhat comically, his jaw drops, and he gestures a halting motion. "Oh no, we just want a few pages. A brief examination of a topic relevant to hospice and palliative medicine," he sputters. "That is way too much."

"Well it is a complex topic looking at the interplay of addictions and end of life care, and it's going to take at least a few more pages...at best." I mutter ominously. A few days later I turn in the paper. There is no formal grade, but I'm told it is satisfactory. It seems like a lot of work for very little feedback. A year later I shorten it some and have it published.

June

June begins on a kinder note. I take a final week of remaining vacation. It will be our extended family migration to the beach. This family vacation began when my mother was 18. For years, cousins both southern and northern gathered at Pawley's Island, South Carolina for a week of sun, beach and drinks. We stayed at the Tip/Top Inn for generations. It was only when my daughter turned five and we learned we'd be paying for her as an adult next year, that we began to look at other options. A year or so later, Hurricane Hugo obliterated the inn.

Both of these factors led to a move from Pawley's to Sunset, North Carolina and eventually Holden Beach, North Carolina. There we have gathered in large family groups and small for over 20 years. My sister and brother and I spend time catching up and the two of them reviewing and trying to understand this past year of my fellowship.

For Gayle, it is sort of a moment of schadenfreude to hear me re-hash my struggles for the past twelve months. My sister Katherine is pleased that I've consulted a lawyer and approves my plan. My brother Rick just shakes his head and wonders about my sanity for taking the fellowship in the first place. Gayle enthusiastically concurs. We golf, we sun, we consume more alcohol than recommended and at week's end, with less than three weeks to go, I head back to Knoxville for yet another interview. This interview is with a hospital nearby that wants me to consider doing do both occupational medicine (what they want) and palliative care (what I want). Apparently, the answer is no, as I hear nothing back after the interview.

My final (presumably) rotation is at a religious based hospital I River City doing palliative care consults. Apparently, I'm on my final effort to pass. We have another conference about my failings. I've been told that I must spend even more time with Howard for his blessing to pass. I hear a few more dire but almost proforma comments about my academic standing drift my way. At this point the repetition makes me feel a bit like Wesley and the Dread Pirate Roberts in the movie- The Princess Bride- *"Good Night Wesley, I may have to kill you tomorrow."* I'm sanguine as we talk, thinking about the lawyer in my 'back pocket.' I solemnly tell any faculty within hearing that I'm prepared to stay until," hell freezes over to finish in good graces." My new enthusiasm seems to set them back a little. Howard spends a couple days with me. Howard thinks I'm OK, and just of a different generation. He didn't really thin he needed more time with me so, after a few days, he passes me on to Naomi for the final weeks.

I wonder how different the fellowship might have gone had Naomi been my first attending instead of my last. Naomi is a cancer survivor and a bit older than the rest. She spends a day with me, watching me with patients and reading my notes as I finish each one. Sphinx-like she makes no comments but returns the next day clutching sheet of paper and prepared to comment and act. "Structure is your friend" she opines gravely.

"You're not stupid; however, all the required and open-ended questions we have to ask invites disorganized reporting. It's no wonder that your notes are scattered. In general medicine, we do a structured interview and we doctors drive the process. I too, had to learn a different way to organize my thoughts because in palliative medicine you're doing an hour or more interview and allowing the patient to drive the process of what's important to them. We give the patient the opportunity to give the information in the form and manner they that they see as important. This forces us to listen to what is important to the patient and build trust that a doctor is actually listening AND hearing. But the patients don't know what is important to us and how we organize. This template will help you. " She passes me her she of paper as if handing off the Ten Commandments.

Continuing she intones, "use this template to be able to go back and assure that you can fill in the gaps in information in the course of the interview. We've asked you to do a common task in a completely different way. This will help. It helped me."

This template helps revolutionize my efforts and improves my notes. The template helps me make sure at the end of the visit that I have what I need. (Maybe that ADD diagnosis wasn't too far off the mark!) Now years later I continue to use an ever-evolving variation of the template Naomi handed me that day to guide my interviews. It is not that I'm forgetful it is that the interview can go in a thousand directions including the illness, the exam, family issues and social issues, Additional issues may arise such as does the patient have capacity to decide care and what do they want and what does the family have to say?

The next day I find myself in the odd spot of being interviewed for the University alumni magazine. With young faculty standing by, Bev and I are both aware of the dissonant appearance that we present to a photo that will offer us as students and the young faculty as our teachers. Bev and I offer vague and supportive comments, conscious that negative comments are not likely to get printed. The only hint of discord I mention is that it has been a bit of a "struggle" at my age to come back to school. Off camera, Marci nods.

Howard comes by a day later to help me with an ER consult. The question is what do we do when consulted too early? Evie was a youngish grandmother showing her grandchildren the joys of card games, as the family explained later to me. When beating her grandchild with a winning hand, she leaped to her feet, "Woo-who" she yelped victoriously and then surprised the grandchildren by collapsing with a cardiac arrythmia. On the way down, she hit her head and being on blood thinners, bled into her brain further complicating her prognosis. The terrified grandchildren went screaming for the parents who called EMS who restarted her heart, she arrived in our ER where the physician receiving her took one look, and consulted neurology, cardiology, pulmonology and palliative care simultaneously. We got there first.

Scans, EKGs and labs had been done. Howard and I surveyed the room littered with medications and equipment. A ventilator now hissing, attached to an endotracheal tube emanating from the patient's lungs through her mouth. We've heard a little of the story from the ER doc. Howard gestures for me to proceed. I come in and gently but politely shake Evie's should assessing her response as I say "Ms. Evie, I'm Dr. Greg from palliative care. This is Dr. Howard. (To this day even if I'm convinced that even if I think the patient might be so far gone as to be brain dead, I try to treat each patient politely and introduce myself on the off chance someone will wake up.)Evie makes no sign of awareness. I then explain to her that I'll be examining her and mention each part as I do so. I'm acutely aware that Howard is behind me again critically evaluating exams I've been doing for 30 years so I take my time. Just as I'm finishing a brusque woman in a lab coat marches in. She is the neurologist as evidenced by a name/specialty and tiny image of a brain on her lab coat.

Avoiding preamble or introductions, she announces "You're wasting your time. I've seen the scan; it is a terminal bleed. There's no one home now." To demonstrate she yanks up Evie's gown and grabs an aged nipple, twists it 360 degrees or more. I see Howard mirror my wince. From Evie, there' no response. The neurologist turns to Howard and says, "she's all yours," and walks back out before we can say a word. The husband is brought back to talk with us. Howard procures several chairs from the nurses' station, and we sit at the end of Evie's bed.

Amidst the beeps and whistles and shouts down the ER hallway, Howard is an oasis of placid calm. Evie's husband is grinding a weathered ball cap in his hands anxiously as he asks how Evie is doing. Howard is reassuring but noncommittal saying she is 'stable' for the moment. "Tell me a little about your wife." Howard encourages the husband. We get the back story, the medical history, and the card game victory that led to Evie's collapse.

Then once letting the husband decompress a little, Howard begins to lay out possibilities saying "There are three ways this could go, Number one, she could stay as she is: unresponsive and on a ventilator. People sometimes can live like this quite a while. This may require eventual transfer to a long-term facility." Evie's husband steps in with a long reminiscence of his wife and her love of her grandchildren. Seeing this is important to the husband, Howard and I wait and nod.

Eventually, undeterred, Howard picks up where he left off. "Number two, she could continue to decline despite our best efforts and die soon." Again, the husband reminisces about how his wife was an active church lady and expresses her hopes for the afterlife. He goes on quite a while. By now I've lost track of three points, but unphased, Howard returns to- "The third possibility although very slim" he emphasizes making eye contact with Evie's husband, "she could improve. We don't know how much. In general, we like to wait three days in brain injury cases before giving up hope of improvement." Evie's husband nods and launches into another reconstruction of his wife's life.

Howard smiles and follows along. I like to think I'm a positive outlier in compassionately hearing family's stories, but Howard has far surpassed my capacity!

Once we walk out, I comment candidly to Howard that I don't think I could have kept my focus on the three points he went through, with all those interruptions, let alone anymore thoughts.

"Oh no," Howard says with a smile, "There are always and only three possibilities, better, worse or the same. Once you know that, the only question is which one you were with, when interrupted. You may not have noticed my hand on my leg counting a finger out each time we moved on. Still," he continued meditatively, "We are hoping the Provigil you started, which we'd discussed earlier, may yet help you focus better." As we come out, the cardiologist comes hurrying in.

We confer at the desk. The cardiologist quickly emerges and agrees that minimal intervention is the best option. Collectively we decide to admit for a watchful three days to ensure any opportunity for a chance for improvement. The husband agrees that if Evie does not show in response after this chance that 'he would want to stop the ventilator and let her move on to heaven.' For the next three days, Naomi, the palliative care team and I spend time with husband, children and grandchildren coming to terms with Evie's probable death After three days, they trust us and are prepared.

"She wouldn't want to be kept like this," her husband reiterates on the third day with no improvement confirming the family decision. We plan the end, the family is present as we turn of the ventilator, extubate her and allow her to die with her family around her. Again, it feels like a sacred moment.

Now, for one final visit to my mother before completing this chapter. During the continuing chemotherapy and radiation, Mom has continued to decline. I need to describe how we got to the nursing home. She had bad lungs from decades of smoking, and now they are worse. The radiation to her throat has caused her to aspirate (inhale food and liquids) more often. Worse than that, she gets confused at night pulling her oxygen tubing off and getting hypoxic. I've had to lock the door to the stairs to the basement, because they are right next to her bathroom door. We figure a fall down the stairs will finish her. Gayle and I are getting exhausted trying to keep up with her during the night. She has been hospitalized several times for pneumonia. The ambulance has worn a track pulling up to the front door by her bedroom. Still we struggle on thinking that we just need to get her through the treatment. After every disaster we look for small upturns that might signal a light at the end of the tunnel. Finally, during yet another hospitalization for aspiration pneumonia a pulmonology friend takes pity on me and escorts me down to radiology for a clinical reorientation to Mom's case, by showing me her CT scans.

"I think you need a reality check," he begins with a kindly tone. "It doesn't matter how the cancer is doing at this point. This is what your mother's lungs look like." The monitor springs to life and he scrolls up and down the scans helpfully making sure I'm oriented to the various views. Usually the lungs are a gauzy white color, bones hard white, absence of lung tissue shows as black. It is all pitch black. There is almost no lung tissue left. "Your mom is receiving Ultra High Flow Oxygen therapy." (I changed the brand name.) This term reflects a new form of high low oxygen technology I've just heard of. (Later it comes to be called the bridge to 'nowhere' as a plurality of patients who are needful of this kind of high flow oxygen die in under a year!) He gently continues, "There's nothing left short of a ventilator, and once we start that..."

"We'll never get her off" I finish. He nods. We make plans to talk to mom about rehab placement and stopping chemo in order to give her a chance to "build up her strength

So, we are back to discussion about the dreaded nursing home. I've mentioned Mom's experience with her mother. Mom had once, years earlier, said she kept a pistol hidden at her home in case anyone used the word 'nursing home' to her. The pistol, however, was in South Carolina. I wasn't sure if she meant it for me or herself.

Once deferred, though the time has come, I remind mom of what she had told me twenty years earlier. The doctors tell her that her stay would be to regain her strength and breath back if possible. It is clear to all we couldn't care for her the way she was. The nursing home and rehab are her best option. Mom listens in silence arms crossed. I brace myself for the coming explosion. To my surprise, that is not how Mom takes it.

To my astonishment, Mom is relieved to stop treatment and go to rehab at a nursing home our hospital owns. A close friend of mine in administration bends the rules to get her in and get Ultra High Flow continued. It takes some extra engineering to make this happen as most nursing homes don't have the oxygen flow capacity to make it work.

Also, to Mom' s credit, I did not receive any no nasty letters and only minimal recrimination. The sting was lessened somewhat by the fact it was a nursing home our hospital owned, and I could and did visit daily during her stay. She was still a little reluctant but consented to go for a 'short rehab stay.' I have since learned this is a common and cruel lie often used by doctors. It is subtle way of blaming the patient for being unable to finish treatment by saying they became 'too weak' and that once they get their strength back, the treatment would likely cure them. In truth most patients at this point never get their strength back. Moving the patient out of sight to rehab, avoids having to say- 'you're dying.' Like these patients, Mom's rehab would end up being a one-way trip.

Rehab did not go well. Mom was bedbound and irritable. To make matters worse her hearing took a sudden nosedive. Looking back, it was probably a combination of diuretics and antibiotics that were ototoxic (damaging to the ear). But shortly after her admission, I came in for my daily visit to the skilled nursing facility (SNF) and said, "Hi mom!"

She responded with "What!? Why are you mumbling?" This was new. My usual problem was Mom's hearing was too good, and whispered asides and *sotto voce*, comments were heard and spit back at me.

Suddenly she couldn't hear squat. That first day I got by putting my stethoscope in her ears and shouting at it. Subsequently, when things failed to improve, we got a headset and microphone. An ear evaluation didn't show anything helpful, and we just continued to get by.

Her biggest problem was poor function in her throat that allowed her to keep aspirating and choking further damaging her lungs. Speech therapy was ordered to help her relearn to swallow. She resisted physical therapy to improve strength and likewise, she fought the speech therapists. It was China all over again. A week into her rehab, I met the speech therapist coming out of the building as I was coming in for an evening visit. Recognizing her from the day before, I stopped her and said expectantly "So how's it going?"

Her blunt reply threw me. "For a sick old lady your mom has got a good right arm!" I was a little mystified until she explained. The therapists use an electric stimulator attached to the neck to try to retrain swallowing. Your mom didn't like it, and after a few minutes she ripped it off and threw it at me… twice.

"Second time it hit me right here" the therapist said indicating a spot on her right forehead. I apologized for Mom, and we agreed we'd postpone that therapy for now. When I confronted Mom, she was unrepentant and strangely satisfied to have shown the therapist who was boss. My efforts to get her to be kinder and gentler and reconsider went nowhere.

Naturally with 'progress' like this, her condition continued to deteriorate. The holidays were approaching with Christmas the next day when I made my nightly visit. The geriatrician in charge of Mom's care met me at the nurse's station. By now Mom knew when I finished up at the hospital and made the 20-minute drive to the facility. Therefore, when I walked up to the nurses' station, I was greeted with "Wow, right on time your mom knows you well." As I started to ask for an update on Mom the geriatrician motioned to a small conference room nearby. "We need to talk." I walked into the tiny room preparing my arguments for why Mom needed more time and needed to work harder on physical therapy. I must admit I wasn't prepared for what came next.

Dropping tiredly into one of the four chairs, the geriatrician came straight to the point.

"Your mom has had enough. She has asked me to call in hospice. She's refusing any further tube feedings, and she wants to be allowed to die."

I hadn't even sat down yet, and I just stood there and gaped, open-mouthed for a moment, then sat down hard. She hurried to press on before I could martial some objection. "Your mom clearly is competent and knows what she wants." A little more gently she added, "It really is you mother's decision. It is her life and her choice."

Thinking with a little time, I could talk Mom out of hospice, so I try to stall. "When will they come to see her? Tomorrow? No that is Christmas, so I guess the next day?"

"We already called, and hospice came this afternoon. It was your mother's wish. She's already enrolled." I sit there a bit- stunned, then a little angry. It is, after all, Christmas Eve when she made this choice.

Then I get back to practicality. "So how long are we talking here?" The geriatrician made the most accurate prediction I have yet to see in years of the work.

"Probably about 14 days."

Having delivered the news and taking advantage of my stunned silence. the geriatrician makes a speedy, but dignified exit. There is nothing left to do but go down the hall and talk to Mom. She's ready, headphones on, amplifier ready, awaiting my expected entrance. I say what first comes to my mind. "Seriously? Christmas Eve? You decide tonight that you've had enough? The whole family is here! All this work and suffering and you give up now?"

To my surprise, she smiles beatifically. She's made her own hard choice and is comfortable with the decision. My objections are water off a duck's back. Her reply makes a certain kind of sense. "I had to do it while the family was all here to be able to say goodbye." In my heart, I have come to see the futility of what she is fighting against. "Greg," she said gently, "When I came here six months ago, I lived alone in my own house and lived my life as I chose. I drove myself here from two states away. I walked under my own power. Now I'm stuck in this bed on this oxygen contraption. All the speech and physical therapy, even if I did it (she smirked here at my obvious irritation) is not going to put me back where I was before. I'm too old, too sick and too far gone. She looks at me a bit plaintively. "I'm sick I'm tired. I'm sick and tired of being sick and tired" Gesturing to the room and the equipment surrounding her she said, "This is not me I'm not going to live like this, I'm done. Just keep me comfortable." I nodded grudgingly.

"Now" she said briskly, "Tomorrow is Christmas, I don't expect a lot of hub-bub tomorrow. Spend it with the kids and your siblings. Time for me after that. I'd like a peaceful Christmas for once, before I go. And, I don't want to spend Christmas Eve or day looking at that face you're showing. Go home." Walking out of the nursing home which was festooned with holiday decorations is one of the lowest points in my life. Lights twinkle and sparkle, staff who know me bid me a 'very Merry Christmas.' My mother who has been my rock and anchor for fifty plus years has decided she'd rather be dead.

It is a mixture of spite and protectiveness that keeps me silent when I get home to the family gathering that night. People are putting on coats and hats getting ready to leave for Christmas Eve services.

"So, how's Mom?" I'm asked by my sister. I refuse to spoil Christmas Eve for her.

"She's fine. She says she'd like to sleep in tomorrow and have a quiet holiday. She's really tired." Everyone nods and clucks in sympathy. I don't break the news until the evening of the following day. Everyone seems to understand why I kept it to myself.

Thus, begins a countdown. I don't share the 14-day prognosis with family. We take it a day at a time. It is a very strange time of candid conversations. Mom has developed an enthusiasm for the medieval novels of Margaret Frazier, so my spare time is spent scouring McKay's used bookstore looking for them. Mom naps and reads through the holiday week. I think she's trying to finish the series before she dies.

"Wow," she says a week in, setting down her book as I enter. "They must be giving me good drugs. I'm not hungry, I'm not depressed." She glances at the book and sets it aside. "I am getting bored. Any chance we can hurry this along a little?"

I sigh and perch on the side of her bed and am equally candid back to her. "No mom. Physician assisted suicide is not legal in this state." She picks up on the phrase 'this state.'

"Is there a state where it is legal?"

"Oregon" I reply with a little acid in my tone." The doc said two weeks. I can't get you there that quick. It's expensive, and there are several interviews a few weeks apart. Quite candidly, you'll die quicker here." I say it hoping to wound her determination, but instead she nods thoughtfully and, undeterred, turns to another topic.

"I want to be cremated and buried next to my parents in Michigan." I nod, I'm hating this conversation but understand she wants to have it and will. She's not satisfied. "I need to know you're going to do it." she persists.

I promise I will, but my word is not good enough. She wants to have me pick out a cremation service, and get it paid for. I agree. Back at the hospital I ask around for advice on cremation. Most of administration knows my circumstances, and they refer me to Fred, 'the cremation guy'. "He's a bit eccentric, but he'll do a good job. Your mom will like him."

I dryly respond, "I doubt she'll be in any condition to form an opinion when she finally meets him."

I call Fred and get a price quote. Mom insists on writing the check for her own cremation. "I want a receipt," she tells me. I promise to hand deliver the check.

The next day Fred and I meet, and he is indeed 'a little eccentric.' Hearing I'm a doctor he wants to give me a full tour of his facility. Gleefully he shows off his morgue and cooling room with slide out drawers, just like on the cop shows. Funeral people are often thought of as a bit dour, but Fred is quite chatty and candidly upbeat, even funny. I hand him Mom's check; he gives me the needed receipt.

That evening at the nursing home, I hand over the receipt. "Great!" Mom, says, "when does it happen?"

"Uh, Mom, there is an intermediate step involved here..."

"Oh yeah," she says unfazed, "I got to die first."

"Yeah," I continue matching her deadpan, "otherwise, it gets kind of messy with yelling and shouting and allegations of homicide." She smirks and says, as if conceding the point.

"Ok, I guess I can wait."

I'm not the only sibling working through the death of our mother. After Christmas, the awful truth has come out. My brother is upset, and my sister is devastated. Worse, both will soon have to depart for other states and return to work and 'normal' lives. My brother and family leave a few days after Christmas. My sister sees them off and goes to the nursing home to say her goodbyes knowing she'll never see her mother with whom she's had a long, loving but complicated relationship ever again. Before she leaves, we hug and commiserate. She gets in her rental car and heads off to the nursing home on the way to the airport. To our surprise, she is back at the house, in a few hours sobbing her eyes out.

"I just couldn't say goodbye while she is smiling and loving me and talking away." Katherine re-schedules her flight for a day later with the same results. She makes three more attempts to leave. Finally, Mom lapses into a coma, and Katherine is finally able to say goodbye and go back to her home. My youngest son, home from college, is the last to see Mom alive. He reports she is unresponsive, and he too heads off back to college. About mid-night, the staff call to tell me that she has died. Filial obligation more than anything presses me to go out for one last visit.

The staff were clearly not expecting me. They apologize and note she is on a gurney, in a body bag with Fred on the way. I unzip the bag and look one last time on my mother and tearily bid her goodbye and much love. It has been exactly two weeks.

The next day, I'm back at work. Our CEO breezes past my office and slams on the breaks.

"Oh, I guess the rumors were wrong!" she says with a note of confusion.

"Depends on the rumor," I say knowing full well where this is going.

"Well I heard your mom died last night, but here you are at work?"

"Yes, she did," I answered, "but it was expected. She lived a full life, and right now she's being cremated. I've got a lot of work backed up and time to do it." Our CEO shook her head, mumbled, "so sorry," and wandered down the hall still shaking her head.

The following day, Fred called to ask if I could meet him at the house. I said I could, and a half hour later Fred came roaring up our drive in a new Corvette, holding a still warm, tastefully fashioned wooden box.

"Figured I'd give the old girl one last thrill ride back home." he said by way of explanation. Gayle and I laughed and accepted the box of ashes. She was explicit in not wanting a funeral, so we held a small memorial service at the chapel of the hospital in South Carolina where she'd lived, volunteered and knit over 1,000 baby caps. Internment beside her parents outside Detroit had to wait until the following spring, once the ground thawed. In between, her ashes roosted on the mantel in our living den. My older son came home from grad school on spring break. I happened on him in the den holding the box he'd just lifted off the mantle.

"Cool box" he said hefting and shaking it, "What's in it?"

"Grandma's ashes" I said with a smirk, as he shrieked and almost dropped the box.

Internment was just family, her children, spouses and my uncle and his family. A small hole for the cremains box had been dug. I knelt in the sodden grass and pushed the box down in the hole and stood up, dusting off my muddy knees. There was an awkward silence. My brother looked around distractedly in the Michigan chill. "Now what"

To his relief, being the religious/spiritual one of the family, I produced copies of the Episcopal rite of burial for our tiny group and we read aloud the liturgy of burial. We all hugged, shook hands, told a few more stories and headed back to the airport where we would all resume our lives.

The month finishes out. Howard, Marci and the rest grudging agree that I should graduate on time. I'll get my letter to take my boards. I've cobbled together two part time jobs for the short term. One is working in the hospital's pain clinic where I'd helped out previously, the other is the hospital's geriatric program. It is enough to pay the bills.

Both Bev and I have finished the year frustrated, burned out and tired. There is no formal graduation ceremony, but the faculty have planned a nice dinner at a local restaurant. Bev and I debate about being boorish and refusing, as one last pointed commentary of the year just passed. However, since Bev still has a final month to go… that and just simple politeness over a kind gesture keeps us burning any bridges. We decide to play nice one last time. Grudges are passed over, kind words are said, and our diplomas are duly handed out. It is raining when I come back to the car. I'd left the back window open in the heat of the day. Getting in the car, I toss the diploma, the object of so much work and suffering, in the back seat where it wafts to the floor and the unseen puddle that formed there, staining it. Like I said at the beginning of this tale- the stain seems only fitting.

CHAPTER SIX

When I finish my fellowship, I close out my apartment and move back to Knoxville. It has been a rough year, and I have a few weeks to lick my wounds and prepare to start again. As I mentioned in the previous chapter, I begin part-time work with two jobs, both hospital based- the Geriatric Assessment Center and the Pain Center. Despite Gayle's misgivings about working with chronic pain patients I find I really relish the challenge. It is a nice change of pace to move from one job to the other, and I enjoy the work. A year and half pass. Gayle and I go to the American Academy Hospice and Palliative Medicine Conference this time in Boston. It is there my cell phone rings. An old friend from St. Mary's hospice who has moved to the University of Tennessee hospice calls.

"Greg," her voiced boomed out of my phone. "Didn't you do a hospice and palliative care fellowship after I left St. Mary's?" I affirm she is correct, still a little mystified. "And I hear you're working part time doing pain and geriatrics...why?" Why not? Knoxville is indeed a small-town and word gets around. I am still not doing what I spent a year training to do.

"Well, wouldja like to come work at a hospice full time?" I would! Shortly, thereafter, I became the medical director for UT Hospice in Knoxville. When I arrived, our average census was 46, when I leave, it is over two hundred. I am given the opportunity to start a palliative care service that quickly grows to over a hundred patients. As the only boarded hospice and palliative medicine doctor in a company of mostly part time physicians, the parent company gives me the opportunity to educate physicians in the larger company all over the US. I have a ball. I do workshops and continuing medical education from the Puget Sound to Fayetteville, North Carolina.

Over the years however, while my work is stimulating and my self-esteem recovers, I am essentially the only doctor and it becomes wearing. After six years, when an opportunity came to move to the Hospice of Chattanooga (HOC) a much larger, not for profit hospice in two states, I couldn't resist. Hospice of Chattanooga was almost twice the size and was not for profit. It has a pediatric service and an in-hospital palliative care service. Most importantly HOC has multiple other doctors to share call. I take the job. This is where I've been ever since. In the few years at Chattanooga, we've expanded exponentially moving into yet another state. I again started a palliative care service and have seen that grow from zero to over 300 patients.

When I come home from the fellowship, a major task is repairing my marriage with Gayle. Given the tensions portrayed here between Gayle and I, it might be surprising to learn we are still married. She was angry at my choice to do the fellowship. She was mad during the fellowship, and it took yet another year for her to get over my absence and willingness to pursue the program despite her objections. But we've always had our differences, often loudly.

Our differences were confirmed fifteen years into our marriage. At church during a Sunday school exercise, the kids and I took the Myers-Briggs personality test from a psychologist who lived in our neighborhood. All our teenage children results were close variants of my own extroverted personality. Gayle missed Sunday school and the test, and she then resisted taking that "touchy feely" test later.

Eventually the kids and I got her to reluctantly acquiesce to having the psychologist neighbor come to the house to administer and score the test. Gayle was, unsurprisingly, our collective opposite, introvert to my extrovert, analytical to my intuitive etc. Getting the results with all of us at the table, she smacks her pencil down hard in disgust. "Great! You made me take this f*#king test, and NOW we're gonna have to get a divorce!" A tense pause, then the kids, the psychologist and I all burst out laughing.

The psychologist hastened to point out the benefits of having a different point of view and perspective on life. "You complement each other in your approach to the world, tempering each other's view. It's perfect." In response Gayle cracks a rueful grin at the kids. Still years later, I'm the perpetual optimist, she the pessimist, and occasional curmudgeon, but it works. We were only a few weeks from our fortieth anniversary when out our blissful union almost stopped

At this point, I'm working in Chattanooga and Gayle is still working as a gastroenterology nurse in Knoxville. We shuttle back and forth and tell friends we live in "Knoxanooga." One weekend she'd muttered about some worsening indigestion. I asked about chest pain signs pointing out that women sometimes had atypical heart disease. "No, just indigestion, Tums helps." I let it go.

Tuesday morning, I get a call from my daughter Tiffany. "Mom sounds awful," she says in worried tones. "She told me she was up yesterday and all night with indigestion. Naturally Gayle didn't say a word to me during our evening, 'not dead yet,' call of the same night. Tiffany and I agree she would divert from work and go over and check on Gayle. Just about the time I'm getting worried, Tiffany calls me out of a meeting with our hospital case managers. She has a slightly frantic tone. "Mom's still having chest pain. She looks awful, sitting by a little pile of different antacids on the kitchen counter and won't go to the emergency room." Health care professionals really are the WORST patients!

I voice a noise between a sigh and a groan, "Put her on the phone." Recalling her fury, over my own recalcitrance with heart problems, driving myself home from Cincinnati years ago, I pull out the one comment I know will motivate her. "Surely", I hiss, "you can't be as stupid as I was with heart problems. Remember how mad you were when I drove home from Cincinnati? Go to the ER…then tell me it was indigestion, and I've got a big bill to pay." The chance to rise above my stupidity and prove me wrong was the one bait I knew she couldn't resist. At the time, given Gayle's minimal risk factors, even I thought it was indigestion but better safe than sorry.

An hour after that, I'm still in the meeting in Chattanooga, Tiffany calls to say Gayle's heart attack markers are positive, and they are going to the cardiac cath lab. I've stepped out of the meeting to take the call. I lean back in holding the door open.

"I'm sorry," I say calmly with a wry smile," I'm going to have to leave a little early, it seems my wife is having a bit of a heart attack."

Apparently, I was calm enough, that the following week a case manager from the meeting asks me if my wife really did have a heart attack, saying, "You were so collected, and you even smiled in apologizing for leaving us!"

I do shed some tears in the 80 mph drive back to Knoxville. I get to the hospital five minutes before the nurses wheel Gayle into what turns out to be quintuple by-pass surgery. When they wheel her back in the room hours later, only slight rise and fall movement of the sheets convinces me she's not the corpse she resembles.

Women are tough, or at least this one is. She took nothing for pain after surgery. She was walking the next day. She told her heart surgeon that she had a beach vacation planned in two weeks and she was going, so his job was not to tell her not to go, but how to go safely. Thirteen days later she drove herself partway to the beach for a slightly delayed Girls' Week at the beach before summer vacation. At that vacation we celebrated her recovery, our 40th anniversary and the baptism of our youngest (fourth) grandchild. Gayle still works at the hospital as a nurse.

Beverly was another key player in my fellowship year. We bonded and supported each other, but then we graduated and went our separate ways. Bev went to her dream job in Bremerton, Washington to do hospice and palliative care for a hospital. We kept in touch with supportive emails back and forth on occasion. The messages were usually about children, grandchildren and the challenges of the new work. Then came an email of a different sort. This one prompted me to hastily call her. She'd been diagnosed with colon cancer, she's had surgery and is now completing chemotherapy, but doing better. (Ironically, she too has waited a few months before telling me!) Another few months later, I happen to be in Washington speaking on behalf of hospices that our parent company owned, and we meet at her home overlooking Puget Sound. It was then I got the whole strange story.

"It began with Himalayan salt," Bev says as we tour her house on a cliff looking down at the water, it is a foggy day, so classic for Washington state. She pauses, points to a couch by the picture window. "This is where I spent months recovering from chemo."

"Himalayan salt?" I prompted.

"Oh yeah, have you ever seen it?" I had, it looked like salt crystals only pink.

"The pink is the key, it's iron. I began craving it and eating more and more pink salt until I was eating multiple tablespoons several times a day. Finally, it struck me that this really wasn't normal, and I went to a doctor for a workup. It turned out I was severely anemic, and my body was trying to get more iron...in an unusual way. The anemia led to additional tests and a diagnosis of colon cancer followed by surgery and chemo, hence the couch."

The treatment seemed to work, and Bev returned to work, then later moved to Oregon to be nearer her children and grandchildren. Sometime later, in an exchange of emails she mentioned she retired early and was hard at work making memories with her grandchildren. I knew what her words implied. Some months later she sent an email that she was in hospice, and then nothing. It is kind of hard to craft an email that says, in essence "are you still alive? So, I waited for a word from someone, I didn't have Jay's contact information and that word was then a year coming when a mutual acquaintance told me at palliative care meeting. After I got word she died, I learned she had a lively on-line Facebook presence documenting her illness and her efforts to find joy in life. I deeply regret I never thought to look there. She was a true credit to our profession.

Now mention to my weight and my health. As evidenced by multiple examples of behaviors documented here, doctors are terrible patients. I already mentioned publishing an article in Medical Economics titled- "I'm Glad My Patients Aren't Like Me." Think about that. I was so bad that even a doctor's magazine accustomed to our many foibles thought I was an entertaining outlier. After my clean cardiac catheterization in October, everyone seemed to lose interest in what to do next. So, I struggled along with intermittent bouts of atrial fibrillation through the end of my fellowship. After I finished fellowship and had a job, I had a new cardiologist and I was tried on this medicine and that, to try to suppress the arrythmias. Some did nothing, some left me on the edge of fainting. None seemed particularly effective. As usual, it was Gayle who called a halt and demanded I try a new approach.

I was out on mountainous country roads seeing patients and had a fierce bout of atrial fibrillation and accompanying tachycardia.

Stubborn and foolish I felt I could push through and finished my calls. Coming into the office afterwards though I looked so grey that the staff got concerned. I tried to wave them off, but in an office full of nurses, this is a hard thing to do. They set to checking me over. My pulse was 170, and my blood pressure.... Well, they had trouble finding it. I was force fed fluids, after refusing to let them start an IV. After a little while my blood pressure recovered, and pulse slowed a little, and they sent me home, first calling Gayle to let her know, since they didn't trust me to volunteer the information. Gayle called my cardiologist and I was diverted to the hospital for another cardioversion. She also demanded another opinion.

An appointment was made to see about a cardiac ablation. This is where a catheter is threaded into the heart and the tissue causing the arrythmias is burned away. At first the ablations seemed to work, but the arrythmias came back. I would also alternate with severe bradycardia, with my heart rate slowing down to 30 beats a minute, or too fast. Like everything else I seemed to tolerate this, but it was concerning, if not to me, to Gayle. Another ablation followed and then I was looking at another. Considering yet another ablation, the cardiologist wanted to see about a new 'hybrid procedure' which included an ablation followed by a flexible scope being pushed into my chest to the backside of my heart, where they would burn lines across the troubled area of my heart on the outside.

The only problem, the cardiologist told me, his face reddening a little, was that I might be too fat for the scope to reach to reach my heart. He made a quick call to the surgeon in the same building and I was hastily sent to suffer a humiliating visit to the thoracic surgeon who poked and prodded my belly. He kneaded my belly fat thoughtfully for a few minutes, brow furrowed in concentration, then announced he thought he could make it work. I dressed and we repaired to his office to talk

"Even I know this is a new procedure," I said, "How many of these have you done?" His reply delivered with great confidence, did give me pause. "By the time I do you next month, I'll have done about ten." I gave him points for honesty and scheduled the procedure. It worked. I have gone years with no atrial fibrillation, and I am forever grateful.

The final point on my health, is the elephant (literally) in the room- my weight. My journal often notes visits to the YMCA gym and the weight I lost- about 40 pounds during my fellowship. As one might guess from the above, I gained it back and then some. Finally, some years and many more diets later, I bit the bullet. I had a 'come to Jesus' moment walking in downtown Asheville with our friends. I had to stop repeatedly on the hilly streets and catch my breath while Gayle and friends looked on concerned. I realized what was obvious to everyone else. I had to not only lose weight but also keep it off or, I was going to die, sooner rather than later. After much research and reading, I had gastric sleeve surgery and lost and have kept off over 100 pounds.

One might wonder if my educational experience was unique, older doctor, new discipline etc., but I'm not the only middle-aged physician who has made this journey. The old paradigm was medical school, residency practice 30-40 years then retire. More doctors though are changing specialties, retraining and/or moving out of medicine to new fields.

It was summer, a year after I'd finished my HPM fellowship. A physician at the medical school called and asked to meet for lunch; he wanted to get my thoughts about going back to do a fellowship in hospice and palliative medicine. A contemporary in vintage with me, we met for lunch, and I relayed my experiences to him. "My program taught me what I needed to know, but (as I've said before) it was like going to learn Shakespeare and being forced back into high school grammar. They really don't know what to do with older learners." I told him.

I suggested several other programs for him to pursue. "Overall," I summarized, "I LOVE what I do. I see it as both ministry and mission, but my experience was probably more painful than necessary to learn what I did. Nonetheless, I've passed the hospice and palliative medicine boards with flying colors and I'm working in the field. So, I'm happy to be here."

He smiled and thanked me for my time. I didn't hear anything until the following Spring when he called me to meet for lunch. "My treat to you" he said, "for giving me sound advice."

We met at a Panera's on a warm Spring day, outside under an umbrella. After we ordered, he started right in, "Well you were right" he opened with a nod in my direction. It had been almost a year, so I had to ask,

"Right about what? Where did you end up doing your fellowship? You didn't…"

He quickly shook his head, "Oh, no, I went to a different program… same results. You were right about pretty much everything. They didn't know what to do with older learners and docs with experience. Your analogy about Shakespeare and grammar was pretty much on target. "It's been pretty miserable."

I did a quick mental check on math and the calendar. "You aren't done yet," I noted, as the March wind ruffled the table umbrella.

"No, but it has been a rough last six months after the 'honeymoon summer'." He came quickly to the point. "I'm thinking about quitting. I'm just not sure I can put up with the bullshit another three months." We talked about his program and his challenges. He was at one of the oldest, premier programs in the country. I found it hard to believe he was having a similar experience, until he gave me all the gory details: He too was blasted with nit-picky reviews on his write ups, questioning judgement and memory, constant reminders he might be too old. Although I commiserated, I encouraged him to hang in for the final three months. He's already invested this much, surely a few more months wouldn't kill him. He grudgingly agreed and said he'd think about it. In the end, he finished and later came back to the university to work.

When I was only a few years out of residency, I entered an on-line program for mid-career physicians for a master's in public health degree focusing on Occupational Medicine. This was really before the internet was a thing. AOL did not exist, and CompuServe was state of the art. An on-line degree, common now, was such a new idea that when I finished in the late 80's, I wrote an article for the AMA News on this crazy new way to go back to school using a computer! Back then, as an introductory part of the program, they addressed the fears of the "Older Learner." Being in my early thirties and the youngest in the class, I thought this was kind of funny.

They talked about how while knowledge doesn't decline, it can take more time and repetition and slower acquisition for older docs to absorb information. But in the end, they concluded while it took more time, older physicians could learn and perform well but needed supporting circumstances to do this. Medical College of Wisconsin promised to provide this platform and support. (and they did)

I now know three other older physicians who have gone back to school for hospice and palliative care in middle age. Two dropped out before completing their program due to "incompatibility over learning styles." Two doctors, myself and the physician I recounted above, completed their programs, albeit with some accompanying psychic trauma. Our conviction though, was that the program and the course of study was essential and that motivated us to finish. All of these physicians, finished or not, found it rewarding enough to remain in the field for years afterward at a time when most physicians are looking to retire. I think this commitment says a lot about the value and importance of care at the end of life and the sense of mission imparted, that all these physicians struggled through. I still find blessing in my work every day.

This issue of physician (and other professional education) is important nationally. NPR estimated there is currently a shortage of 18,000 hospice and palliative medicine trained physicians. This statistic flies in the face of an expanding senior population that grows by 10,000 -every day! Medicare, insurance for elderly and disabled pays for graduate medical education for most specialties such as internal medicine, surgery and cardiology. The two specialties Medicare has not supported, bizarrely enough, are geriatrics and palliative medicine.

Many doctors come to the specialty mid-career, and unlike me, they cannot afford to quit work for a year to re-train to sit for the HPM boards.

Congress is looking to improve training with the PCHETA Act (Palliative Care and Hospice Education Training Act) but while the bill has passed the House on several occasions, that is as far as it has gotten as of this writing. Many HPM physicians come from mid-career changes to HPM. This means the HPM physicians skew older than the average age of physicians which is about 51. Since the only way to be board certified is to do a fellowship and there are few of these fellowship positions compared to the demand, the number of certified hospice and palliative medicine physicians is declining at time of rising need. Hopefully PCHETA and other innovative training may reverse this trend.

Similarly, education about end of life care in medical school is grossly under-represented.   Curriculum   needs   to   adapt   to   changing circumstances. All medical students are required to do hundreds of hours in OB when only a small percentage will deliver a baby. Likewise, students must take pediatrics, psychiatry and others when they may never work in those realms again. But death and dying is an experience that every doctor will participate in. Even OB doctors!

Even now, most med schools may provide only one hour of a modified Elizabeth Kubler-Ross- "Death and Dying" talk. River City Medical School was among six schools to get a pioneering grant to require med students participate in hospice and palliative training. In May 2017, University of Tennessee Health Sciences began mandating similar education and those students in Chattanooga rotate in our hospice and palliative care services. Many medical schools still do not have any end of life required rotations.

Some years had passed after I finished my fellowship. I had worked at University of Tennessee Medical Center Hospice and then Hospice of Chattanooga, (now Alleo Health Systems) I ran into Howard at a conference. We'd had a nodding relationship for some years after my fellowship but standing in the hallway we had our first substantive chat. We'd just finished discussing, remembering and commemorating Beverly.

Howard looked me in the eye. "You know it took a lot of guts not just for her but you as well. You left a successful job to come study with us. I know it was hard and while you struggled, you hung in there and finished. I have a lot of respect for that." I nodded and thanked him. It was nice to hear the effort acknowledged. We shook hands. I felt, somehow complete. I no longer needed to be validated, ten more years of practice had done that, but it still felt good.

FINIS-

D edications: For the women in my life

First to my wife Brenda Gayle Knotts Phelps RN BSN. Love of my life, she has hung in there with me for over forty years. The good times greatly outweigh the bad.

Second: My mother Cynthia Calkins Lange Phelps MLS- who formed me, educated me, passed along her love of books and taught me how to face death with a smirk and a quip.

My daughter: Tiffany Celeste Phelps Vargas BA who was often my sounding board and supporter

My sister: Katherine Lee Phelps Jackson PhD who was her younger brother's champion though it all.

Robin Howe who edited and re-edited this manuscript. As I've mentioned I was NOT an English major. Any errors left are mine not hers.

Katie Baker friend of over 30 years who repaired my diploma and did the cover for this book

Finally- in memorium Beverly Jeff-Steele DO who supported me as I supported her as we worked though this fellowship.

CPSIA information can be obtained
at www.ICGtesting.com
Printed in the USA
JSHW022114230520
5838JS00008B/15